WHY STORIES MATTER

The Political Grammar of Feminist Theory

CLARE HEMMINGS

DUKE UNIVERSITY PRESS Durham & London 2011

© 2011 Duke University Press
All rights reserved

Printed in the United States of America
on acid-free paper ∞

Designed by Jennifer Hill
Typeset in Arno Pro and Avenir
by Keystone Typesetting, Inc.

Library of Congress
Cataloging-in-Publication Data
appear on the last printed page of this book.

Why Stories Matter

NEXT WAVE:
NEW DIRECTIONS IN WOMEN'S STUDIES
A series edited by Inderpal Grewal, Caren Kaplan,
and Robyn Wiegman

To Helen, for her insistence . . .

CONTENTS

ACKNOWLEDGMENTS

As with all writing, that this book is in print is down to more people than can be acknowledged. The project came first out of a love of narrative and a desire to play with it: in this ongoing endeavour, David Hansen-Miller is always my main partner in crime. It is a privilege to be surrounded by feminists who generate hope out of hopelessness, not by turning away from reality but by grappling with it. Here I simply do not know how to thank Amal Treacher, Anne Phillips, Fran Tonkiss, Helen Crowley, Hilary Hinds, Jackie Stacey, Jane Rowley, Jo Eadie, Kate Nash, Laleh Khalili, Nadje Al-Ali, Ros Gill, Rosi Braidotti, Ranjana Khanna, Robyn Wiegman, Rutvica Andrijasevic, Sara Ahmed, and Tina Campt, whose combined intellectual and personal connections I cannot do without. Readers of and responders to my work at key moments kept me going and persuaded me this was a book worth finishing: particular thanks to Sadie Wearing, Tyler Curtain, and Vron Ware. Ken Wissoker and all the team at Duke University Press managed my hysteria beautifully. Merl Storr was a gift of an indexer.

I am fortunate to be working in feminist projects that provide community and critical engagement in equal measure. The Feminist Review Collective and all the members of Travelling Concepts provide contexts of furious engagement with what it means to think and act as a feminist inside and outside the academy. Working with colleagues and students past and present at the Gender Institute is an amazing experience—curse me if I ever take the intellectual vibrancy and humour of this environment for granted! And each year, the Abersoch crew remind me of the importance of collective living and shared stories that connect us to one another.

I am as fortunate to have parents who assume I will do all the things I claim I will and don't hold it against me when I don't.

INTRODUCTION

This book is on how feminists tell stories about Western feminist theory's recent past, why these stories
matter, and what we can do to transform them. It
explores their narrative form and charts their inter-
action with other stories about feminism and social
change. It asks what might be at stake in feminist
storytelling, and most importantly it seeks to intervene in these stories, to realign their political grammar to allow a different vision of a feminist past,
present, and future.[1]

The work starts from the assumption that how feminists tell stories matters in part because of the ways in
which they intersect with wider institutionalizations
of gendered meanings. For example, stories that frame
gender equality as a uniquely Western export, as a
way to measure or enforce economic and democratic
development, resonate disconcertingly well with feminist stories that place "feminism" as a radical knowledge project firmly in the Western past. When feminists celebrate the move beyond unity or identity,

when they lament the demise of a feminist political agenda, or when they propose a return to a feminist vision from the past, they construct a political grammar that is highly mobile and does not belong only to feminists. It is not enough for feminists to lament what is most often perceived as the co-optation of feminism in global arenas. Feminist theorists need to pay attention to the *amenability* of our own stories, narrative constructs, and grammatical forms to discursive uses of gender and feminism we might otherwise wish to disentangle ourselves from if history is not simply to repeat itself.

This book is a claim for the continued radical potential of feminist theory and for the importance of telling stories differently. If Western feminists can be attentive to the political grammar of our storytelling, if we can highlight reasons why that attention might be important, then we can also intervene to change the way we tell stories. We can interrupt the amenability of the narratives that make up dominant Western feminist stories and tell stories differently.[2] Throughout this work I am pulled in two directions. One pull is the interest in highlighting overlaps among a range of stories about gender and feminism usually held apart. I want to examine commonalities across antagonistic Western feminist narratives, between these and postfeminist positions that reject such narratives, either in media and cultural contexts, or within the growing area of gender policy. Another is the belief that feminist theory is particularly well positioned to challenge these intersections because of its deep history of attention to differences, intersections, lies, and silences (Ware 2006). Feminist theory is certainly bound up in global power relations, particularly when we consider the various ways in which a presumed opposition between Western gender equality and non-Western patriarchal cultures is mobilized in temporal and spatial modes, but it also occupies a position of reflexive non-innocence that can break open those relations. Starting from invested attention to silences in the history of feminist theory, then, I suggest several ways of making the stories we tell both more ethically accountable and potentially more politically transformative.

This position is perhaps untenable—that feminism is both caught and freeing—but I hold it nevertheless and revisit this position throughout the work that follows. In this belief, I acknowledge the influence of other feminist theorists whose work, words, and lives have insisted, and continue to insist, on the potential of non-innocent theorizing for change. I read Rosi Braidotti's *Patterns of Dissonance* nearly twenty years ago, and was transported then by her certainty that passion was the point of theory, and that without that passion, feminist theory could have no real value (1991). I have always loved feminist theory for its utopianism, and I hope to contribute to the tradition of dogged optimism that allows its practitioners to understand and experience life differently. In this spirit, there are three overlapping strands to this work, all of which seek to allow for a different kind of feminist political thinking: the laying out of Western feminist storytelling in this intellectual space I call home; the exploration of the political grammar of feminist narratives that make up these stories and their consistency with other stories about feminism and gender; the sketching out of interventions that start at the level of political grammar and propose ways of breaking open dominant narrative forms. Of these three strands, the last one is the most important, as it constitutes a starting point for a reflexive Western feminist accountability that shuttles back and forth between past and present in order to imagine a future that is not already known. My interventions focus specifically on citation tactics and on textual affect as starting points for unravelling the stuff of Western feminist storytelling to transformative effect.

STORYTELLING

So what are these stories I claim are told about Western feminist theory's recent past? The surprise that motivated much of the early research on this project was the uniformity of representations of Western feminist theoretical trajectories. Despite the complexity of the last few decades of feminist theory—its dizzying array of authors, objects, disciplines, and practices—the story of its past is consistently told as a series of interlocking narratives of progress, loss, and return that oversimplify this complex history and position feminist subjects as needing to inhabit a theoretical and political cutting edge in the present. Let me give a flavour of these common threads here.

One: Progress. We used to think of "woman" or feminism as a unified category, but through the subsequent efforts of black and lesbian feminist theorists, among others, the field has diversified, and feminism itself has become the object of detailed critical and political scrutiny. Far from being a problem, difference within the category "woman", and within feminisms, should be a cause for celebration. Postmodern feminism has moved us still further towards a focus on political effect over identity politics and highlights the exclusions and inclusions social movements, including feminism, produce. In the process of intellectual and political advances, we have developed a variety of epistemological and methodological tools and critiqued the scope, reach, and ontological narrowness typical of Western feminism's earlier preoccupations and subjects. Since "woman" is no longer the ground of feminism, and the relationship between subject and object of feminist theory has been destabilized, an intellectual focus on gender or feminism alone may indicate an anachronistic attachment to false unity or essentialism.

Two: Loss. We used to think of "woman" or feminism as unified, but progressive fragmentation of categories and infighting have resulted in the increased depoliticization of feminist commitments. Conservative institutionalization of feminist thought and the generational popularity of "post-feminism" are empty parodies of a feminist social movement that has incontrovertibly passed. The demise of feminism can be understood as part of a more general political shift to the right that has also killed the viability of a left-wing alternative. Feminist academics and a new generation of women have both inherited and contributed to this loss, particularly through their lack of interest in recent feminist history and an acceptance of political individualism. Whatever the failings of previous feminist commitments, it was better to have a feminist movement than none at all. We need to risk academic and political marginalization by asserting uncomfortable truths about ongoing gender inequalities in the West and elsewhere.

Three: Return. We have lost our way but we can get it back, if we apply a little common sense to our current situation. We may have been convinced by the turn to language, a poststructuralist capacity to deconstruct power and value difference, but we know better now. We know now that critique does not alter power relations and indeed that these have endured and strengthened. We know now that postmodern feminism leads to relativism and political incapacity, while women everywhere remain disadvantaged. Perhaps earlier feminist theories might still have something to teach us about what we have in common as women, despite the valuable critiques of essentialism that have come since. On the bright side, we do not have to accept the opposition between fragmentation and unity; we can combine the lessons of postmodern feminism with the materiality of embodiment and structural inequalities to move on from the current theoretical and political impasse.

Despite each story's proclamations of difference from the other accounts, there are striking narrative similarities that link these stories and that facilitate discursive movement between them without apparent contradiction. I provide an initial sense of these overlaps here, a sense I develop in subsequent chapters that analyze the narrative structure and techniques of each story in turn. All three stories divide the recent past into clear decades to provide a narrative of progress or loss, proliferation or homogenization. Stories of return are equally invested in these distinctions to argue for what it is that we need to return to in order to rescue Western feminist theory. You may know without me telling you that "the past" most often refers to the 1970s, that reference to identity and difference denotes the 1980s, and that the 1990s stands as the decade of difference proper, as that which must be returned from in the noughts. The stories part 1 of the book is concerned with tracing are thus "common stories."[3] Implicitly or explicitly too, each decade is understood to house particular schools of thought and particular theorists, irrespective of whether or not their work spans much longer periods. Thus Marxist or radical approaches give way to identity politics, which give way to deconstructivist critiques, which are replaced in turn by (new) materialism. And no doubt we have not seen the last shift. Whether positively or negatively inflected, the chronology remains the same, the decades overburdened yet curiously flattened despite each story's unique truth claims.

These stories describe and locate feminist *subjects* as well as events or schools of thought, of course, and this also makes them affectively saturated for both authors and readers. They are not neutral and do not ask us to remain neutral. They position their teller as a heroine of the past, present, and future of Western feminist theory. To dispute where we have ended up in the present is to dispute not only a given account of feminist theory, but also its proper subject. So in a progress narrative as described above a radical or socialist feminist is not and cannot be its transcendent subject; she is left behind. Neither can a poststructuralist feminist be the ideal subject of a loss or return narrative; she needs to change her mind. In this respect claims for what has happened in feminist theory are also claims about individual status. One's own intellectual and political commitments are always at stake in these stories, as one sees oneself by turn marginalized by the passage of time, or at the cutting edge of contemporary thought and practice. These commitments also form the basis of generational claims of progress or loss, allowing for the deflection of personal hopes and regrets onto collectivities or general trends: previous generations made certain understandable mistakes; a generation of academics contributes to and pays the price for professional institutionalization; youth in general has no awareness of history, is apolitical, bored, or self-interested.

To return to one of the characteristics of the three stories of feminist theory, that of the decade by decade fixing of shifts in feminist theory, one key issue is who is identified as belonging to which decade. As I will explore in further detail in the next two chapters, in progress narratives, black feminism frequently acts as catalyst for a more general, *later*, move to difference as proliferation. In the process, the former is consistently cited as taking place in the 1980s, while an essentialist radical feminism or myopic socialist feminism occupies the 1970s, and poststructuralism moves forward into the 1990s and sometimes beyond, free of both essentialism and identity restrictions. In a related vein, lesbian feminist theory is called to account by the pro-sex demands of the 1980s, with the 1990s belonging squarely to queer theorists. In loss narratives, the seventies are equally uniform, the 1980s an important decade of identity contestation but one ambivalently related to both 1970s radicalism and 1990s fragmentation. Whether politically brave or misguided, identity politics have given way completely to the professionalization of feminist knowledge in the 1990s, and we have yet to return from this lamentable state of affairs.

In all versions of this story, postmodern and poststructuralist feminism are understood to mark a break from feminism proper through their attack on the category "woman."[4] The separation of these theoretical traditions from their feminist genealogy has some important narrative and political effects. The first is that "other" critiques of unified womanhood (from identity politics perspectives, for example) become teleologically bound and their challenges transcended in turn. Thus black and lesbian feminist engagements become firmly identified with the past, become anachronistic, as do their presumed subjects. A second, related, effect is that the separation of postmodernism and poststructuralism from their complex feminist histories means that the former too emerge oddly subjectless and without reference to contests that characterize their own inclusions and exclusions. Such an imaginative separation is essential for return narratives to function, since postmodernism and poststructuralism need to be rendered as wholly abstract in order for the plea for a return to "the body" or "the social" to make sense. Indeed, these imperatives are recast in return narratives as the very reason we need to move away from postmodernism and poststructuralism: repeated cries of "Wither the body? Wither the material?" are not meant to be resolved but serve as rhetorical gestures that anchor Western feminist historiography.

MOBILIZATIONS

To begin thinking about this question of narrative amenability, I want to emphasize that it is not only feminists who tell us (feminist) politics has been lost. The intellectual and temporal separation of feminism from postmodernism and poststructuralism resonates with more general understandings of feminism as "over." Broader social and cultural theory reproduces the same story in relation to its own "lost politics" of the past, as Wendy Brown (1999) and Lisa Adkins (2004), among others, have pointed out. Indeed, much of what I argue in this book might be seen as offering ways of critiquing stories about the teleology of social theory more generally. These strands overlap in the sense that social theory's storytelling is also governed by progress, loss, and return narratives that champion, lament, or advocate revisiting a unified past vision of social change. And feminism is characteristically located both as part of what has been surpassed, but also as part of what contributed to the fragmentation of the Left in its downward narrative trajectory. In social theory's stories about the recent past, then, feminism is anachronistic, and the desire to hold onto it—and its objects and methods too—misguided. But in social theory's return narratives, feminism is usually stranded or straddled, as social theory seeks its own salvation by prioritizing either a return to orthodoxy or a transformation that transcends partisan distractions.

More directly still, it is within Western media and popular culture that feminism is most consistently rendered as old-fashioned, and indeed stereotyped as unnecessarily aggressive or misguided. In popular media, as feminist commentators have highlighted in considerable depth, feminism is understood to have achieved its primary goals of equality in the West, leaving young Western women free to flaunt their femininity and sexuality as part of a contemporary gendered agency (McRobbie 2000; Gill 2007). Where feminists insist that equality has not been properly achieved, or that feminism may not only be about formal equality (Gill 2000), they are vilified as angry and humourless and blamed for creating a generation of fearful, unsuccessful, metaphorically castrated men (Faludi 1992; McRobbie 2004).[5] The stereotype of the feminist subject here, as in earlier postfeminist texts that pitted new against old generations of feminists (Paglia 1992; Roiphe 1993), is familiar. She is masculine, unattractive to men, prudish, humourless, and badly dressed: in short, she is a lesbian. And lesbianism itself is marked as anachronistic, unless combined with a palatable mainstream femininity, since there is simply no need to be hostile to men in contemporary Western culture (any more). Why be so churlish to men now that our equalities have been achieved?[6] Not only has feminism "been expelled . . . [to] a retirement home in an unfashionable rundown holiday resort," as Angela McRobbie caustically notes (2004: 512), the fear of "her return" is framed as threatening young women's social and sexual capital.

If the lesbian is left behind in the postfeminist West, non-Western women are left behind in popular discourses of culture and tradition that reference the global South and postsocialist West (and never the twain shall meet). As Gloria Wekker notes in the context of the Netherlands: "The Minister of Social Affairs . . . officially proclaimed in Nov. 2003 that the emancipation of 'autochthonous,' read white, women had been accomplished . . . Now is the time to devote all our energies to the emancipation of 'allochthonous,' read black, migrant, and refugee women" (2004: 490). As she further comments, such a position represents "white Dutch women as the epitome, the teleological endpoint of emancipation, the example for black, migrant and refugee women" (2004: 490).[7] The project of modernization itself is thus profoundly gendered at both an imaginative and material level, since attention to gender inequality (within a specifically economic framework) is frequently levelled as a prerequisite for financial investment/aid from governments, international corporations, or transnational organizations such as the World Bank and the World Trade Organization (despite their own unequal gender practices).

The insistence on Western gender equality as *the* marker of progress does complicated and damaging work in terms of fixing non-Western cultures as backwards (as premodern) and in need of help from Western philanthropists and experts (as postmodern), as many feminist and post-colonial authors have observed (Grewal and Kaplan 1994; Narayan 1997; Puri 2006). And indeed, imagining gender equality as a postmodern export also does important work in securing gender equality as the preserve of capitalist democracies in relation to the former socialist West (Gal and Kligman 2000; Ousmanova 2003; Kašić 2004). In all these contexts, gender equality discourse carries and deflects cultural, ethnic, and racial differences while appearing to operate to reduce the same in the name of a global free market. This work is achieved partly through representation—who speaks or is spoken for (Suleri 1992; Alcoff 1995), who is cast as an individual or representative of their "culture" (Spivak 1988; Mohanty 2003 [1988])—which remains a key concern for feminists interested in exploring global manifestations of gender inequality in ethical and sustainably transformative ways (Spivak 1993b; Alexander 2005; Duhaček 2006a).[8] Feminism itself, insofar as it is assumed to be over in the West, does not need to be exported, only the equality that one needs to take care to ensure does not go too far.

The insights of the above literatures cover enormous ground and ask questions about the role of Western feminism in relation to some of the problematic mobilizations of gender equality from a global perspective. I want here to flag the significance of thinking in this vein for this project. First, it seems worth saying again that the use of gender equality as a marker of an economic and regulatory modernity marks the subject of gender equality as Western, capitalist, and democratic, and the West, capitalism, and democracy themselves as sites that create the possibility of, and reproduce, rather than hinder, gender equality. Critically, they position the objects of gender equality as non-Western or postsocialist, and such contexts, and particularly cultures or economies, as creating and perpetuating traditional gender inequalities not part of the modern world. A gender agenda is thus consistently harnessed to cultural or economic difference from Western subjects and sites. Second, feminism is placed in the past, irrelevant to contemporary Western and non-Western sites and subjects, ensuring both that any ambivalence about feminism's achievements in the West are sidelined, and that the subject of modern gender equality has a nonfeminist subject and expert. Here is where geography and sexuality, media and international policy come together so productively: that subject is not only Western, capitalist, and democratic, but also heterosexual and feminine (Annfelt 2002). Freed from the burdens of (historically understandable, but no longer necessary) bias, gender equality can finally be achieved impartially. Learning the lessons of Western democracies, we can skip that unpleasant bit in the middle and propel the culture-bound and unliberated directly to the emancipation part, directly to the freedom to participate in global markets part, which is to say without upsetting families, or challenging a democratic imaginary.

Varieties of these postfeminist, gender-equality discourses resonate very close to home for those of us working as feminists in Western academic institutions, too. In institutional terms the broader discursive positioning of feminism as misguided, limited, or anachronistic—within social theory, postfeminism, and gender agendas—makes academic feminism extremely vulnerable. As the Feminist and Women's Studies Association (U.K. and Ireland) discovered while documenting justifications for closures of women's studies departments in the U.K. (Hemmings 2006), success and failure of feminism are alternately cited as reasons for not needing such departments, courses, or academic appointments any more. Anecdotally, there are repeated examples of Western feminist progress narratives in particular being used institutionally to justify non-investment in feminist knowledge projects. The success of feminism (as both social movement and knowledge project) in the West is understood to make its intellectual importance redundant, and its failure to speak to a current generation cited as the primary reason for any low enrolment, as well as evidence for its lack of a future. As Gabriele Griffin and Jalna Hanmer note ironically, such stories allow deep changes in British Higher Education— the move to fee-based enrolment, increasing instrumentalization of learning and the dominance of audit culture—to remain unexamined (2001).

Importantly, the one success likely to be institutionally validated is that of a transition from women's studies to gender studies, where gender studies is understood to reference the transformation of politics and bias into rigor and neutrality or objectivity, in other words where gender studies is also perceived as free from an anachronistic feminist past.[9] In particular, in a U.K. context, gender studies is most likely to be institutionally supported where it is harnessed to globalization and seen as producing future gender mainstreaming or gender and development experts. Indeed, I teach at the London School of Economics' Gender Institute, a site that might be accurately described in this very way. The institutional validation of the institute relies on our capacity to highlight the degrees' "global value" within this discursive ordering, and produces tensions and misunderstandings that crosscut the staff and student body and are not easily resolved (an issue I return to in chapter 3). In this respect, gender studies is understood to be relevant in a U.K. context primarily where its institutional formation reinforces the split between times and places where gender equality is understood to have been, or not been, achieved. In discursive terms, if not in terms of what is actually taught, feminism remains in the past once more, as gender expertise is encouraged in terms of its capacity to export the lessons learned from a necessarily *now over* Western second wave feminism.

These critiques of postfeminist or gender equality discourses are not new, as indicated by the range of relevant theorists cited throughout this section. It is certainly urgent to engage with how what we might call "the temporality of gender discourse" functions as a central mechanism for securing rather than challenging global inequality in the name of freedom. But the separation of gender equality and feminism, the recoding of gender discourse as neutral and its analytics as objective, and its mobilization as political alibi for economic or military intervention, are usually lamented as direct co-optations, as a series of moves away from a feminism necessarily critical of such discursive duplicity (e.g., Grewal and Kaplan 1994; Duggan 2003). And indeed it is no doubt essential to hold these separate in order to retain the political potential of feminism in relation to global power relations (Grewal 2005), to think of feminism as more than those relations. We need feminism's critical tools to highlight the hetero-sexism and racism central to the contemporary mobilizations of gender discourse, to show us, as Vron Ware puts it, "how to navigate the various pitfalls of racism, ethnocentrism, cultural relativism, and plain ignorance that flow from using 'culture' as an explanatory tool" (2006: 532). But we also need to examine the ways in which Western feminist stories about the recent past coincide unnervingly with those that place Western feminism firmly in the past in order to "neutralize" gender equality in its global circuits. In particular, we need to think carefully before presuming that the simple presence of a feminist subject will be enough to mark the difference we may desire.

In the context of this book, this question of amenability is key, because it also points to the ways in which the mobilization of gender equality discourses within and for global markets and regulation is not as uniform as the above description might suggest. Campaigns for gender equality globally can improve the lives of women and men and are used knowingly and strategically by local and transnational groups, for example, community groups and NGOs, in ways that alter the meanings of gender's temporality in turn. Indeed, the assumption that feminist theory is simply 'co-opted' in a global arena preserves both the innocence of "feminist theory," and the hegemony of "gender equality"; instead, it seems productive to work through their mutual implication in space and time, to think carefully about what an accountable feminist theory might foreground in that relation and who its contradictory subjects might be. To begin with, we might want to continue to explore the links between postfeminism's heterosexualizing imperatives, a free market's violent passing as women's liberator, and Western feminist narratives that underscore a similar linearity, even—or perhaps particularly—where these shifts are lamented.

CORRECTIVES

My damning presentation of Western feminist storytelling thus far might lead a reader to wonder what I am suggesting as an alternative. If Western feminist stories of progress, loss, and return share aspects of postfeminist political grammar that make untangling contemporary uses of "gender equality" difficult, what might a willing feminist theorist do? Tell different stories perhaps? Put together an alternative historiography that can tell a better story, one with fewer, or less harmful, exclusions? One that refuses to leave feminism behind, for example? I could, to paraphrase Hayden White (1992), marshal corrective efforts to set the story of Western feminist theory straight. I could point out the errors, as I have been doing, and suggest other pasts. I could, as many interlocutors at different stages of this project have suggested, prioritize difference over similarity and look for moments, and of course they are myriad, when these stories are not reproduced, or not reproduced faithfully. I could intervene at the level of truth telling, then, and leave us with a fuller, richer version of the recent past of Western feminist theory than these dominant narratives allow.

Such projects are indeed important. Feminist historians have consistently sought to tell stories other than dominant ones, both in response to mainstream records, and as part of enriching feminist historiography.[10] I also have a great deal of respect for projects that seek to tell alternative stories that highlight what has been left out and endeavour to reinsert those omissions into the historical record. For example, Becky Thompson shows how retelling the history of Western feminism from a multiracial perspective would see the 1970s less as a heyday and more as a "low point of feminism—a time when many women who were committed to an antiracist analysis had to put their feminism on the back burner in order to work with women and men of color and against racism" (2002: 344).[11] Significantly, Thompson's work points to the importance of assuming not just that there will always be exceptions to the norm of any given historical account, but that these exceptions provide an epistemological challenge to accepted teleologies. Indeed, my own entry into this project arose partly from the experience of disjuncture between the linear stories told about the recent past of Western feminist theory and my encounters with multiple feminisms and feminist debates through this forty-to-fifty year period. I still remember my surprise when I first visited a feminist archive, perused newsletters and magazines from activist groups, and realized that discussions about sadomasochism in the lesbian community had been raging long before the "sex wars" and that black feminist and transnational critique had been a consistent component of feminist theory, rather than one initiated in the late 1970s or 1980s. For me, that moment of realization not only emphasized the importance of personal experience, luck if you like, in one's relationship to history, but also precipitated an ongoing discussion in my head about the best way to respond to absences from contemporary accounts.

Yet despite this genuine pull towards the corrective and the multiple, I do not finally think that attempting representation of this kind can be the answer to the particular problems of repetition and grammatical transferability identified in this book. One reason for this resistance is that I have been persuaded by feminist historiographers' insistence that which story one tells about the past is always motivated by the position one occupies or wishes to occupy in the present. As Antoinette Burton (2001), Elizabeth Grosz (2002), Gayatri Spivak (1999a), Jennifer Terry (1991; 1999), and Eve Sedgwick (1991) all variously indicate, since fullness in representations of the past can never be reached, a corrective approach will always be likely to erase the conditions of its own construction, particularly if it purports to give us the final word.[12] To correct the story which writers should we choose? How would this happen without reification? Who will tell this story? What methods might be proposed for fullness (Campt 2004)? In an early article outlining my concerns in this project, these questions are abruptly answered by a rather out-of-place footnote in which I provide a list of black feminist writers from the 1960s and 1970s as a way of making clear that the dominant stories I am critiquing are not only politically injurious but also inaccurate (2005b: 132, n.7). As one critic of this piece points out, the footnote both authenticates the desire to critique the existing ways of telling stories and reveals a more corrective approach than I otherwise claim to endorse (Torr 2007: 61). The stranded footnote remains uncontextualized and proposes an alternative history without fully delineating it, or being accountable for it. It hints at multiplicity but cannot find a way to represent it.

Similar problems arise when the Western feminist stories I have been sketching are set against geographical alternatives. In one strand of argument progress, loss, and return narratives are framed not as Western in general, but as Anglo-American in particular. Thus, the story that feminist theory has moved from radical or socialist feminism, through identity politics and into postmodernism and thence a "postcultural" turn, is sometimes critiqued by continental European feminists for positing Anglo-American trajectories as descriptive of the entirety of Western feminist theory. In this line of argument, the European alternative, often through the (re)claiming of sexual difference as current rather than surpassed, is offered as the corrective.[13] A fuller, more geographically representative theoretical reach is advocated and the story retold. Yet in the process, of course, only certain kinds of "European alternatives" can be incorporated: those standing in contrast to ones perceived as Anglo-American.[14] Not only does the "European alternative" thus posed risk simplifying the difference that it makes, but the Anglo-American centre remains static, too. In the volume *Italian Feminist Theory and Practice*, for example, the future may be Italian, but the Anglo-American feminist past continues to comprise a familiar move from sex to gender, from essentialism to deconstruction (Parati and West 2002). And in Chrysanthi Nigianni and Merl Storr's collection *Deleuze and Queer Theory* it is Anglo-American versions of the latter that are constraining, while continental inflections promise mobility (2009). In this respect, it is often the particular that is fleshed out, while the dominant that is corrected remains intact. Correction is bound to treasure what is found at the stereotyping expense of what is jettisoned.

What such geographical correctives miss are the ways in which dominant stories (Anglo-American or Western) traverse boundaries and operate in relation. They tend to substitute literal location for a politics of location (Rich 1986), and in doing so perpetuate stereotypes about who lives where and how stories travel.[15] Thus, the geopolitical power of located publishing and English as the global *lingua franca* means that feminist theory produced in an Anglo-American context is always likely to exceed its geography (King 1994). More importantly, conceptualizing of Anglo-American feminist theory's travels as direct *dissemination* fails to capture the transitions and translations that mark its movements back and forth and that highlight the nature of international engagement with its various forms (Bal 2002; Vasterling, Demény et al. 2006). For example, Sabine Hark's careful work on the discursive life of Judith Butler's *Gender Trouble* in Germany (2002) explores the ways in which dismissal of *Gender Trouble* by powerful feminist academics on the basis of its "seductive Americanness" masks and displaces central anxieties about queerness that the text also brings with it when it travels. Neither do what I continue to call *Western* feminist narratives of progress, loss, and return emerge only from Anglo-American sites, or even ones with English as a national language; they are produced and endorsed much more broadly than that. Journals such as *Nora: Nordic Journal of Women's Studies* and the *European Journal of Women's Studies* generate the same stories about what has happened in Western feminist theory, even where this does not fit with the specific institutional context or political history at issue. To see these stories as geographically bounded, then, is to suggest that they do in fact accurately describe the history of feminist theory in Western (or indeed Anglo-American) contexts and that the failure is primarily one of inclusion rather than representation. Difference from dominant accounts is thus always elsewhere rather than within. In terms of the marginalization that those dominant narrations effect for particular subjects and histories, a belief in their geographically descriptive accuracy redoubles the racial and sexual exclusions that permeate those sites.

The realization of feminist theory's multiplicity, then, leads me to want to analyze not so much what other truer history we might write, but the politics that produce and sustain one version of history as more true than another, despite the fact that we know that history is more complicated than the stories we tell about it. Although I am always bound by my desire to see more multiplicity represented, this desire does not have to be approached from the perspective of plugging the gaps, as if this could ever be finally achieved, or as if which gaps one prioritizes were in need of no further explanation. Holding in mind multiple histories that remain un- or under-represented in the present should not determine the mode of one's response to that representation and does not automatically point to corrective redress as the most appropriate means to address the problem of omission. The moment, that snapshot of the discursive dissonance that makes up feminist history, might operate instead as a reminder that all histories are selective and motivated histories, even if they can make plain their "contested authorization" (Hemmings 2007a: 73). In line with my interest in what storytelling reveals about the politics of the present, my responses to Western feminist storytelling in this book start from, but do not conclude with, the multiple erasures and investments of the present. I seek to flesh out the substance of Western feminist stories and to intervene by experimenting with how we might tell stories differently rather than telling different stories.

TECHNOLOGIES OF THE PRESUMED

The three chapters that comprise part 1 provide a detailed mapping of the narratives of progress, loss, and return that I have sketched out in this introduction. I focus on the ways in which Western feminist stories are secured in a selection of interdisciplinary feminist journals and a smaller range of cultural and social theory journals published in English. Because I am interested in the *dominant narratives* that emerge in the telling of Western feminist stories about the recent past, my aim is to highlight which aspects of these stories are presumed to be held in common, which statements or glosses do not require evidencing. I home in on that which tends to pass unnoticed in the telling of the story, or assumptions that are framed by particular certainty, such as accounts introduced with phrases like "we can all agree that x or y has happened in feminist theory . . ." or "as we all know. . . ." These common sense glosses suggest views that are generally rather than only individually held, and an examination of these offers insights into the dominant narrative forms governing our perception of the recent Western feminist past. Importantly, they are *pervasive* stories that feminist and other theorists participate in, reproduce, and embellish.

My intention is to identify the repeated narrative forms that underwrite these stories by analyzing the textual mechanisms that generate coherent meaning and allow for author, context, and reader agreement. Thus, for example, I pay particular attention to the subject/object relationship, binary pairs and the excluded outside, embedded temporality and hierarchy of meaning, citation practices, and textual affect. The purpose of this discursive analysis of journal glosses in the telling of Western feminist stories is to uncover the political grammar through which we come to believe in narratives of progress, loss, and return. It is my contention that this kind of close attention can enable both an important tracking of how these narratives function intertextually and how certain strands of thought and subjects come to be understood as past or present. Further, it goes some way to explaining how it is that we reproduce these narratives in ways that fly in the face of the complexities we otherwise cherish.[16] This mapping of the overall narrative forms and techniques through which they are secured enables a more detailed understanding of the narratives themselves: why and how they work. It also allows me to draw out some of the potent absences produced in the present by these narratives and thus provide a grounded starting point for beginning to tell stories differently.

The journals I have chosen to analyse in detail are *Signs: Journal of Women in Culture and Society, Feminist Review, Feminist Theory, Nora: Nordic Journal of Women's Studies, European Journal of Women's Studies*, and *Australian Feminist Studies*. These were chosen in order to provide some geographical as well as interdisciplinary range within the Western feminist context I am concerned with. They are all English language journals, although editorial practice may include translating articles not originally written in English, and they are all concerned with Western feminist theory's development. The analysis of these journals took two main directions. The first involved a focus on special issues on the history of feminist theory, often published around the millennium, or on individual articles from the same journals that take up the question of the history of feminist theory directly as part of their overall argument. But while giving a useful overall sense of the different narratives drawn on, this direction felt limited by the kinds of issues such articles addressed. I felt increasingly that these sources gave a clear sense of developments in Western feminist theory because they took this as their primary object or goal. They could not, however, give a good sense of the *implicit* stories told about Western feminist theory's development, whatever the overall direction of argument. They could not, in other words, give a real indication of "commonly held" positions about the recent past, since their object was precisely to interrogate that past. And so the second direction the analysis took was of the journals chosen as a whole, rather than only of the special issues concerned with similar themes to my own. This more general focus involved reading all the articles in each journal from 1998 onwards, in order not to presume where, or in which kinds of articles, understandings of changes within Western feminist theory might be represented. Throughout this mapping I focused in on gloss paragraphs, introductions or segues in articles that told a story about feminist theory's development, whether or not the article otherwise centred on that development.

To complement the analysis of these journals, I also consulted a range of articles from *Feminist Studies, Women's Studies International Forum, Gender, Place and Culture* and a handful of social and cultural theory journals, *Theory, Culture and Society, Critical Inquiry, Differences, Economy and Society, Body and Society,* and *Cultural Studies,* again from a similar starting point of around 1998 (occasionally earlier). In these cases, I read articles particularly addressing the development of feminist theory or feminism, or special issues and debates in the same area. My main interest here was in crosschecking that similar patterns were in evidence elsewhere, that the dominant narratives I had identified were not coincidental or particular to the key journals for the mapping. I concluded the analysis of the core journals in June 2007 for fear that the process was starting to resemble *Groundhog Day* and that I would still be in the midst of the process at retirement; I stopped analyzing additional journals at the point that new examples of the same phenomena seemed unnecessary to be sure the case I was making was not entirely eccentric.

At several points during the mapping process I considered broadening the scope of the analysis to include single-authored texts, textbooks, or readers that develop similar themes and utilize indicative tropes. In genre terms such overviews would seem ideal for the kind of analysis I am proposing; a cursory investigation suggests narratives of progress, loss, and return do centrally structure many such publications (Jackson 1993; Nicholson 1996; Robinson and Richardson 1997; Davis, Evans et al. 2006). And there are now a series of memoirs in which individual feminist theorists and activists weave together the personal and the historical in their accounts of the recent history of Western feminism and feminist theory and lament or celebrate its trajectory in ways that resonate very clearly with this project (Brownmiller 1999; Rowbotham 2000; DuPlessis and Snitow 2007; Segal 2007), as well as a surge of edited collections that mull over the question of "wither feminism?" and its relationship to institutionalization of feminist knowledge practices post-millennium (Bronfen and Kavka 2001; Messer-Davidow 2002; Wiegman 2003). These texts form the intellectual backdrop to the discussions at the heart of the book, and I draw on many of these thinkers directly through the book as a whole.[17] These texts, and many more besides, are worthy of critical attention in their own right, but are limited for my analysis here in similar ways to journal special issues on Western feminist theory's fortunes, in that they represent direct attempts to account for change over time. In this respect, as with journal special issues, these general publications are less useful for uncovering what I think of as the *technologies of the presumed* within Western feminist theory because they take those presumptions as their analytic object. In addition, textbooks, readers, and edited collections draw on a more limited range of community input than journals, particularly where the latter practice peer review as part of accepting an article for publication (this is true for all the journals I analyzed). Journals draw on a far greater number of participants in the field as part of deciding which aspects of an article need rewriting and which do not, as the usual list of the hundred or more of people involved in peer review in a given year at the back of a given journal attests.

Returning for a moment to an issue I raised in my discussion about the pull of the corrective, there is a danger that in focusing on repeated rather than anomalous stories I may in fact be further bolstering the monotony of the progress, loss, and return narratives I identify as so problematic. And indeed, on several occasions when I have given papers including such mapping, questions from the floor stressed that I had ignored multiplicity in my own single-minded focus on dominant patterns. I could not agree more that the stories I map and analyze here are not the whole story of Western feminist theory. Many of the glosses I analyze are in fact the prelude to innovative, unique arguments that characterize the particular interests of the individual author concerned. This diversity of argument is not at issue; indeed, as I indicated earlier, the knowledge of what is left out of these stories underwrites the structuring tension between corrective drive and corrective refusal throughout the project. But this is not a descriptive project, nor one that seeks the argument that will set our story straight. My interest in the rehearsed rather than the creative is both to account for the former's pervasiveness *despite* the inventiveness of other positions, their co-presence even when they seem directly at odds, and to get at the politics of the rehearsed in a range of ways. The presence of alternatives does not, in itself, make a dent in the relentless persuasiveness of the presumed. And indeed, one of the underlying principles in this mapping is that if we can identify the techniques through which dominant stories are secured, through which their status as "common sense" is reproduced, that political grammar may also offer a rigorous point of intervention through which Western feminist stories might be transformed.

INTERVENTIONS

Two particular storytelling tactics have emerged as central to my interest in the transformation of progress, loss, and return narratives throughout this project: attention to citation and to affect. I have mentioned both of these in passing thus far, but want to conclude this introduction by drawing out some of the threads of both approaches as they run through the text as a whole. Both citation and affect, I argue, are key techniques through which these narratives operate, through which they are secured and made believable. As I will demonstrate in some detail in the following chapters, who is or is not cited as evidence in the case for Western feminist theory's recent past as a story of progress, loss, or return underwrites the decade by decade approach I have already begun to critique here. It is the primary technique through which people and approaches are assigned an era, positioned as pivotal to key shifts in theoretical direction, or written out of the past or present. Affect is similarly germane to the narratives I analyze and how they function. One of the ways in which the glosses I scrutinize appeal to the common sense of their reader without detailed discussion is through the mobilization of affect. Alternative ways of narrating the recent past of Western feminist theory are foreclosed in progress narratives, for example, through their celebratory tone that provides little space for dissent. Loss narratives, as laments, express and produce negative feelings that also allow a slide over what might be missing in a given account, and that paradoxically enough, might be said to underpin a positive affective state in the subject whose version of history is thus consolidated. As I outline further below, I am interested in affect as a core part of political grammar and, following Lauren Berlant (e.g., 1997; 2007; 2008), understand it as producing internal textual and external community cohesion that is difficult to resist. Both citation and affect seem like good places to start in thinking about my own storytelling tactics too, then, precisely because of their centrality to the dominant narratives I want to intervene in.

I have developed several ways of experimenting with citation in my analysis of Western feminist stories throughout the book. The first shines a spotlight on these stories as held in common irrespective of what else a given author may be arguing. Anyone who has ever published a piece of writing knows that which aspects of an article are assumed to need referencing, which ways of telling stories need further explanation or argumentation, are never individual decisions alone. As an editor or reviewer for more than one of the journals I examine in the book, my reading practices are shaped by the knowledge community within which I operate. When I review articles, my eye alights on certain things and not others; some parts of an article stick out, and there is a lot that passes my notice. Thus, my citation practice here combines with my choice to focus on journal articles rather than textbooks, single-authored books, or edited collections as a way of foregrounding knowledge practices as shared rather than individual. The primary tactic I employ is to cite the *source* of the extract I introduce—the journal and year—rather than the author, throughout. This tactic is intended to emphasize the role of journal communities— editors, boards, peer reviewers, and responses to publishing conventions and expectations—in the establishment of feminist (and broader academic) knowledge practices. It also provides a way of being able to focus on patterns across the journals, seeing them as a set, rather than being distracted by resonances across an individual oeuvre.

Citing place and time of publication in this way also underlines my commitment to non-corrective approaches to engaging Western feminist storytelling. It is intended to shift priority away from who said what, away from thinking about feminist theory in terms of "good" and "bad" authors, and away from the lures of prior agreement. In relation to the latter point, for example, a given author may well utilize aspects of a loss or return narrative despite the fact that they are more generally known (and liked or disliked) for endorsing progress narratives. Taking the authors out of the citation frame is thus a way of focusing attention on repetition instead of individuality, and on how collective repetition actively works to obscure the politics of its own production and reproduction. Other feminist authors have suggested similar moves. Christine Hughes, for example, suggests that we look at feminist texts not in terms of what is right or wrong about them, but in terms of their conditions of production, institutional resonance, and interpretative possibilities (2004), and Gayatri Spivak consistently warns us against the individual author-blaming that mitigates against real recognition of historically and discursively constituted speaking locations (1999b). In this spirit, I also hope that the sustained approach to citation I take here works against the tendency to produce work that largely consists of extended critique of key authors: back and forth we go, arguing about who got it right. Instead, I see the narrative strands I analyze as creating stories that we all participate in and that constitute a process of collective knowledge production that locates us in particular ways. This citation tactic allows me to track the commonalities of utterance, the remarkably similar affects mobilized and produced, and to suggest that there is no "outside" of these processes, no single (or even multiple) alternative story one could tell that would finally "get it right," even while there remain ways of thinking stories differently.[18]

My second citation tactic in the book similarly intervenes at the representational level, though in a more assertive mode. In part 1, I examine citation practice in narratives of progress, loss, and return, focusing particularly on its role in temporally separating strands of feminist thought that could as easily be cited as co-extensive. Citation is important because it anchors an overall chronology, provides a semblance of detail, and has an appropriate status as evidence. This or that text will certainly have been published (or sometimes reissued) at the date cited, but this empiricism masks the selective nature of that evidence. The repeated choice in narrative glosses to cite black feminism as an eighties phenomenon, for example, tells us not just about that decade, but forms part of an overall chronology. Similarly, it is an indisputable fact that Judith Butler's *Gender Trouble* was published in 1990, but its relentless citation as that which precipitates feminism into a new era of critique serves a much broader narrative function. In these and many other cases, citation works to position feminism as part of the past and contemporary work as apolitical or more political depending on textual affect. In my analysis of citation in part 1, I focus both on the political productiveness of these practices—the kind of Western feminist present they instantiate—and on what is excluded through these practices. This examination of citation as key to the politics of the present forms the basis of the first major tactical intervention into Western feminist storytelling in this book. In part 2, chapter 5, I develop an approach to narrative I call "recitation," which seeks to disrupt dominant narrative grammar and open up multiple re-readings of the present. Starting from what is precluded in dominant citational practice, I fold these hauntings back into the political grammar of Western feminist theory to produce a set of potential feminist realignments. I ask what happens when we recite stories in which feminism has been left behind by poststructuralism, by forcing absent presences back into the narrative, beginning from affective investments in what has been half-forgotten. One might describe this process as one that mobilizes my ambivalent corrective impulses as a starting point rather than endpoint of imagining otherwise. What kinds of historical and political possibilities does such a move allow us to imagine or temporarily inhabit? Recitation, then, combines with my other citation tactic of de-authorization to constitute a consistent intervention into the political grammar of Western feminist storytelling that runs through the book.

My introduction of tactical recitation, above, states that I start from "what is precluded in dominant citational practice" and move forward, as if identifying absent presences were not itself a selective process. If citation is selective in ways I have suggested, then so too must be my own identification of what is lost. This is the danger of correctives I have been warning about throughout this introduction, of course. Consideration of this problem has lead me both to clarify that recitation is limited by its original frames of engagement (i.e., it is not an "anything goes" approach) and to explore more fully the importance of a motivated relation to Western feminist theory as the basis of a reflexive, accountable historiography. Feminist theory is filled with passion and with passionate attachments. Their expression forms the very stuff of feminist language, makes feminist theory alive, and produces passionate responses in audiences in turn. And one need only look at the hostile online responses to feminist writing in news media to see that these responses are just as motivated as their originals. Indeed, fury is one of the primary modes of antifeminist expression, despite its frequent claim to have moved beyond politics. Attempting to answer that question of motivation—in the stories I tell as well as those I analyze, and the relationship between these—has lead me to integrate questions of affect as central both to how narratives of progress, loss, and return function and as key to effective intervention at the level of a transformative political grammar.[19]

Affects of despair and hope, resentment and passion form the very currency of Western feminist narratives of progress, loss, and return. They presume a shared affective state, if not shared emotions.[20] Thus, loss narratives work through appealing to that sense of loss the narrator assumes is already present in the reader, providing a shared affective platform. Who is to blame for this loss, what needs to happen next and so on, is often less significant than this shared starting point, which overrides differences in historiographic interpretation. Progress narratives similarly presume a shared sense of pleasure at having overcome the worst excesses of a unified feminism, however we may have come to this present, more sophisticated, state of affairs. In this respect attention to the affective registers of Western feminist storytelling allows me to concentrate on the politics of the present in ways that are crucial for this project. Further, the use of emotional appeals in Western feminist narratives positions the teller of tales as heroic, triumphant, wounded, or marginalized in turn, bolsters this affective underside, and actively works to create agreement through identification. Indeed, lack of identification risks readerly positioning as the antiheroine: as self-interested, privileged, or narcissistic instead. Western feminist theorists make narrative judgements and foreclose other narrative possibilities, set subject up against object, theory against politics, now against then, and here against there, in part through mobilizing affect. Thus, although I am wary of being drawn into a critical process that privileges affect over politics in my reading of narrative, it is also clear to me that affect is part of the *texture* of narrative and political investments in feminist theory (Sedgwick 2003).

Following Gilles Deleuze and Silvan Tomkins respectively, Brian Massumi and Eve Sedgwick conceive of affects as having an ontological life that cannot be analyzed through epistemological frames or through their reduction to social structures (Massumi 2002; Sedgwick 2003). Yet perhaps they might also tell us something about the affective life of those same social structures, particularly when conceived of in terms of investments in past and future collectivities, as is the case in this project. Indeed, in following affect through the book what has struck me most is how this attention can reveal aspects of narrative meaning otherwise obscured, rather than revealing something outside of narrative altogether (Staunaes 2010). In this sense, alongside Lauren Berlant (1997; 2004) and the Jacques Derrida of *The Politics of Friendship* (1997), I understand analysis of affect as key to reading the relationship between the epistemological and the ontological. Elspeth Probyn's work on the tension between gendered epistemology and ontological experience as the basis for a reflexive feminist politics might indicate affect as a key object for a reflexive feminist criticism.[21] Further, attention to affect may take us along different paths because its presence often represents a substitution of one motivation for another (because direct reflection on affect is often too difficult) and thus needs to be analyzed through *association* rather than through opposition or exclusion.

If attention to affect is important in reading narratives of progress, loss, and return in all their complexity, it is also important intersubjectively in terms of how it positions me as well as other readers. As Sara Ahmed has indicated, the affective nature of intersubjective formation means that there is no "outside affect," no place to retreat to in order not to be moved (2004c; 2004b; 2004a). Indeed, it is partly through trying to trace my own relationship to Western feminist stories that I have become convinced of the importance of affect in the sustaining of critical attachment to one version of the past or another. Throughout this introduction and the mapping in part 1, for example, I represent my own priorities as concerned with the pertinent racial and sexual absences that occur when feminist theory is understood to have left feminism behind and with the relation of these absences to larger social and political mobilizations of gender equality discourse. This is a rather admirable set of investments, I am sure you will agree, one definitionally likely to uncover less worthy aims in the texts I read. Yet it proposes my critical position as outside of the narratives I examine, one invested in exposing their exclusions as if they were not also my own. Tracking my own affect is instructive, in that this "admirable neutrality" is of course impossible to sustain throughout the book. I am most unable to maintain this distance in my mapping of loss narratives, where I am directly implicated as a "co-opted professional feminist" in the accounts I read. My rage at being misrepresented is expressed as scorn, a set of emotional registers that enable me to preserve the prior convictions about poststructuralism as *not this* that I bring to the text. Intellectually and politically enlivened in the 1990s by queer, postcolonial, feminist poststructuralist theories, I see my past self, and the life and times of my pomo-comrades, dissolving in narratives that evoke "those days" as ones of critique alone. In loss narratives, we are not only subject to feminism's demise, we are also responsible for it; hence the spilling over of rage evidenced in textual tone. My smug interest in racial and sexual exclusions is thus tempered by a prior interest in their inclusion remaining part of the poststructuralism I need to remember myself by.

And perhaps too my own reticence at revealing these attachments from the outset has something to do with not wanting to be dismissed as anachronistic in this era of "post-poststructuralism": far better to be rescuing something or someone else. I too have an affective state to preserve it seems, one that positions me fully within rather than outside of these debates, saturated with epistemological–ontological tension. This tracking of affect as revealing of something brought to as well as revealed in the text is also central to the last chapter of this book, where I explore the limits of a Western feminist fantasy of its own progress through a focus on affective excess. In this second experiment I intervene in dominant political grammars of Western feminism by starting from stasis or explosion as a failure of linguistic representation. As with recitation, my second experiment of part 2 is to imagine a history of feminist theory in which the affective consolidation of the subject is disrupted for a moment and to explore how this subject puts herself back together again. I propose this approach as a way of exploring both what is preserved when narrative fails and what new formations might emerge between the cracks of what we think we already know (and feel) about one another. Such an approach also centres affect without figuring it as outside narrative or beyond the text. Both interventions—recitation and affective mobilization—constitute experimental approaches to telling stories differently so that feminist theory might be less amenable to co-optation. Both experiments start from textual and political absences in the stories we already participate in, explicitly folding these back into narrative in order to reconfigure the political grammars of Western feminism. They offer ways of *approaching* feminist stories and politics over the temptation to produce a more correct account and thus prioritize the unknown over the known and refusal over acceptance. In this respect, both interventions develop new qualitative approaches that require attention to memory, desire, and uncertainty as central to feminist practice and radical politics, and that are intended for use, should you find them useful.

PART ONE

PROGRESS

1 The following statement from *Feminist Theory* is as uncontroversial as it is typical of accounts that describe Western feminist theory's development over time:

There is no disputing that feminist theory, methodology and practice have undergone substantial change since the heady days of the late 1960s and early 1970s. Pressure from within and outside and rapidly changing contexts have resulted in a multiplicity of theoretical and practical approaches to the issue of how to challenge and change the gendered nature of everyday life. (*Feminist Theory* 2003)[1]

It is self-evident—"there is no disputing"—that the last four decades of feminist theorizing, together with the uneven but tangible emergence of academic feminism, have resulted in an increased range of theoretical frameworks to draw on, as well as an increased number of feminist texts published. It is not only the proliferation of approaches and methods that we can be certain about, but, as the extract below makes clear, the displacement of one set of approaches by others, the move from natural, essential truths to the uncertain pleasures and dangers of post-structuralist approaches:

As we all know, the study of gender and sexualities in the humanities and social sciences of the past 15 years has been characterized by the prominence of post-structuralist analytical approaches that challenge the biology-based naturalness of genders and sexualities, and emphasize, in different ways, the socio-cultural and discursive construction of sexual categories and identities. (*Nora* 2005)

Further, not only do "we all know" that this trajectory accurately describes what has happened in the study of gender and sexualities, but we can also all agree that such theoretical transformations are in line with, in fact propel, transformations in the object of study—gender and sexuality—itself:

Without question, certain historical developments, technologies and theoretical insights have forced gender's slide from sexed bodies. Ranging from queer fantasy and transsexual surgeries to critiques of essentialism, these developments make it seem that there is little which is true, fixable or stable about gender meanings. (*Feminist Theory* 2003)

Where we used to accept natural, biological givens, perhaps because things were simpler back then, we now need and have theoretical insights and practices that are more appropriate to the complex world we currently inhabit, one our theoretical insights have played their part in creating. As I hope is clear from the extracts I have introduced thus far, such assertions about the transformations understood to typify both theory and the world it engages (or produces) leave no room for doubt; indeed the more assertive the statement—"without question"—the more singular the story about the recent past of Western feminist theory appears to be.

But what if we do not "all know" the same things about what has happened in Western feminist theory's recent past; what if we were to understand the "we" of the address as inaugurated by rather than inaugurating this repeated certainty? What if we start to dispute that which there "is no disputing" and begin to query its relentless rhetoric? What if we approach the question of Western feminist theory's recent past with greater hesitancy and ask both what is missed in the certainty of such progress narratives and what some of the effects of the same certainty might be? What does such incontrovertibility tell us about the present and those "heady days" long past, beyond what we are already expected to know?

How might the development of a sceptical relationship to what Megan Jones characterizes as "the conceptual truth-claims of feminist thought" (1998: 118) provide insights into what these descriptions do and how they do it? As indicated in my introduction, I want to start the analysis of Western feminist storytelling here with a dual approach: on the one hand, holding in mind that such narrative insistence can never be entirely accurate, is always at least contested; and on the other, asking after the work that this narrative momentum effects, what it inculcates, particularly in its authoritatively descriptive guise. In this approach, I have been particularly influenced by Robyn Wiegman's careful readings of the multiplicities that make up U.S. academic feminism's institutional history, and her insistence that singular feminist narratives about that history actively work to depoliticize the field (1999a; 2002; 2004).[2]

In this chapter I extend my line of inquiry by mapping, sceptically, Western feminist progress narratives, with particular attention to how the meaning and momentum of this aspect of Western feminist storytelling is textually secured and mobilized. This first chapter will provide the building blocks of my subsequent analysis of loss and return narratives, which use similar markers to complicate the story, and reinflect these to different ends. Let me provide a range of initial examples from some of the journals I have analysed to get the discussion underway:

Over the past decade, general theorists within feminism have developed increasingly sophisticated responses to questions about how best to theorize power and subjectivity. . . . (*Signs* 2000)

The development of Women's Studies occurs through crucial shifts in the theoretical paradigms of feminism and the political preoccupations of the women's movement. These shifts have both deconstructed the founding premises of feminist theory and generated a greater depth to feminist thinking and research. (*Feminist Review* 1999)

During the 1970s we could argue straightforwardly that women were marginalized and subordinate—that women lived and suffered under patriarchy. This claim now requires some urgent refiguring in order to move towards a more nuanced understanding of how and why marginalization and subordination continue and how they were changed. (*Feminist Review* 2000)

The breadth of feminist issues is now much broader than ever before and intersects with a number of theories about gender, race and ethnicity, sexuality, class, corporeality and popular culture, to name just some areas of current complex feminist discussion. (*Feminist Theory* 2002)

First, the question of universal female subordination is set in focus, then the second phase, when eyes are opened for "the differences of the difference," and a third deconstructivist phase where multiple genders, floating gender boundaries and the body become the key issues of interest. (*Nora* 2001)

Identity politics has overcome the homogenizing tendencies of second-wave feminism by acknowledging the differences among women and, most significantly, attacking the hierarchy concealed in the category "woman". (*Feminist Theory* 2000)

The most interesting and far reaching of the rethinking of theoretical frameworks and of feminism itself would be the rewriting of the mind-body split and the rethinking of the sex/gender distinction. These poststructuralist feminist arguments had radical consequences for the understanding of the gendered nature of knowledges, and even more significant consequences for the ways in which identities came to be understood as multiple, unstable positions which could therefore be negotiated and possibly changed. (*Australian Feminist Studies* 2000)

I have included the above examples all together to give a sense of this narrative of progress told across journal sites on either side of the millennium as one that is general and repeated. It is, I expect, a story familiar to many readers, and one that we are likely to reproduce ourselves in teaching or writing contexts. It is a story I was told as a student in the mid-1990s, and one I find myself telling students now, whatever my intentions. In one way or another, through curriculum design, through what is included in an "advanced" or "introductory" academic feminist class, or through the narratives we produce in lectures or in our readings and corrections of student work, we reproduce this understanding of Western feminist theory as having progressed, and in a particular manner. We have moved from a time when we knew no better, a time when we thought "woman" could be the subject and object of liberation, to a more knowing time in which we attend to the complexity of local and transnational formations of gender and its intersections with other vectors of power. Further, in the extracts above, this is a familiar account of the institutionalization of feminist knowledge and thus describes the development of "Women's Studies" (from the second extract) as well as feminist theory more generally. Indeed, in both progress and loss narratives, academic feminism is often understood as an agent, one that has acted upon and transformed Western feminist theory and practice.

I will return to some of the more intricate themes represented in the above extracts later in the chapter, but for now I want to outline some of the more striking features of a progress narrative. First, it is clearly a positive account, one told with excitement and even relish. It is a narrative of success and accomplishment and positions feminist theory, and its subjects, as attentive and dynamic. Second, it is a narrative with a clear chronology: we are taken from the past—in one extract explicitly the 1970s—via key shifts in politics, theory, and feminism's subject, and towards a complex feminist present. The shifts represented are from singularity of purpose and perspective to understandings that emphasize multiplicity, instability, and difference. The enthusiasm for these shifts is enacted through the use of terms describing current approaches as "interesting," "far reaching," "complex," generative of greater "depth" and nuance, "increasingly sophisticated," and so on. Indeed, the epistemological shifts referred to are consistently rendered as possessing the urgency and eye-opening capacities of a new political moment. Third, these shifts in time and approach are not represented as an inevitable flowering of difference and multiplicity, but are the outcome of that critical energy, directed explicitly at older approaches seen as lacking. In the extracts cited above, "founding premises" are "deconstructed," assumptions about women's subordination require "urgent refiguring," and "homogenizing tendencies" must be "overcome." Feminist theory has moved away from, indeed has directly distanced itself from, earlier preoccupations with "patriarchy," "woman," and "female subordination," focusing instead on intersections of power—"gender, race and ethnicity, sexuality, class"—the "gendered nature of knowledges," and the limits of earlier approaches. Thus, a Western feminist progress narrative transforms rather than merely adds to existing approaches, deconstructs and moves beyond as well as forward. The story is one of change brought about through displacement: of feminist objects, epistemologies, and subjects. Integral to the momentum in the above extracts is the enthusiasm about these transformations in both object of inquiry and methodology. Western feminist progress narratives position their subjects as energetic and analytically astute, as generative of and residing in a well-earned state of positive affect.

How do these common glosses work to persuade their reader that the shifts they describe are both accurate and desirable? How do they produce the enthusiasm we are likely to want to share? We can already see that the work is not achieved by direct citation of particular theorists, or by analytic attention to debates over any of these issues. Instead the narrative certainty is textually achieved by techniques of comparisons that propel the momentum described above, that combine time and critique to create the appealing endorsement outlined above. We can see this textual technique already in the above extracts, which describe a trajectory from sameness to difference, singularity to multiplicity, or simplicity to complexity. Further, these relationships are temporally secured, where the former term belongs to the past and the latter term to the present. The shifts are complete; the past is over. Neither is the move from sameness to difference a neutral one occurring gently with the passing of time. Sameness is consigned to the past precisely because of the critical efforts of those who occupy the present position of difference, as indicated above. Thus the characterization of feminist sameness or singularity is as not only over but as necessarily over, dusted as well as done. In this respect, a critical as well as temporal hierarchy is established between textual comparisons between terms. Laying claim to being the subject of this Western feminist progress narrative, laying claim to being on the side of complexity and multiplicity, enthusiasm rather than nostalgia, one thus adopts a shared past, and crucially, one that is displaced through that very enthusiasm in the present. In narrative terms, one is not given the opportunity to choose homogeneity or singularity instead, because we will want to be on the side of sophistication not homogenization, proliferation not unidimensionality, intersectionality not intractability, and thus belief not defeatism. We will want to take up the opportunities these narratives provide to be an optimistic subject of Western feminist theory.

To take up the desired position of subject of this critical displacement, the required shift is not only from one set of objects or concerns to another, but also from one set of perspectives, approaches, or methodologies to another. These reveal and effect the displacement necessary to produce the present narrated in progress narratives. Shifts are not only from sameness to difference, then, but also from the epistemological and ontological assumptions central to their logic. As the above extracts emphasize, instead of an emphasis on and investment in female experience as the ground of feminist knowledge and action, we must insist on the irreducibility of gendered experiences, and thus on the instability of experience as a term and ground for Western feminist inquiry. And instead of an investment in sex/gender as a critical tool to reveal kinship norms and social structures, we insist on deconstruction as the primary tool for revealing sex/gender's exclusions. In contrast to asserting women's universal subordination and the importance of its transformation into action, we focus on power as diffuse and changing, and the subjects and objects of violence or marginality as not fully known in advance. These shifts do more than describe the terms sameness and difference themselves. They describe shifts in critical investments and methodologies that transform what we mean by the key terms—and related terms such as power, subjectivity, and agency—as well. In effect, in charting moves from sameness to difference, and singularity to multiplicity, Western feminist progress narratives also chart a move from one set of schools of thought—radical or socialist—to another—poststructuralist or postcolonial.[3] As an attempt to represent the complicated relationship between sameness and difference and other related textual pairs, I often denote this as sameness → difference. I do so to highlight the epistemological and temporal direction of the comparison, in which the latter term critically transforms rather than merely comes after the former.

The binary relationships described and instantiated here not only anchor theoretical, political, and temporal shifts, but disciplinary ones too. If we have displaced experience as the ground of feminist knowledge production, we have also displaced empirical observation as a primary feminist method for accessing and transforming the social world. If instead we celebrate the possibilities opened up by a focus on what was excluded in these former accounts, then we come to prioritize textual deconstruction as a method too. How we understand power will thus also determine what we think comprises an effective intervention. This next, rather early, extract is particularly explicit about the methodological underpinnings of the Western feminist progress narrative:

Empirical studies conducted from a range of theoretical perspectives (radical, socialist and liberal feminist) have all in some way affirmed the existence of women's experience as a source of privileged understandings, if not the basis of an alternative social science. Now, however, the deconstruction of "women" is having profoundly destabilising effects upon feminist theorising and research. . . .

With the turn to post-modernism many of the certainties of a feminist research practice have been dislodged. This has liberated a plethora of exciting philosophical, political and cultural endeavours that tackle the essentialism around women embedded in both feminist and non-feminist texts. At the same time, however, feminist social analysts find themselves confronting an ironic impasse as what have been seen as the unifying objects of our research dissolve before our eyes. (*Gender, Place and Culture* 1994)

Empiricism, women's experience, and essentialism are fused in this account, such that a change in methodology and an interdisciplinary "post-modern" perspective can be framed as uniquely able to "tackle the essentialism" and the "certainties of a feminist research practice" of the past.[4] In the process the objects of inquiry also alter; a focus on "culture" rather than "social reality" references these overlapping epistemological transitions. As indicated in the final line of the above quotation, uncertainty about this move from the social sciences to the interdisciplinary humanities becomes an important rallying point for Western feminist return narratives that stress the need to recover not only lost objects of feminism that seem to "dissolve before our eyes," but lost disciplinary methodologies as well.

WHEN IS THE PAST?

To return to the chronological aspect of this story, temporal transitions are combined with assumptions about the theoretical, epistemological, methodological, or political shifts discussed above to ensure that the latter can be assumed to have happened once and for all. Western feminist progress narratives produce a clear sense of what comes when in feminist theory, what is displaced, what takes place in the present, and what the future holds. What takes place in the past is cast as irredeemably anachronistic, in order that the present can represent the theoretical cutting edge.[5] A key concept for the chronology of Western feminist progress narratives is "essentialism," which is both that which has been transcended and the political and intellectual reason for that transcendence. Essentialism is, as we know, never a good thing; its negative characteristics are so self-evident that uncovering evidence of it in any school of thought or text has the potential to consign it to an intellectual backwater from which it cannot return.[6] In progress narratives, essentialism and anachronism are frequently tied up with each other, mutually constitutive of the need for difference, the very opposite of what constitutes theoretical rigour and accountability in the present.

But to say that essentialism is anachronistic, or that it is over, does not give us a very precise sense of when these essentialist ills are assumed to have taken place, or when they were critiqued and overcome. In the series of extracts I introduced above, only one names a precise decade—the 1970s—as the site of this particular anachronism. The overwhelming majority of progress narrative glosses do not name the 1970s directly; instead changes are more euphemistically temporalized, as is the case in this extract from *Feminist Theory*:

There are, undoubtedly, some feminist (and other) approaches which take absolutist and essentialist approaches to questions of difference and social location. Yet, one of the heartening developments in feminist theory and practice over the past few years has been the increasing take-up of positions which are concerned to build temporary, strategic alliances across differences. (*Feminist Theory* 2000)

"The past few years" remains obscure, the phrase's function less to explore that past than to reassure its reader that the present is a time of proliferation. So accepted is this view that neither the past nor its transitional phase need citation or discussion: once the business of reiterating the credentials of the present is out of the way, we can move to more controversial considerations. Yet despite this lack of direct decade naming, we do know that it is the 1970s that carries the weight of essentialist anachronism in Western feminist progress narratives. Intertextually and imaginatively, the 1970s is consistently marked as thoroughly unified in its aims, unreflexive in its theorizations, yet bold in its ambitions. By intertextually, I mean that texts outside of the glosses I am analyzing here often do explicitly name the 1970s as "already composed in a fairly fixed way, and this with particular effects" (Bashford 1998: 51). Megan Jones notes that "the feminisms of 1970s Australia are often perceived as a unitary, simplistic and predominantly uncomplicated whole . . . [that] constructs an unsophisticated feminism at its beginnings in the 1970s and progresses to the supposedly sophisticated feminisms of the 1990s—feminisms of plurality, multiplicities of meaning and complex specificities" (1998: 117). By imaginatively, I mean that "the 1970s" as a decade may be referred to through its presumed essentialist dimensions in part because this fits with our broader sense of what has happened in Western feminist theory and our attachment to not being essentialist any longer. I should note here that I am not contesting the idea that many 1970s texts might be deemed "essentialist" and that essentialism all too frequently has problematic effects; indeed it does. But I am struck nevertheless by the textual containment of essentialism in the 1970s in progress narratives and in ways that this (irredeemable) ill attaches to the 1970s *as a decade.*

More than through intertextual or imaginative modes, however, our knowledge that the 1970s is "the essentialist decade"—whether or not it is named—is secured in Western feminist progress narratives through other, more precise, decade naming. Thus, we often know that the 1990s (or later) is the site of difference and multiplicity, both because this is often the time of writing and because it is directly cited as representing these self-evidently good things. But this naming of the 1990s is patchy too and heavily reliant on the role of the 1980s. In Western feminist progress narratives the 1980s is the most directly named decade, burdened with the responsibility for moving feminist theory from a generalized, generalizing past to a differentiated, differentiating present. The following example from *Women's Studies International Forum* is typical:

During the 1980s there was another, compelling, reason for questioning the category "women," in that it served to conceal differences among women and to privilege definitions of womanhood framed from White Western viewpoints. Once this ethnocentrism was exposed it became clear that "women" has never been a unitary category (Brah, 1991). (*Women's Studies International Forum* 2001)

The 1980s takes on a kind of explanatory role in progress narratives, temporally anchoring the growing realization of difference, bringing to light the problems of unity, acting as a stepping stone to postmodernism or poststructuralism, however understood. The transformation of feminist theory is serialized, with the 1980s acting as the pivot or transition point for the emergence of a fully realized focus on difference. The direct mention of the 1980s, more consistently than any other decade in progress narratives, ensures that anachronistic essentialism belongs to the 1970s, as suggested, but it also ensures that it too is transcended by what comes afterwards. Thus, we see that contemporary approaches to difference were unquestionably "shaped by a post-1980s pendulum swing within feminist theory and research" (*Feminist Review* 1999) and that,

By the eighties, changes were taking place that laid the groundwork for the third phase of feminist criticism, which I will call the engendering of differences. (*Critical Inquiry* 1998)

These last two quotations make clear that in progress narratives (within and beyond interdisciplinary feminist journals) the 1980s functions as a catalytic decade rather than as a decade of arrival: the changes taking place then pave the way for something else; a pendulum swing finds its level only after several swings back and forth. It is consistently "identity" that is positioned as that which moves Western feminist theorizing away from universal claims about "woman" and sisterhood (see citation from *Feminist Theory* 2000 above), but also as that which itself needs to be moved on from for fragmentation not to result in reification. Identity, as I explore below, is thus rather strangely located as poststructuralist ally, and simultaneously as difference's antonym.

The combination within Western feminist progress narratives of textual pairings and chronological ordering that assumes the essentialist past belongs to and resides in the 1970s, with difference proper taking place in the 1990s and beyond, means that we can tell this story without needing to include all of its component parts. Thus, in very general glosses of Western feminist theory's development, even those that contest some of its presumptions such as the those below, utilize familiar markers:

I reject the argument that there are insuperable chasms between the knowledges of different communities, and am against settling for the defeatism and isolationism of forever partial and situated knowledges. (*Feminist Theory* 2000)

What [remains] . . . unexplored are questions of how to formulate in explicit terms the relation between female subjection and multiply positioned, unstable female subjects, between patriarchal power and the regulation of female self-difference. (*Feminist Studies* 2001)

While both extracts make the case for bridging the gaps between different schools of thought and do not prioritize one framework over another, they do nevertheless reinforce the temporality I am discussing here. In the first quotation, "knowledges of different communities" are counterposed to "partial and situated knowledges"; in the second, "female subjection" is compared to "regulation of female self-difference," mirroring the techniques of singularity → multiplicity, sameness → difference that underpin the chronology I am interested in unpacking. In fact, these general state-ments only make sense insofar as we understand them as already tied to a chronology comparing the 1970s with the 1990s. In considering the tech-niques that make up the political grammar of Western feminist progress narratives, then, I am also struck by the fact that not all parts of the chain of associations that make up the narrative as a whole need to be present in a particular gloss for the others to become resonant. Indeed, this is how the different components signify, as standing in for the narrative overall and as concomitantly reliant on that whole for singular meaning.

DIFFERENCES A DECADE MAKES

If the 1980s is the decade of transition in these narratives, it marks a very particular kind of transition. In Western feminist progress narratives the 1980s is marked as the decade of critique of universal categories and essentialist presumption as we have seen, but it is also marked as the decade of located critique. The 1980s offers an interrogation of 1970s exclusions from particular positions, and with particular, and often multi-ple, differences in mind. The following two extracts are typical of the ways in which a variety of subjects and critiques come to occupy this overburdened decade:

Perhaps the most important legacy of 1980s feminism is the crucial concern with difference: differences between women in race, class, sexuality, and nation; and differences within particular women, with gender conceived as one of a number of social categories that are coarticulated in female subjects. (*Feminist Studies* 2001)

Since the early 1980s, lesbians, feminists of color, postcolonial critics, and queer theorists, as well as postfeminist and antifeminist women, have exposed the ethnocentric conceits and consequences of the foundational categories of West-ern feminist thought—women, gender and sex. (*Signs* 2000)

In both excerpts the 1980s is marked as the decade where proliferation and interrogation coincide. The "crucial concern with difference" in the first extract emphasizes gender's "coarticulation" with "other" axes of differ-ence, typically "race, class, sexuality, and nation," while the second extract focuses on the subjects articulating these critiques, namely "lesbians, femi-nists of color, postcolonial critics, and queer theorists." In this respect, the

1980s is represented as the decade in which critical mode and subject of critique coincide. Thus, differences of "race, class, sexuality, and nation" are exposed by subjects whose identities are formed through their marginal locations. In other words, it is "lesbians . . . and queer theorists," and "feminists of color . . . [and] postcolonial critics" who reveal "ethnocentric conceits and consequences" of "women, gender and sex." This is a common pattern across the journals. As part of a Western feminist progress narrative, the 1980s is heralded as the decade of emergent black feminist and lesbian critique in particular, both in terms of what constitutes the appropriate object of analysis and of its speaking or writing subject. Yet as I indicate later, these subjects and objects of inquiry are not positioned entirely equally. Although most work identifying the 1980s as the site of the emergence of complex Western feminist analysis frames this period as one of attention to multiple differences, what is overwhelmingly focused on is the critical assessment of white, Western feminism as endeavoring to represent all women. The extract from *Signs* above is instructive in this respect as it includes a range of subject positions making critiques of "the foundational categories of Western feminist thought," but what is critiqued by all of them is the same problem: ethnocentrism, rather than, say, heterosexism and ethnocentrism.

The 1980s attention to racism and ethnocentrism in prior feminist work constitutes a dominant theme in progress narratives. Progress narratives thus reflect the importance of critiques of white, Western feminism and reiterate the significant damage caused and privileges maintained when feminists assume that white, middle-class women are the *de facto* subjects of feminism. The critique provided, as progress glosses make particularly apparent, precipitates feminist analysis into a more enlightened era of interrogation of Western feminism from within. The two following excerpts give a flavour of how these glosses scan:

During the 1980s . . . the notion of "woman" that had been the focus of feminist study was recognised as colour, class, and nation specific. The result of this critique was a new or increased emphasis on differences among women. (*Australian Feminist Studies* 2000)

For example, the writings of black women in the 1970s and 1980s were concerned to get difference debated by white as well as black feminists (Bryan et al., 1985; Mirza, 1997; Sudbury, 1998). (*Feminist Theory* 2000)

As in the prior examples from *Feminist Studies* and *Signs*, a range of differences are brought forward in the 1980s to critique homogeneity, and a range of subjects are implicated as needing to shift their own critical attentions. Yet what interests me about these examples is the temporality that anchors the narrative and contains the critical direction it represents. In the *Feminist Studies* and *Signs* examples, difference is a 1980s "legacy," inaugurated after the 1970s and brought forward into the present of writing. And in the above extracts, too, the 1980s marks a shift away from the problematic previous emphasis on "woman" as the singular object of feminist inquiry. As discussed earlier, this is a common technique of rendering the present more sophisticated and multiple than the past and a way of dismissing the 1970s as anachronistic and essentialist. This is straightforward in the first example. In the second, even though (unusually) black women's writings from the 1970s as well as the 1980s are mentioned, note that the citations included are from the 1980s and 1990s (reprints in anthologies rather than original publication dates are chosen here). The momentum is thus forward rather than backward even where citation practice is more ambivalent.

Such historiographic practices have several effects. First, they mark the 1970s (or before) as the decade that contains the problems highlighted in the 1980s. One effect of this I have already flagged is to code the essentialism of the 1970s not only as a misplaced belief in sisterhood but also as a primarily racially exclusive one. The anxiety of being labeled essentialist or anachronistic within Western feminist theory is thus a more precise anxiety of being understood as racist; this historiographic narrative tactic more than any other ensures a Western feminist disidentification with its imagined past. Second, the temporality of such glosses fixes black feminist critique in the 1980s from the other side too, allowing Western feminist theory to represent itself as *increasingly* attentive to difference—particularly racial difference—as well as coding the past as notably inattentive to the same. In the above extracts it is feminist theory as an enterprise that has shifted as a result of these critiques, resulting in "increased emphasis on differences" in the first and debate about difference across racial locations moving into the 1990s in the second. In the first two examples the 1980s leaves a "legacy" for the present and inaugurates Western feminist theory's increasing sophistication and attention to multiplicity. In this respect, black feminist critique is frequently inscribed in Western feminist progress narratives as *catalyst* to a more general focus on difference.

This forward momentum from exclusion to inclusion is achieved by a variety of techniques of comparison and citation that situate black feminist critiques as essential to the transformation of Western feminist theory, but ultimately as transcended. The following extract provides the typical chronology:

Initiated by feminists of color who called attention to their exclusion and/or misrepresentation by mainstream feminist accounts of "women", the focus on women's differences was underwritten as well by poststructuralist feminism. Both critiques have produced the most recent object of feminist theoretical inquiry: the female subject who inhabits diverse cultural locations and for whom gender is dynamically engaged with numerous other social categories and discourses. (*Feminist Studies* 2001)

In this example the "focus on women's differences" is once again framed as a legacy, one that enables a fuller consideration of a different kind of object, one who is not in fact named, but is "a subject who inhabits diverse cultural locations." In this quotation the shift in emphasis is "initiated by feminists of color" and "underwritten . . . by poststructuralist feminism"; it is a combined move that leads to the present subjective mobility of our research focus. Note too that, by the end of the extract, "exclusion and/or misrepresentation" have been replaced by a "dynamically engaged" female subject. The transitions Western feminist theory has made have also transformed the object of inquiry into an agent rather than a victim of power. This shift is essential in order that the present be a space of positive affect, of celebration at the accomplishments of Western feminist theory, rather than a space of conflict or irresolution.[7]

The next excerpt makes this framing of racial critique as a developmental stage clearer still:

Two related intellectual debates provided the impetus for critical reflection on "the subject" of feminist thinking. First, women of color and Third World women feminists critiqued "the subject" implicit within most feminist thought at the time, a subject that normalized the experience of white, middle-class, first-world women (hooks, 1984; Trinh, 1989). This critique stimulated greater interest in the multiplicity of oppression and fractured the notion of "woman" and her experience(s). Second, a growing interest in post-structural psychoanalytical perspectives (e.g. those of Lacan and Derrida), as well as Foucault's notion of power/discourse, also profoundly affected feminist theory. Feminists appreciated post-structural attempts to deploy an anti-essentialist world-view, reject totalizing 'grand' theory, and embrace multiplicity, difference and the "decentred" subject (Sarup, 1988). (*Gender, Place and Culture* 1999)

While black feminism and "post-structural psychoanalytic" accounts are on one level represented here as of the same era (all citations are from the 1980s) and as having related concerns, the temporality I am tracing is reinforced through the ordering of critiques: "poststructuralism" comes "second." Further, the "first" set of critiques is described as stimulating "greater interest in multiplicity," rather than evidencing that interest *tout court*. This ordering of theoretical engagement is reinforced by the use of the past tense in describing the critiques of women of color and Third World feminists, while the "growing interest" in poststructuralism is linguistically active, allowing its proponents to continue to "deploy," "reject" and "embrace." Thus, poststructuralism imaginatively spills over into the next decade, while the critiques of women of color and Third World women are temporally fixed by their frames of citation, becoming tropes in the service of a teleology they are no longer the subjects of. In the extract from *Signs* cited earlier (on page 42), the ordering of critics is similarly instructive, though perhaps less immediately evident. Here, critical exploration of "foundational categories" has been occurring "since the early 1980s" from "lesbians, feminists of color, postcolonial critics, and queer theorists, as well as postfeminist and antifeminist women." My analysis in this section has suggested that this ordering is pivotal rather than accidental, leading from identity politics to epistemological and ontological challenges to authenticity and further to the rejection of feminism altogether.

It is not entirely accurate to suggest that these shifts to difference are always represented as occurring first in the 1980s, however, while this is certainly a common trend. Alongside narratives that directly highlight the transitional role of that decade in the achievement of a contemporary era of flexibility and difference in both feminist object and subject, there are others that locate this focus more firmly in the 1990s. Thus, to extend a quotation I included a fragment of earlier in this chapter:

Over the past decade, general theorists within feminism have developed increasingly sophisticated responses to questions about how best to theorize power and subjectivity. . . .

To this end, theorists such as Joan Scott (1988), Elizabeth Spelman (1990), Iris Young (1990), Chantal Mouffe (1992), Anne McClintock (1995), Leonore

Davidoff (1995), Nira Yuval Davis (1997), and Ruth Lister (1998) have begun to formulate various ways of addressing the multiplicity of subject positions that women, as bearers of classed, racialized, national, ethnic, sexual, and aged as well as gendered identities, occupy in relation both to men and to each other. (*Signs* 2000)

Here all citations of theorists attending to the "multiplicity of subject positions" are from the 1990s except Joan Scott, who is thus marked as rather precocious (as Haraway or Spivak often are in other contexts). A further example from the same journal suggests similarly that:

"Radical" feminists usually do acknowledge racism and economic marginalization as factors that render some women especially vulnerable to sexual and other forms of exploitation. However, they do not even begin to engage with the insights of 1990s post- or neo-colonial feminist theory, which teaches that "race, gender and class are not distinct realms of experience, existing in splendid isolation from each other; nor can they simply be yoked together retrospectively like armatures of Lego. Rather they come into existence in and through relation to each other—if in contradictory and conflictual ways" (McClintock 1995, 5). (*Signs* 2000)

There are several features of interest to me in this passage. The first is the routine association of "radical" feminism with a focus on women's oppression and marginalization, which here can address racism and classism, but only as what makes women vulnerable to "sexual . . . exploitation" (rather than as agents). The extract then jumps straight to the failure of such an approach to reach the giddy heights of 1990s sophistication in theorizing intersections within and across differences. Again it is McClintock from the 1990s who is cited. But what has happened to the 1980s in this formulation? Why is the 1990s credited with these insights when the dominant narration of change in Western feminist theory locates the beginning of these same insights in the previous decade?[8]

My reading of this apparent contradiction has to do with two issues mentioned earlier. The first is that in its role as the decade of theoretical and political catalyst, the 1980s is also historicized as concerned with identity rather than "difference proper." Thus its absence in such glosses serves as further evidence that these early attempts have been surpassed. The second is that, in line with the narrative techniques linking sameness → difference and singularity → multiplicity with empiricism → decon-

struction, the 1990s has to be understood to address these issues of difference in a fuller, more sophisticated manner, in order that the narrative
remain one of progress rather than stasis. Reading across all the examples
given in this section, the 1990s thus stands for an epistemological and
methodological plurality begun but not achieved in the 1980s, whether or
not the latter decade is explicitly mentioned. This temporality is reinforced in the following fragment:

Recent decades have seen the academic feminist discussion on decentring and
pluralizing the (white, western, heterosexual, middle-class) categories of gender
and woman by examining how other intersecting categories such as race, ethnicity, nation, class, generation, sexuality and disability shape or constitute gender
and women (see, for example Anthias and Davies 1992; Collins 1998; Crenshaw
1994; Lorde 1980; Oyewumi 2002; Young 1997). (*Nora* 2003)

Once again, the 1990s and onwards are cited as the intersectional de-
cade(s), moving us well beyond the "white, western, heterosexual, middle-
class" past. The citation of Audre Lorde as a very early exception (it is so
frequently Lorde) serves two functions here. It marks a threshold point
that reinforces our knowledge that this exclusionary past comes before
1980 and positions her as notable exception, separated from her closest
citational ally by over a decade. For me, it is particularly in these excerpts that pass over the 1980s that one of the most problematic effects of
"decade-fixing" of black feminist theory can be most fully appreciated: that
it allows for its subsequent textual and historical erasure or tokenization.

SEXUAL SUBVERSIONS

In Western feminist progress narratives, the 1980s is not only represented
as providing necessary critiques of white, Western feminism. This decade
also frequently carries responsibility for inaugurating the critique of feminism's heteronormativity. Where this is the case, the terms of the comparison mirror those already discussed above, with the 1980s signalling a
progressive move away from sexual as well as racial myopia. To return to
two extracts cited earlier, we are reminded that the 1980s represents a
transfer of attention in both object and subject of feminism:

Perhaps the most important legacy of 1980s feminism is the crucial concern with
difference: differences between women in race, class, sexuality, and nation; and

differences within particular women, with gender conceived as one of a number of social categories that are coarticulated in female subjects. (*Feminist Studies* 2001)

Since the early 1980s, lesbians, feminists of color, postcolonial critics, and queer theorists, as well as postfeminist and antifeminist women, have exposed the ethnocentric conceits and consequences of the foundational categories of Western feminist thought—women, gender and sex. (*Signs* 2000)

The 1980s thus opens feminism up to a range of newly appropriate objects and draws previously marginalized subjects, including sexual subjects, towards its centre.[9] As I discuss in more detail below, however, racial critique will always be prioritized in contexts where more than one form of critique is introduced or understood as competing, as the second extract above implies.

As with representations of black feminist critiques, the inclusion of sexuality in Western feminist progress narratives similarly pivots around the 1980s and contrasts the singularity of the past with an increased openness in the present. Thus, and typically:

From the feminist "sex wars" of the 1980s to the queer theory and politics of the 1990s, debates about the politics of sexuality have been at the forefront of contemporary theoretical, social, and political demands. In feminism's sex wars of the 1980s, pro-sex feminists argued, persuasively I think, that radical feminism's representation of women as disempowered actors fails to see women as sexual subjects in their own right. . . .

While radical feminists see "female sexuality" as repressed by "the patriarchy," the pro-sexuality movement sees repression as produced by heterosexism and "sex-negativity"—cultural operations often seen as institutionalized in feminism itself. (*Feminist Review* 2000)

In by now familiar ways, here radical feminism implicitly occupies the demonized 1970s and is imagined primarily in negative terms. While radical feminists "fail" to recognize sexual subjectivity, reducing "female sexuality" to repression, the pro-sex feminists of the 1980s are expansive, indeed are "at the forefront" of an impressive range of demands. Importantly, pro-sex feminists see women as "sexual subjects in their own right" rather than a patriarchal dupes. This emphasis on agency as marking temporal transition in progress narratives is most marked around sexual subjectivity, in fact. It indicates a shift from a concern with oppression and violence (and the concomitant need for liberation) and towards a focus on agency and pleasure (and thus new modes of political engagement). If the placing of pro-sexuality concerns in the 1980s (and later) were not enough to remind the reader of the inadequacies of what has been left behind, we might notice that the radical feminist claims in this passage are all in scare quotes, while the pro-sex positions remain unqualified (with the exception of the "sex wars" that brings together both perspectives in antagonistic relationship), a technique that underlines the extract's forward momentum. Again, however, as with the containment of black feminism, those pro-sex feminist positions themselves give way to the "queer theory and politics of the 1990s," the "wars" of the 1980s having been resolved in the latter's favour. Indeed, perhaps the scare quotes around the "sex wars" in the extract also signal precisely this inevitability: they are not really "wars," because they can only be resolved in one direction in Western feminist progress narratives.

This chronology of Western feminist sexual politics allows the specific steps that underwrite it to be easily passed over in much the same way as we saw in relation to black feminism. Thus:

Whereas the earlier generation of feminist scholars challenged patriarchal ideologies that reduced women's prime contribution to society to their "biological capacity" for nurturing and reproducing, the new gender theorists are fundamentally concerned with the historical subjectivity of sexed individuals and the embodiment of sexual identity, seen as indeterminate, ambiguous, multiple (Morris, 1995). For Judith Butler (1990, 1993), who argues that sexual identity is lived as a highly regulated performance, one is not female; one can only "do" female. (*Theory, Culture and Society* 1998)

The excerpt represents the familiar opposition between the challenges to "patriarchal ideologies" of "the earlier generation" and the "indeterminate, ambiguous, multiple" focus of the 1990s. The "earlier generation" needs no direct reference in the above quotation, its response to those "patriarchal ideologies" locating it firmly in the 1970s as we have seen. The narrative skips over what we can only presume happens in the 1980s, with the "new gender theorists" and their focus on indeterminacy and multiplicity remaining the only ones cited and temporally located in a direct way. Indeed, not only are Morris and Butler brought into the text, but Butler's texts are also lent precision by their differentiation from one another. As with black feminist containment in the 1980s, here "the sex wars" and sexual identity have been displaced by a move into difference proper, difference without fixed sexual object or subject.

While the role of sexual critique in Western feminist progress narratives mirrors that of racial critique in many ways, its taken-for-granted subjects are rather more ambivalently positioned. Thus in the extracts from *Feminist Review* and *Theory, Culture and Society* discussed above, we might also want to call attention to the fact that lesbian feminism and lesbian feminists are nowhere directly mentioned. They are not named in relation to a "pro-sex" feminist turn in the 1980s, despite the centrality of debates about lesbian sexual practices to those "sex wars," for example, in contrast to black feminists who are assumed to carry racial critique in the same era. And they are clearly not part of the 1990s, with its focus on indeterminacy and performance, rather than named identity. Perhaps we might find a lesbian resting somewhat uncomfortably under the term "female sexuality" instead? Or perhaps one can hear echoes of lesbian identity through its implicit challenge in the statement "one is not female; one can only 'do' female"? If this is the case, lesbian subjects may be more associated with the 1970s than their superficial inclusion in the "turn to difference" of the 1980s might lead one to believe. Certainly this dynamic is true of the following example, in which the 1980s is imagined as both the time of lesbian critique and the time of its undoing:

In 1980, Monique Wittig challenged lesbians and gay men to deny the divisive power of heterosexuality by refusing to think of themselves as women and men. More recently, postmodernists and queer theorists have questioned the twofold divisions of gender, sexuality and even sex, undermining the solidity of a world built on men/women, heterosexuals/homosexuals and male/female (Butler, 1990; Garber, 1992, 1995; Sedgwick, 1990). (*Feminist Theory* 2000)

Again, the extract produces a familiar chronology in which the 1990s figures as the bold inheritor of previous perspectives. But here Monique Wittig's role is ambiguous. As a lesbian theorist her citation marks the 1980s as a time of lesbian critique, yet her challenge is to "lesbians and gay men" to move beyond dualism. Both her injunction and the deconstructive call of the 1990s take sexual identity as their target, as that which must be surpassed, even while providing it with a history that crosses over several decades. More candid critiques of the accuracy of this picture of "redemptive inviolate lesbian feminism" as "something invented *about* the 1970s during the major sex wars of the 1980s" (*Feminist Review* 1999) nevertheless retain dominant assumptions about where the 1990s has taken us that retrospectively code previous decades as stages in the development of a taken-for-granted multiplicity and fluidity. This point echoes the one I make in the introduction that reformist histories do not necessarily attend to the problematic politics of the present, and thus offer revisionist rather than radical challenges to accounts of the feminist past.

Any ambivalence about the temporal, epistemological or political location of lesbian feminism is resolved when brought directly into comparative tension with black or postcolonial feminism, however. While both sexual and racial critique give way to "difference proper" in the 1990s and beyond, and while both lesbian and black feminist subjects give way to radical postmodern or poststructuralist indeterminacy, so too is their own encounter temporally and hierarchically ordered. When brought together, black feminists or ethnocentrism/racism as subject and object of critique take priority over lesbian feminists or heteronormativity/homophobia. We saw this in the example from *Signs* cited earlier, in which all manner of subjects expose ethnocentrism, rather than a range of exclusions produced by "the foundational categories of Western feminist thought." Here is the passage again as a reminder:

Since the early 1980s, lesbians, feminists of color, postcolonial critics, and queer theorists, as well as postfeminist and antifeminist women, have exposed the ethnocentric conceits and consequences of the foundational categories of Western feminist thought—women, gender and sex. (*Signs* 2000)

Further, when a direct critical relation is expressed chronologically, it is lesbian identity or politics/theory that is surpassed by black feminists or critical race feminism. This example from *Signs* demonstrates that relationship quite clearly, I think:

Beginning in the 1980s, the scholarship of feminists of color in the United States challenged lesbian studies as monolithic . . . (Moraga 1985; Lorde 1984; Anzaldúa 1987). (*Signs* 2003)

In the above excerpt, "feminists of color" are familiarly positioned in the 1980s (more explicitly than usual, indeed), as underlined by the chosen citations. But here this scholarship is pitted against lesbian studies rather than radical feminism more generally, a move that reinforces the ways in which "radical feminism" and "lesbian feminism" often come to stand in for one another in Western feminist progress narratives. Thus although in some versions of the progress narrative, feminist essentialism of the 1970s is rendered as *both* racist and heteronormative, in others lesbian essentialism is critiqued for its own racially marked exclusions. At no point did I come across a progress narrative gloss in which lesbian critique in the 1980s is represented as challenging prior black feminist exclusion; where the two are framed in sequence rather than coextensive, black feminism is always the one challenging exclusion and holding the temporal as well as moral high ground.[10] The above excerpt is interesting for another reason, too. The challenge to lesbian studies that takes place in this gloss is inaugurated by "feminists of color," but importantly the authors cited are all well-known *lesbians of color*. On the one hand, that would indicate a more complex relation and temporality than I have suggested here, one internal to rather than displacing of lesbian studies. But on the other, I am struck by the fact that their scholarship is textually represented as that of "feminists of color" and precisely not "lesbians of color," again prioritizing a singular, racialized, aspect of critical identity. In the process, these authors are utilized to effect their own erasure from their participation in feminism in the 1970s ("beginning in the 1980s" the text insists), in order that "lesbian studies as monolithic" signals a racial exclusion subsequently corrected.

A Western feminist progress narrative that moves from lesbian feminism to black feminism and on to postmodernism or poststructuralism chimes unnervingly with some of the broader cultural representations of lesbians, and of second wave feminism as anachronistically lesbian, that I outlined in my introduction. We are familiar with the stereotype of a 1970s feminist as an unfashionable, angry, man-hating lesbian. From tracing the relationship between black and lesbian feminists and feminism in Western feminist progress narratives, we can also see how this stereotype finds intertextual, intercultural validation in representations of that figure as white and/or racist as well. In the progress narratives I have been tracing here, in other words, the character of the lesbian feminist is not only anachronistic, but the very essentialism that she represents is also coded in racial terms. As Victoria Hesford notes in her astute essay on "feminism and its ghosts," "as the 'flannel shirt androgyne, close minded, antisex puritan humourless moralist racist and classist ignoramus essentialist utopian' [Zimmerman 1997: 163], [the lesbian feminist] often stands as a symbol for the limits of cross-class and cross-race alliances in second wave feminism" (2005: 228). I want to argue that this linear account of feminist development also provides the perfect alibi for implicit or explicit homophobia in both feminist and postfeminist accounts, marking lesbian feminist politics as particularly inattentive to racial exclusion historically, and therefore as ignorable on those grounds. This is one of the ways in which Western feminist progress narratives uncomfortably reinforce postfeminist accounts of "an earlier generation" as inattentive to the complexities of contemporary social, political, and interpersonal life, as dated, as nothing to do with the present. It is this kind of amenability—of one form of feminism narrative with another—that makes the political grammar of Western feminist stories significant both within and outside feminist theory.

CITATION TRACES

Representations of Judith Butler's work are key to securing the Western feminist progress narrative I have been mapping in this chapter. As is no doubt clear from many of the extracts above, Butler is frequently credited with being *the first* to move feminism on from the political and intellectual traps of both an exclusive prioritization of "woman" as the ground of theory and activism (through her critique of the sex/gender distinction, in particular) and the related problems of identity politics, however multiplied. While not taking issue with Butler's importance for feminist theory, in conducting the research for this book I could not help but be struck by the repetition of Butler as responsible (occasionally alongside others, often on her own) for the most extraordinary range of transformations in and of feminist theory. Importantly, for this point in the analysis, it is Butler who is consistently understood to move Western feminism beyond both essentialism and identity reductionism in ways that often precipitate her to a location outside feminism itself.[11] The following examples are typical of the position Butler's work occupies in the glosses I am interested in here:

It is difficult to overestimate the extent to which Butler's compelling reformulation of these theoretical impasses [between theorisation of the psyche and the social] has succeeded in pushing feminist thought on gender identity on to new conceptual terrain. (*Theory, Culture and Society* 1999)

For such feminists as Judith Butler, Joan Scott, and Denise Riley, it is the refusal of *women* as a foundational referent that gives to feminism the internal critique necessary to rethink its own historical emergence. Such rethinking functions to revise accepted notions of power, politics, and subjective agency, thereby challenging the foundational assumptions of certain activist agendas common to feminism's earlier practices. (*Differences* 1999/2000)

Judith Butler's (1990, 1993) deconstruction of the strategic division of gender from sex rejecting the notion of prediscursive materiality . . . (*European Journal of Women's Studies* 2004)

At least since Judith Butler's seminal book *Gender Trouble*, published in 1990, feminist and gender studies have been concerned with how new conceptions of the body affect and reform disciplinary questions in the humanities, as well as to some extent in the natural and social sciences. (*Nora* 2002)

Butler "pushes" feminist thought forward, "refuses" to get caught in the traps of a focus on "women" that mark earlier periods of feminist theorizing and politics, rejects an essentialist view of the body or the social as outside discourse, and carries academic feminism into a new era. Because of Butler, feminist theory now has the epistemological and methodological tools to deconstruct or "revise" previous understandings of "power, politics, and subjective agency" and to take its own history as object of inquiry. In such accounts, Butler is positioned as critiquing both the "foundational assumptions" of earlier activism (1970s) and identity claims (1980s) in order to take feminism into a broader realm of relevance too (1990s and on). In this respect, citation of Butler, accompanied by a striking lack of engagement with anything she writes, performs Western feminist theory's move fully into deconstructive approaches to the subject and the social world, and away from assumptions about feminist sameness and the reification of difference. More specifically, citation of Butler marks essentialism and identity as in the past, and the subjects of a feminist theoretical present as different from and opposed to these earlier approaches. In the process, iterations of her *threshold* role in a Western feminist progress narrative erase any previous challenges to "womanhood" as an unqualified ground of feminist knowledge.

Looking more closely at how Butler signifies as this threshold figure in Western feminist progress narratives highlights many of the central problems I have already indicated attend Western feminist progress narratives. In discussing how black and lesbian feminisms and feminists are positioned in these narratives, I identified two main modes through which identity politics (associated with the 1980s) are represented as an important stage in Western feminism's development. The first mode cites these interventions as important, but ultimately and necessarily as surpassed; the second skips straight to the 1990s or later without direct citation of what has been transcended. In the former, identity politics is separated out from 1970s feminism; in the latter the previous two decades are folded into one another, and the past is more euphemistically referred to. Both modes allow postmodernism, poststructuralism, or deconstruction to variously emerge as more concerned with difference than what has come before and thus as heroic in the celebratory tone of these narratives. Citation of Butler, as indicated in the above extracts, tends to reinforce the second mode, moving us beyond generally "accepted notions of power, politics, and subjective agency" through a critique of "certain activist agendas" that remain unspecified. In the process, the specific contributions of black and lesbian feminists are not simply transcended, but entirely erased, as Butler's critiques appear to emerge out of the blue. Such citation of Butler allows poststructuralism to emerge as both *more* concerned with gender, sexuality, race, and class and as *less* dependent on feminist theory in general to explore power relations, since feminism can be represented as the worst of the essentialist offenders left behind.

Western feminist progress narratives are not neutral about the transformations Butler inaugurates. Progress narratives inflect their achievements positively, of course, expressing these shifts enthusiastically and as something we should all celebrate. This positive affect is achieved through the emphasis on newness, transformation, and proliferation; the present is an exciting time of possibility, and we are invited to explore this "new conceptual terrain" with appropriate attitude. Such positive affect is also achieved through the combination of narrative tactics I have been exploring throughout this chapter. Any potential discomfort at the generational logic that homogenizes the past in order to discard it is allayed by the particular framing of what we are being encouraged to leave behind. We are being enjoined to leave behind homogeneity and essentialism, which we now know are racist and homophobic as well as anachronistic. To be ethical subjects of feminism, we *must* leave the past behind, then. All that is narratively required is to bracket out specific reference to what has otherwise been assigned to the 1980s, namely the black and lesbian feminist epistemologies and ontologies whose absent critiques haunt the theoretical present. Feeling good about where we are can also attach to Butler in other more precise ways, because citation of her obliquely references the rejection of lesbian identity in favour of strategic mobilization of sexual alterity: a queerness that has no a priori subject. In this respect, I do not think it is too much of an over-reading to suggest that citation of Butler brings both the general temporality of progress narratives into textual play, as well as a temporality that will abandon lesbian feminism more easily than black feminism.[12] I hope I have been able to illustrate that these problematic figurations of race and sexuality are key rather than tangential to how feminist progress narratives operate and that erasure of a complex past is a necessary condition of their positivity. Our celebrations have historiographic and political consequences that are not always immediately visible, then, ones that fold us into narrative logics that figure race and sexuality in particularly problematic ways. These historiographic representations imagine an anachronistic feminism in singular terms that resonate with postfeminist or antifeminist accounts, and provide "difference alibis" we should be exceptionally wary of.

L O S S

2 As this nicely acerbic quotation that follows suggests, I am certainly not the only critic of the Western feminist progress narratives explored in the previous chapter:

When you make your reputation by suppressing those old feminist traditions of the collective, or when you abandon the politics of citation, as it was called, as you seek to deliver your own hand-stamped version of "strategies," or when you write feminist theory that politely overlooks its social application, just remember: The Party means you never have to say you're sorry. (*Signs* 2000)

Other accounts insist that descriptions of Western feminist theory as moving from singularity to difference, static uniformity to sophisticated proliferation, are over-simplified and take a tone of scepticism similar to my own in the last chapter. To introduce another example:

"In the past," the implication is, there were the "theory wars" between Marxist feminism, socialist feminism, radical feminism, liberal feminism and so on. But "in the present," there is a body of developing "feminist theory"—a feminist social theory that has shed those earlier naiveties—and, in spite of a few remaining internal fractures, all right-thinking (non-essentialist) feminists adhere to this new sophisticated form. And implicitly, but sometimes also explicitly, people who do not agree or who advance considerably different ideas and ways of working are implied to be deficient in their scholarly and/or political credentials. (*Feminist Theory* 2000)

Where in progress narratives it is common to put scare quotes around terms associated with the 1970s, such as "radical feminism," "the patriarchy," and so forth, here the dynamic is reversed. What constitute past and present and the presumed relationship between them are challenged, as are the assumptions about what counts as feminist theory in the present. The above excerpt emphasizes the limits of such a progress narrative—I particularly like the ironic "in spite of a few remaining internal fractures"— and, importantly, the impact that such certainty about the past and present has on subjects of feminist theory. If, the text suggests, particular eras and schools of thought are understood to be essentialist in comparison with the "right-thinking" present, individual writers holding views other than those "right" ones are likely to be tarnished with the same brush. Essentialism becomes something that sticks ontologically as well as theoretically and historically, such that one might be, or think another to be, "an essentialist feminist." On the basis of arguments made in the previous chapter, I would also add that this characterization raises the spectre of essentialism as racism in particular, making the doubled accusation one feminists will want to transcend rather than embody.

Critiques of a Western feminist progress narrative from this perspective tend to underscore its mythic status, countering the conviction that feminist theory has become ever more multiple with correctives that emphasize instead the lost multiplicity of the past. For example, in its specific disciplinary context, the following extract stresses that the past was always already concerned with the sophisticated questions wrongly understood as the unique property of the present:

I should emphasize that this early work, contrary to some of the myths about the evolution of feminist criticism . . . was already concerned with the intersections of literary form and the structure of gender relations. (*Signs* 2000)

Importantly, such correctives stress that what has been left out of Western feminist progress narratives should be understood at the level of episte-mology as well as in terms of object of inquiry. Thus "early work . . . was already concerned with the intersections of literary form" and gender, not just with what literary texts were being read in a more conventional critique of the male canon, say. While I am in considerable agreement with many of the questions loss narratives raise in relation to representations of the recent history of Western feminist theory as one of progressive evolu-tion, the counter-claims of loss narratives create their own relentless histo-riography in turn. These narratives are not so much interested in a history of Western feminist theory as one *of multiplicity*, but as one that has aban-doned multiplicity for increasingly singularity, leading to present myopia. Thus loss narratives both emphasize past complexity and reinflect celebra-tions of its advances, indicating instead that fêted theoretical trajectories have in fact contributed to feminist criticism's demise. Again in the context of literature, for example, we hear that:

Indeed, there are reasons to consider a number of developments in the eighties and nineties a hazard to the vitality of feminist literary studies. (*Critical Inquiry* 1998)

In this respect, I am as sceptical of many of the central presumptions of the counter-claims of loss narratives as I am of progress narratives. These alternative shows of certainty do not disrupt the logic of progress narra-tives other than superficially: they retain the same history, revising its movement as one from multiplicity to singularity, openness to narrowness, and so on. And as we shall see, in so doing they too create their own favorite feminist demons to replace the vilified "radical feminist" whose stereotyping in progress narratives they are right to contest.

Western feminist progress and loss narratives are thus locked into a mutually reinforcing battle for meaning within a common storyline. While they each represent their own logic as singular and as running directly counter to the other, their use of similar markers and points of transition might better be read as a debate within the same terrain. Even in the few extracts engaged with in this chapter thus far, it is clear that we are deal-ing with a call and response mode in both narrative forms. In this sense, my own division of Western feminist storytelling into discrete narrative strands through the book is something of a misrepresentation. It gives a false impression of their independence, perhaps, and makes it difficult to gain a flavour of the ways in which they circle round one another or intersect in context. For example, an author may make use of a progress narrative at one point in a text, only to introduce aspects of a loss narrative later on in the same article, without this disrupting their overall argument. Special issues of journals on a common theme may include pieces that endorse one or other narrative, but otherwise reinforce a third position. In teaching contexts we may—I know I certainly do—provide accounts of feminist theory that emphasis its progress, while cautioning students not to abandon past accounts as uniform. Look how diverse feminist theory has become, there are now so many "feminisms" we might say; yet let us be careful not to jettison feminist classics too soon, our foremothers have much to teach us. Importantly, these different inflections do not appear contradictory—if our foremothers have much to teach us, might there not be a question mark over the assumption of increased diversity?—precisely because they employ similar markers and operate with a similar temporality. It is the closeness of these narratives, their mutual imbrication, that allows for such slippage and performs the conditions necessary for return narratives to spin their own version of Western feminist storytelling, as I will explore in the next chapter.

In their "pure form," both progress and loss narratives refute the possibility of the other version, of course, and this lends to a consideration of them independently. Both inflect their rendition of Western feminist theory as common to all and precisely not one version of a story that might be differently inflected. Both present their own narrative as a truth tale that foregrounds complexity over singularity and that offers the best present and future for feminist theory. Both assume a reader who recognizes herself and her history in the narrative and who is both the subject of the tale told and thus also the subject of feminist theory. She may need some coaxing, but she will recognize herself in the narrative, or, if not, she will become its antiheroine, potentially locating herself outside feminism altogether. In other words, while the narrative forms do actively speak to one another and are intertwined, their mode is emphatically singular. While the presence of different narratives is of course acknowledged, these are consistently managed through a generational discourse that I examine in more depth later in the chapter.

Given their intimate appeal to a particular subject of feminist theory, it is not surprising that both progress and loss narratives are also powerful in affective terms. They both construct a heroine who inhabits a positive affective state or a negative affective state in progress or loss narratives respectively. Both require emotional attachment to the tale told in order to remain its subject and continue to safeguard or transform feminist meaning in heroic mode. Both make use of prior, atextual attachments to feminism, assume that the reader wants to be a "good" feminist and not a "bad" one, and propose that there is only one way to be properly feminist in the current moment. Narratives of progress and loss in Western feminist storytelling presume an active reader, then, one who wants to contribute to the health rather than demise of feminism and who will tell a tale that allows her to occupy the present in ways she can be content with. These narrative appeals draw me in and spin me round, sometimes spit me out. My relationship to loss narratives, in particular, seems governed by profound ambivalence, as I indicate through this chapter. On the one hand, I feel pleased when loss narratives counter what I also perceive as misrepresentations of feminist theory written in the 1970s. I approve of the mission to rescue feminist theorists mischaracterized as essentialist and too casually dismissed on that basis. I know well the ease with which a progress narrative is taken up institutionally to mitigate against support for academic feminism in the present, how quickly celebrations turn. But on the other hand, as will become clear through this chapter, I am not the ideal subject of a Western feminist loss narrative, by any means. I am also interpolated as its antiheroine, an example of a generation of academic feminists who do not, cannot by virtue of age in fact, remember what has been lost. And this makes me cross, of course, because one prefers not to be demonized. That crossness in turn sets me up in opposition to my forced narrative exclusion, and that has its own curious, resistant pleasures too. My ambivalence in relation to loss narratives makes it impossible for me to occupy one affective state or the other, so instead I have to be content with trying to transform restlessness into reflexivity, to see if this failure might provide some useful reflections on feminist knowledge.

WHAT HAVE WE LOST?

Many of the general characteristics of Western feminist loss narratives can be traced in the following passage:

"Then and there," back in the 1970s, we saw ourselves, as many other feminists did, as "producers of feminist theory" which then informed and was changed by our practice as feminists; and we entered the academy . . . "to know and therefore to change the world." Over the period that has led to "now and here," it has been interesting to observe the gradual assimilation of academic feminism, and the entry into it of successive cohorts who "came to feminism" through the text rather than through political practice. One of the results of the passing of time and the perhaps necessary correlates of assimilation has been the rise of a distinct category of "feminist theory" and a distinctive professional category of "feminist theorists." What has supported this is a gradually decreasing awareness of the earlier feminist critique of theory as "ideas" produced through material practices cross-cut by the operations of power. (*Feminist Theory* 2000)

In this extract the 1970s is reclaimed as a site of energy and praxis, while the present is marked by its "assimilation" (a term used twice) and political memory loss. The loss narrative uses similar markers to the progress narrative, but highlights rather different aspects, framing them through opposing values. Rather than embodying sophistication, then, later periods of feminist theory are represented as co-opted, professionalized, and peopled by indistinguishable "successive cohorts" who lack a political practice to inform their feminist knowledge production. As in Western feminist progress narratives, it is generational inflections that allow the narrative to make sense. Where feminist subjects of the political past are naïve or exclusionary in progress narratives, in loss narratives it is feminist theoretical subjects of the present who fail in their feminist radicalism. Further, in loss narratives, generational rhetoric allows the narrator to remain distinct from the "feminist professional" of the co-opted present, even where she occupies the same institutional terrain.

In both this example from *Feminist Theory* and throughout loss narratives momentum is produced through binary comparisons and a consistent temporal frame. Similar oppositions work through the glosses, but where in progress narratives the relationship between terms such as practice and critique, activist and professional, or sameness and difference charted a positive development towards sophisticated present multiplicity, in loss narratives they chart the opposite. The move from practice to theory, for example, is a sign of contemporary myopia, and the move from activist to professional concerns marks a reduction rather than expansion of feminist possibilities in the present. In each case the first term is imbued with integrity and the latter with opportunism. In this respect, representing these relationships in hierarchical as well as temporal terms as practice→theory or world→text, as I also did in the last chapter, maps a downward trajectory within Western feminist theory, a loss of its potential rather than a celebration of its institutional or epistemological successes. This renarration of relations between binary terms is most explicit where they are not only reinflected as suggested, but are inverted, such that we move not from singularity to proliferation as suggested in progress narratives, but from proliferation to singularity, as suggested in the following example:

"Against two decades of an incredibly rich multiplicity of theorising, feminist theory is now increasingly becoming a singular entity" (in *Australian Feminist Studies* 1998)

As I flagged in the introduction to this chapter, the binary relation of multiplicity → singularity is the primary textual opposition through which loss narratives are expressed as laments. We move from richness to a singularity that poses as multiplicity, and these poses themselves constitute a sign of feminism's demise. This primary opposition governs a range of other oppositions that describe this lament and codes the nostalgia of loss narratives as ironically pivotal for hope. We must look back to have a future. In that we are clearly enjoined to identify with multiplicity over singularity, loss narratives also require identification with the past. The true subject of feminist theory remains the same as in the past, but that position is currently occupied by a pretender.

These textual oppositions are also governed by their temporality. Western feminist theory moves from an implicit or explicit 1970s richness to a 1990s narrowness, a chronology that charts the move from a concern with political transformation to a concern with professional advancement. In the example from *Feminist Theory* above, the lamentable present is arrived at through a euphemistic "passing of time"; in the example from *Australian Feminist Studies,* the barren 1990s and beyond is explicitly counterposed to a fertile 1970s and 1980s. In both cases "the passing of time" takes us from radical to mainstream, from vibrant to domestic feminist theory, such that its capacities can now be said to have become severely limited. A further example from *Australian Feminist Studies* underlines the point:

The feminist theory which in the 1970s and 1980s gained its energy from a marginal speaking position outside institutional, intellectual, and disciplinary power structures, has now generally become mainstream, orthodox, successful, and powerful. (*Australian Feminist Studies* 2000)

In this excerpt similar radical weight is given to the 1970s and 1980s as precursors to the "orthodox" 1990s. Indeed, in loss narratives the 1980s is rarely directly engaged with, either sandwiched between the 1970s past and the present (1990s or 2000s, depending on time of writing) or identified with rather than against that earlier period. Institutionalization and the diminution of feminist theory more generally are thus consistently rendered as a recent problem.

Yet we know from our analysis of Western feminist progress narratives that there are real difficulties with glossing over the 1980s, given what this decade is deemed to include above all else. The euphemistic glossing over the 1980s, or its association with an earlier political integrity, references a profound ambivalence about the place the identity critiques that occupy that decade have in both progress and loss narratives. On the one hand, Western feminist loss narratives tell a story of feminism's demise, a downward trajectory from vibrancy to stasis. On the other, they must take care not to dismiss black feminist or lesbian critiques of essentialism, since this would only confirm the accusations of racism or heteronormativity made about the 1970s (or "earlier feminisms") in progress narratives. Such an error would resonate back and forth across loss narratives, calling past multiplicity into doubt and begging questions about the integrity of the current lament, as well as the subjects of nostalgia. Loss narratives' caution in relation to the "difference critiques" that both progress and loss narratives locate firmly in the 1980s is aptly expressed in the next extract:

Universities have clearly offered opportunities to many students of Women's Studies and provided careers for academic feminists. They have also afforded spaces in which ever more sophisticated feminist thinking can be produced. But there has been a price to pay in terms of depoliticization and exclusion. . . . Issues are no longer as clear as they were once imagined to be and feminist work may have a tendency to become inward-looking. . . .

Critiques of essentialism have brought contradictory possibilities. On the one hand, there have been positive gains from the recognition of difference whilst, on the other, loss of the imagined community of "sisterhood" has led to fragmentation and disrupted political cohesion. (*Feminist Review* 1999)

While "opportunities" and positive gains over time are here acknowledged, "the price" remains the same as in more condemnatory glosses, referencing "depoliticization and exclusion" alongside the political uncertainty such critiques have wrought. The excerpt simultaneously asserts the importance of critiques of essentialism and laments a loss of cohesion, a potentially untenable contradiction enabled here by the framing of the "sisterhood" as always having been imagined. Further, it is "loss of the imagined community" that is grammatically active in causing "fragmentation," not the subjects of those "critiques of essentialism," or even the critiques themselves. I take both the ambivalence and the use of active and passive voices in the above passage as emblematic of the uncertainty of where to place identity critiques in the story of Western feminist theory's demise. It is a particularly good account of what is at stake in loss narratives. We know that the fantasy of "sisterhood" cannot be sustained, the extract seems to suggest, but perhaps this risk is inevitable for the maintenance of feminist imagination.

HOW DID WE COME TO LOSE WHAT HAS BEEN LOST?

As we can already begin to see, what is supposed to have happened in the 1980s is textually managed in two main ways in Western feminist loss narratives. It is glossed over and not mentioned, except implicitly, or it is retrospectively fused with the 1970s, represented as part of the political vibrancy the 1990s abandoned. In both extracts from *Australian Feminist Studies* introduced above, for example, the "two decades" of rich theorizing are contrasted to its current mainstream failures. The 1980s— that represents black, postcolonial, and/or lesbian critiques in both stories—is thus claimed for radicalism in loss narratives, where it is claimed for poststructuralist or postmodern politics in progress narratives. There are several intersecting ways in which any anxiety about temporality and politics is allayed in loss narratives. One central way is to indict increasingly abstract and obscure language use within feminist theory as constituting both *the sign* of a current lack of political engagement and as actively *creating* an elite culture of feminist theorists willing and able to share this language. The following example from *Signs* is a particularly strong version of this tendency:

I am baffled at what I view as one of the disadvantages of having the feminist movement institutionalized in the academy—namely, its apparent need to adopt one of the worst characteristics of that institution, its separating, alienating, exclusive, and, to my mind, often ugly and off-putting language. (*Signs* 2000)

The "ugly and off-putting language" constitutes Exhibit A in the case against current feminist theory. This evidence can be assessed by every-woman. "Look at how (obviously) ugly and off-putting this language is"; "Yes," agrees the jury, "it most certainly is." Indeed, it is frequently the tone of feminist theory more generally that is the object of scorn (or, rather coyly, bafflement here) in loss narratives. Not only "separating," "alienat-ing," and "ugly," theory in the present lacks the passion of early feminist knowledge production, a sad state of affairs that directly represents its lack of political commitment. The following extracts underline this point:

Critical election, abjection, and obscurantism perform a disservice to the liber-tarian politics and pedagogies endorsed by many of those whose astute ideas play a justly prominent part in feminist thinking. (*Critical Inquiry* 1998)

In place of cynicism, academic feminism ought to be considering ways to recap-ture at least some of the spirit of our earlier political action. (*Signs* 2000)

There is something interesting going on here concerning the relationship between language and politics, expression and action. In part, the rather uncontroversial assumption that language and politics have a direct rela-tionship to one another is underwritten by a prior assumption, namely that we already know what politics is and that it is clear therefore what kind of language should be used in the production of a politicized feminist knowledge. But this insistence that ("ugly," "obscurantist") language con-stitutes *the* sign of the depoliticization of feminist theory is also one way in which loss narratives can ensure that it is academic feminism rather than identity politics that acts as catalyst for the turn away from feminist theory as activism. It is the increase in theoretical production and abstraction and not the critique of "woman" as the ground of knowledge and transforma-tion that leads to the problems inherent in the apolitical present.

I am particularly struck by the emotional registers used to express this aspect of loss narratives. As we see above, the descriptions of and re-sponses to loss of theoretical accessibility are not at all neutral. Not only are they "ugly" and so forth but they also express "cynicism" and "abjec-tion" in a direct inversion of the positive registers claimed for the same theoretical moves in progress narratives. It is progress narratives that express lack of hope then, in truth, and loss narratives that express appro-priate anger at the loss of "the spirit of our earlier political action." The affective appeal here asks its reader to consider if they too may have felt "stupid" in reading theory they did not feel included in and offers the possibility of reframing exclusion as indignation and political acumen. Affectively, then, loss is transformed through textual displacement in ways that allow the subject of what has been lost to occupy the present despite her attachment to the past. Through a focus on off-putting abstraction, the "universality" critiqued so roundly in progress narratives is reclaimed in loss narratives not as exclusionary, but as the basis of a revitalized feminist theory accessible to all.[1]

It is but a short step from the identification of abstraction as sign of depoliticization to the identification of the academy itself, and more particularly academic feminism, as responsible for what has been lost in feminist theory. The move from an active, thriving feminism—including feminist knowledge production—to a myopic, singular "Feminist Theory" is thus also, and primarily, narrated in terms of a move from politics to institutionalization. As the extracts below emphasize, Western feminist loss narratives must work to insist that feminism's original interest in producing work that challenged the status quo has dwindled with its increasing location inside the "ivory tower," and with it the very purpose of feminist theory:

For what was once the subversive, intellectual arm of a thriving grassroots movement has been institutionalized and professionalized, while the movement that launched our enterprise is far less activist, confident, or popular. (*Signs* 2000)

Has this once dissident interdisciplinary body of theories and practices mutated into a corpse? What use is insubordination and defiance that has morphed into compliance and conformity? (*Feminist Theory* 2003)

Where feminist theory was once "dissident" and "subversive" due to its links with a grassroots feminist movement, now we are witnessing a "growing separation from ongoing social, cultural, and political developments" (*Australian Feminist Studies* 2000). Academic programmes that have institutionalized feminist knowledge production have prioritized university procedures and expectations. In doing so, what was previously the "intellectual arm" of the feminist movement has moved further and further away from its foundational aims. This is a hugely common theme that is probably familiar to many readers as the dominant account of what has happened in feminist theory, where this is a tragic tale. To give just a couple of additional examples then:

These programs are far from the origins of women's studies, which was to use the academic arena to deepen our understanding of the problems women face and to encourage women to be activists. Maybe some women's studies programs do still see it that way, but I am not sure that the evolution of feminist theory has furthered these goals. (*Signs* 1996)

Since its beginning, feminism was meant as a social movement, having political tasks and achievements. Feminism seems now to be more strictly connected to academic research and institutions. What does this mean? Is feminism becoming less political and more theoretical? (*European Journal of Women's Studies* 2003)

Both of the above excerpts are sure that these shifts have occurred, and both express this certainty in similar ways. Despite being separated by seven years and with different publication venues geographically speaking (the first speaks to an international, but predominantly U.S. audience, the second an international, but predominantly European audience), both glosses assume that the original goals of academic institutionalization of feminism were shared and that these goals have now been abandoned. As with the questions at the end of the prior example from *Feminist Theory*, the questions at the end of the second extract here do not represent real ambivalence, since feminism's new allegiance to institutions over "political tasks" has already been established in the previous sentences. And the acknowledgment that not all women's studies sites have changed position, while seeming to offer qualification, is not an endorsement of a multiplicity of differently political women's studies site, but instead only affirms that there is one clear way that feminist theory can be and remain political.

Central to the coherence of all of the above fragments are the familiar oppositions between activist and institutional locations, theory and practice. In Western feminist loss narratives, theory's efficacy is always to be judged outside of itself, in locations other than those where it was produced. Thus,

The test [of feminism and other social movements or theories] must ultimately be their success in identifying the conditions of existence and of coming into being of less oppressive forms of social and intellectual community. (*Feminist Theory* 2000)

On one level, I think few academic feminist writers, myself included, would take issue with the belief that feminist theory assumes a political life and meaning beyond the page or the academy. That there might be tests of feminist theory other than its institutional validation is not particularly contentious. What is particular to Western feminist loss narratives, however, is the certainty that this success can be measured along the lines of a theory/practice split that privileges the latter and sees the two as mutually exclusive.[2] It is an *a priori* opposition, one that lends weight to the earlier critique of abstract language as a major contributor to feminism's losses. A politics of theory thus always comes from its use and recognition "elsewhere," in other words; politics is always external to "the academy." These mutually exclusive terms are overlaid on a chronology that locates politics and feminist activism firmly in the past, and the present as devoid of community attachment or responsibility. In contrast, we are told,

There is an older feminist approach that sees ideas as the shared social productions of epistemic communities and their gatekeepers and hierarchies, and not as the unique production of "great minds." In this more subversive vein of feminist thinking, what counts as "knowledge" is seen as a dominant discourse. . . . This older feminist analysis has resonant implications for the state and status of feminist theory. It questions how "the theorists" get created as well as how "(real) theory" is seen to be formulated and its knowledge-claims articulated. (*Feminist Theory* 2000)

This "older feminist analysis" interrogates the politics of institutional knowledge practices, is community focused, and is less self-interested than the work of contemporary feminist "theorists," those "great minds" supported by a system feminists were previously disinvested in. The use of inverted commas, as in so many progress and loss narratives, underscores the declared scepticism at the current state of feminist theory. These are emphatically not "great minds"; this is not feminist "knowledge"; these are not even perhaps feminist "theorists" at all. Interesting to me here too is the insistence on collaborative, politicized approaches as belonging to the past (twice represented as "older"), despite their linguistically active—"resonant"—ability to question what counts as "(real) theory" and how "knowledge-claims" are formulated in the present. This presumed move from collaboration to individual authorship within feminist production makes sense because it chimes with the overarching shift from multiplicity → singularity that governs loss narratives.

As Robyn Wiegman has argued in her excavations of what she terms

"apocalyptic feminism," the dystopian chronological view is always nostalgic, always seeking rectification of ills through a reinstitution of similarity
(1999/2000; 2002; 2003). The capacities of past political critique can only
be achieved by a reintroduction of its (identical) concerns, objects, and
subjects. As I have been exploring thus far in this chapter, a dystopic
approach is also always looking to displace its "bad feelings" onto other
spaces and subjects, retaining the lament but divesting itself of mal-intent.
Loss narratives resist an appreciation of any contests over the meaning of
that key term "the political," either in the past or the present; deviation
from these "older approaches" is always to be placed outside of the political rather than as an engagement with what the political might be (2004).
Academic feminism is thus inauthentic, not-actually-feminism—"Theory,"
remember—rather than a feminism of a different, if disputed, kind. Yet in
order for the lament of the loss narrative to make any sense, even within
this rather narrow view of what constitutes politics, feminism must first be
understood as over, as having had its day, and the imagination of the
political that the loss narrative relies on must have been abandoned.[3]

As I suggested in the introduction, and as numerous other commentators have noted, nothing seems to be announced quite so consistently as
the death of feminism (Ferrier 2003; McMahon 2005). As Mary Hawkesworth shows us, "Between 1989 and 2001 . . . a Lexis-Nexis search of
English-language newspapers turned up eighty-six articles referring to the
death of feminism and an additional seventy-four referring to the postfeminist era" (2004: 962–63). Indeed, statements such as

Perhaps I am just mourning what I sense is the end of feminist activism, at least
among that large group of feminists who now reside behind the walls of the
university (*Signs* 2000)

are extremely common in loss narratives. As Hawkesworth further insists,
the acceptance that such declarations are simply descriptive "erases the
social justice activism of women around the globe while covering the
traces of the erasure" (2004: 983), but knowing this does not seem to alter
the certainty such announcements engender. One the one hand, and as I
have already argued, it can be useful to debunk such assertions with
reference to the growth of feminist movements globally, the temporally
and spatially uneven international life of feminist projects, and the problems of thinking about activism and indeed knowledge in linear, rather

than cyclical terms, say. But a sole focus on what is left out of Western feminist loss narratives can only go so far. It misses the importance of that "feminist death" for the internal coherence of the Western feminist loss narrative. Loss narratives *require* the "death of feminism" in order to retain a static and familiar object to be lamented, in order to ensure at all costs that they do not encounter that object in the present, and in order to imagine a future in which that familiar feminism can be recovered by the same subjects as those who keen for its current internment. Where in progress narratives the temporality is forward looking and active, and the past stolid and inward looking, in loss narratives the temporal gaze moves both backwards and forwards, anticipating the return that is the focus of the next chapter. The present has to be evacuated of feminist political value (otherwise why the lament?), the past has to be that which has been lost, but also, and importantly, a good object worthy of being recovered (otherwise its loss might not be lament-worthy). And the subject of loss narratives must be mournful but hopeful, bitterness the property of those other (anti- or quasi-) feminists who would narrow feminism's prior uto-pian reach because of their own deluded critical attachments. The current problems central to the loss narrative will be resolved then, but—and always—not just yet:

We look forward to 10 or 15 years' time, when feminist theory is as thoroughly informed and transformed by feminist principles and practices as is feminist work on epistemology, methodology and ethics. (*Feminist Theory* 2000)

The future, as the next chapter on return narratives further delineates, must belong to the subjects of the past if the loss narrative is to be resolved. Feelings of pain and abandonment that typify loss narratives must be reproduced in the present, to ensure that future (and no other) is the one validated. Lisa Adkins provides a critique of discourses that mourn the "passing of feminism" that is similar to my own and that locate this as problematically reproducing broader social stories of feminism as over (2004: 40–41). Yet Adkins also places those she critiques as "out of time," that is, anachronistic, because of their attachment to previous ways of doing things (both political and theoretical), which is the point that I depart from her analysis. Instead, I think of these backwards glances as central to what enables subjects of loss narratives to occupy a particular present, whose future must always be deferred.

Thus far in this chapter I have been concerned with how loss narratives write the present of Western feminist theory in negative terms, and in particular what must come before in order to ensure that this present is a lamentable state of affairs. Anxieties about the place of identity critiques of essentialism are displaced or fused with characterizations of earlier decades as activist, creating the academy both as responsible for increased loss of feminist vision and as the origin of abstractions that constitute depoliticization's primary sign. Yet as my reading of some of the above extracts has already indicated, institutionalization is not represented simply as something that is externally imposed on academic feminists; it is something that shapes them, creates them, even mirrors their own apolitical investments. If the subject of loss narratives is to remain the subject of a past-to-come, is to remain innocent in other words, someone else must take the blame for feminist theory's intractable demise. We have seen in the section above that "the academy" is rendered as always already apolitical in Western feminist loss narratives, allowing for the displacement of conflict over the proper subject of feminism onto that site. Such a move constructs an entirely abstract vision of "the university," one unable to delineate any of its actual conflicts or institutional politics, let alone any geographical or hierarchical specificity in this regard.[4]

To return to an earlier extract from *Australian Feminist Studies*, loss narratives produce the conditions appropriate to the assertion that

The feminist theory which in the 1970s and 1980s gained its energy from a marginal speaking position outside institutional, intellectual, and disciplinary power structures, has now generally become mainstream, orthodox, successful, and powerful. (*Australian Feminist Studies* 2000)

Note once more that this displacement of the "becom[ing] mainstream" of feminist theory allows the 1970s and 1980s to be reunited, iterated as identical platforms for "marginal speaking position[s]" because of their shared footing *outside* the academy. Yet if "feminist theory" has "become mainstream . . . and powerful" then we might also wonder what has happened to its subjects. We know that the subject of the loss narrative looks on bewildered from the sidelines, of course, but what of the subject of this "orthodox . . . successful" feminist theory? How are her struggles to survive within Western higher education contexts over this period represented? How, I wonder, are her own attempts to negotiate increased institutional demands on her time, increased demands for productivity represented most potently by the U.K.'s Research Assessment Exercise,[5] and increased job insecurity in the context of neoliberal rolling back of public funding for education dealt with in loss narratives?[6] With empathy and an attempt to keep feminist *theorists* themselves separate from the "feminist theory" that has become mainstream in the above extract? Indeed not.

Let us take a look at an indicative range of excerpts that inform us most explicitly who rather than what is to blame for the decline and fall of Western feminist theory:

Particularly dispiriting to those of us old and confessional enough to admit that we once naively endorsed the slogan "sisterhood is powerful" is the fact that these days an almost unimaginable oxymoron spearheads many of these attacks—a highly vocal, articulate cadre of anti-feminist academic "feminists". (*Signs* 2000)

Feminist theory currently lacks the kind of meta-theoretical thinking that so excited many of us in the early 1970s; and . . . an elite group of international feminists are creating travelling theory at a remove from the real world. (*Feminist Theory* 2001)

In my view academic feminists don't seem sufficiently concerned about the problem of how to gain access to outlets which will give feminism a voice. We used to be concerned about such issues. We (those of us on the Left) analyzed media, and worried about how we could wrest control of the distribution of information away from those who controlled and profited by their ownership of the means of communication. (I am struck by how quaint this language now sounds.) (*Feminist Studies* 2001)

Feminist scholars, perhaps not surprisingly, have been absorbed into the vanity-envy culture of higher education—the pursuit of careers, competitive individualism, star systems, and hierarchies of privilege. On balance, some of us have come to wonder, How [sic] much have feminists changed the academy, and how much has it changed us? (*Signs* 2000)

In the above passages, the slips between feminist theory and feminist theorist, with both constructed as increasingly co-opted, make clear precisely *who* has produced abstract, apolitical theory and gained from the professionalization of academic feminism. Feminist theory "currently lacks" the theoretical tools and political will to continue its previous aims of knowledge and social transformation, to the extent that feminists theorists themselves have been transformed by personal desire for glory. The academic subjects who occupy the mainstream do not resist, they are "perhaps not surprisingly" unconcerned, preferring to accrue to themselves the benefits of "the vanity-envy culture of higher education," occupying elite, privileged positions and trading in the "star-systems" and "travelling theor[ies]" that benefit their careers. Such a view of academic feminists is not particularly new, of course. Mary Evans identified the myth of the "selfish academic" as essential to allow her equally mythic politicized sister to retain her position as "the true believer" almost thirty years ago (1982: 70). In these more recent accounts that form the loss narrative I am tracking here, however, the "true believer" has all but lost her cause. The "selfish academic" has, it seems, completed her task. A politicized language critiquing the ownership of "the means of communication" is now parenthetically "quaint." What remains is a by turns wistful and resentful memory of how things were before an international feminist elite used their considerable communication skills to bolster rather than challenge "competitive individualism."

Where in Western feminist progress narratives it was feminism and feminists of the 1970s that lacked political integrity, in loss narratives it is professional feminists of the "now and here" who bear primary responsibility for the demise of feminist activism. In the above glosses, the demonized feminist theorists are, of course, presented as "other" to the narrator, who is "dispirited" where she used to be "excited," "concerned" about rather than "absorbed into . . . vanity-envy culture," the object not subject of contemporary "attacks" on real feminist analysis. The elite are elsewhere, no doubt traveling around as well as creating "travelling theory," fully taken over by their priorities of reaching the top, not caring whose shoulders they leave footprints on. Any potential difficulty about the narrator being confused with the "selfish academic" who is the object of her ire—the narrator is likely to be an academic too in the journals I am analyzing, after all—is resolved by the use of *generation* to keep the different kinds of feminist theorists apart. Notice in the first extract from *Signs*, above, that we have two kinds of academic feminists, the antifeminist ones in scare quotes—"feminists"—and the "old" ones who "endorsed the slogan "sisterhood is powerful," however "naively." The subjects of loss narratives, of political feminism, use "quaint . . . language" and remember the 1970s because they were there then, not only because they identify with the past, although this is also important. To return to part of an excerpt from *Feminist Theory* cited earlier in this chapter, academic feminists are thus separated from feminist praxis by their entry point into feminism:

Over the period that has led to "now and here," it has been interesting to observe the gradual assimilation of academic feminism, and the entry into it of successive cohorts who "came to feminism" through the text rather than through political practice. One of the results of the passing of time and the perhaps necessary correlates of assimilation has been the rise of a distinct category of "feminist theory" and a distinctive professional category of "feminist theorists." (*Feminist Theory* 2000)

While there is nothing to prevent a feminist from a previous generation being changed by "vanity-envy culture," a young feminist is stuck in the present it seems.[7]

Not only does the present "articulate cadre" not engage in an appropriate political fashion, with appropriate objects and tools, but those who make up its ranks are often unfamiliar with the nature of political practice in the first place. "Cadre" is a resonant term here, I think, using its distinctly military resonance to indicate absolute separation and hostility between "feminist camps." "Cadre" is a term frequently used to refer to professional militia or a group of mercenaries; it conjures images of counter-insurgency, of the fight against a false enemy. Instead of a just war against the patriarchy this "articulate cadre" picks fights with the naïve (and implicitly defenceless) advocates of the sisterhood. No doubt a member of the "cadre" will as soon turn from and on her peers to vouchsafe her own competitive self-interest. Our antiheroine is not only misguided, then, she is duplicitous, using any advantage she accrues to increase her own power rather than for the greater feminist good. Like the postfeminist, the academic "quasi-feminist" or "professional feminist" will "[arrogate] the global terrain to [herself] without a clear basis of legitimation from local constituencies" (*Feminist Theory* 2002). The feminist professional is doubly to blame: she has no mandate, and she has harnessed feminist fragmentation for her own ends. Importantly, loss narratives often use the term "professional feminist" to bring together gender mainstreamers and academic feminists as similarly problematic. Both have made careers from gender (in)equality, both are other to the real feminist political subject who longs for a pure activist past. The battle has already been won, and feminism lost; the only hope for its recovery is for a return to the optimism, energy, and transparency of the past and its subjects.

POLITICAL ATTACHMENTS

You may have noted already the intensity of my own response to Western feminist loss narratives thus far? Any attempt to map loss narratives from the sidelines on my own part has already begun to falter. The ambivalence towards and provoked by loss narratives that I flagged in the introduction to this chapter has by this point resolved itself into a righteous irritation, it seems. In the previous sections I ironically imagine "evidence" of post-structuralism's obscurantism deliberated on by a jury, and mock loss narrators' lack of empathy for their overworked "sisters." I should also say that I am really beginning to enjoy myself in this chapter, drawing out techniques of othering in loss narratives and running with possible textual resonances of the term "cadre." I feel at home in these kinds of critiques; I know exactly where I am. These moments might be taken to indicate my stakes in the terrain I seek to delineate, a kind of "sceptical echoing" that reminds my reader that I (and they) are likely to be participants in rather than mere observers of these discourses. In this respect I think these strong feelings are worthy of further investigation.

The "echoes" I have sketched thus far highlight the call and response nature of Western feminist storytelling: they literalize struggles over who can claim to be the subject of Western feminist theory. Thus, in response to the demonization of academic feminists as selfish and myopic, I am at pains to reference the political context of higher education in the U.K. that has blighted the professional lives of younger academics in particular. I highlight the lack of attention to the material conditions of university life in loss narratives, trumping its subjects' own call for attention to real politics in my own mind. I include a longer footnote than is usual for me on the nature of the Research Assessment Exercise (RAE) and Research and Excellence Framework (REF), should anyone not already be familiar with these blots on the U.K. academic landscape, and I would also want to affirm here that its impact on the self-assurance and morale of a generation has indeed been devastating. Where, I want to know, are these confident, powerful, institutionally validated academic feminists, particularly when generationally defined by loss narratives? My initial response, then, is to want to provide a political history to academic feminism in the context of neoliberalism, as suggested, and in particular to shine the spotlight on its impact on my generation (and later) of academic feminists. We are, I want to insist in turn, surviving not thriving, an abandoned generation of wounded feminist souls. Wounded, yes, but also enraged, much like the heroines of loss narratives, in fact.

And now, having established the material basis for my own pain and marginality, I can really let rip, can give a fuller voice to those sceptical asides in equally generational terms. It is all well and good for those established professors to complain about younger feminists, I mutter to myself, for them to complain about the privileges of academic life my own generation has in fact never had access to. Much less a newer generation, who have to struggle for any jobs at all, let alone gender and women's studies jobs, much less transnationally where there may not be a place for academic feminism at all, or where academic jobs only emerge when professors retire or die, if then. It is bad enough, I continue, that we struggle with the legacies of a manifest audit culture our feminist foremothers in the academy did not protect us from. Meanwhile, while they take another funded period of research leave to work collaboratively on projects that will only further convince them of their own moral high-ground, a current "cadre" (we know how I feel about this term) of feminist academics has to bear not only their abandoned teaching loads but apparently also the responsibility for everything that has gone wrong with academic feminism. And another thing . . . is it only the 1990s that produced feminist stars in love with the sound of their own voices? Ever heard of Kate Millett, Germaine Greer, Betty Friedan? And another . . . just because you don't find yourself part of a thriving political milieu any more, don't assume there isn't one. . . . Wow. Who knew my rant would feel so cathartic! You! You're the one who has let feminist theory down, not me! I'm the one who is displaced; you're the one with power!

As I suspect is clear, a desire to be the heroine not the antiheroine of feminist theory produces the momentum in both sets of narratives, as we project any lingering anxieties about critical truths we might otherwise have to negotiate onto the other pretender. The generationalism I otherwise say that I resist seems to be working rather well for me here, in the struggle for political and intellectual relevance that characterizes both loss narratives and my own charged response. So in my rant above I am delighted to cast myself as the poor, neglected feminist academic rather than the Director of the Gender Institute at LSE, a role that would fit ill with my emotional outburst in which I imply it is other people who determine my teaching load. In the battle over who is the "real feminist theorist" we each pose as the more sidelined and put-upon, we each imagine ourselves marginal to the institutional contexts that provide us with authority to speak, write, muse, or rant, because feminist heroism can above all not be seen to derive from privilege. But is that all there is to be said about this contest for relevance? That it is simply not accurate and needs to be qualified or abandoned on the basis of the empirical evidence? I would say not, since such a position is as likely to authorize a scramble for empirical examples of marginality versus authority to settle the question of feminist institutionalization that I want to keep open. What I want to suggest instead is that my rant might reveal something interesting about the ways in which we inhabit the political grammar of Western feminist storytelling that this book analyzes. And further, it may indicate some of the ways in which a focus on affective entanglement may get us closer to that occupation than direct critique alone.

We might recall that my overarching commitment expressed in the introduction to this book was to theorize the taken for granted nature of Western feminist stories about the recent past that I believe we all participate in. While we may individually prefer a progress tale over a loss one or *vice versa*, this is usually because of the ways we are biographically or theoretically implicated in these narratives: unsurprisingly, we usually prefer the tales that present us in a favorable light over those that do not. But as I have been attempting to show so far in this book, Western feminist progress and loss narratives are in fact intimately linked. They divide the recent past up into the same periods, construct similar versions of theoretical and political developments, albeit differently inflected, and cast a past or present abstracted feminist subject as their antiheroine in order that the generationally overdetermined author of the narrative in question can remain its heroine. Within this context, the exchange of emotional registers allows the subject of each narrative to retain their "positive affect," either through a straightforward smugness or through a slightly more circuitous enjoyment of an abjection appropriate to a heroic status that must deny its hierarchical designs. This is the nature of glee in this context, I think: a pleasure in negative affect that has the power to transform it into positive affect while obscuring that move.

Yet the same affective play that reinforces generational linearity and the separation of loss and progress narratives also disrupts that separation. The righteous anger expressed in loss narratives and my own response is always overstated, cannot be reconciled with that which it purports to describe; it is too absolute and cracks from its own posturing. It does not make sense to blame an entire generation for the demise of feminist politics, just as it does not makes sense to blame one for the demise of prior academic freedoms. The insistence that it is I, I who should be mournful, not them, pushes me into making claims I cannot sustain about my own institutional marginality, for example. If the mobilization of "generation" as narrative technique works to create a singular feminist subject who emerges triumphant (or miserable, which is the same thing here), then it also acts to obscure the complexity of the present and its competing subjects. That emotional excess points to the sheer affective labor required to secure these narratives as generational, the work needed to ward off "the other" in both narratives. In this respect, it also indicates the difficulties and frustrations of shared space rather than of clean transfers from the subject of one narrative to another. It expresses irritation at the persistence of the "other," who is always nudging up against the subject and cannot simply be dispensed with through a too-blunt generational rhetoric.

This dissonance between the appearance of narrative (what it appears to describe) and the work it can or cannot do is registered in loss narratives at the textual level, too. Just as the tension between generational rhetoric and the institutional contexts depicted cannot be sustained affectively, neither can it be sustained chronologically. The very mode through which "the other" is consigned to a different place and space confuses the subjects and objects it seeks to hold apart. In the loss narratives I have been reading above, the author of each excerpt is positioned as a commentator upon rather than participant in the academic feminism that is the object of critique. "Academic feminists" are always other people, while the narrator, since she cannot be the same as the reviled object of interrogation, has to place herself somewhere else. The past becomes this subject's true home, her critical claims rendered "quaint" in the present she cannot be both a part of and distant from. Yet, to return to two of the excerpts I have already included, the requisite temporality of loss narratives breaks down, since the narrator most certainly *does* occupy space in the present. She is not in a different time or place, but inhabits the present space of writing as we read: she is our guide to the present she claims to have been forced to abandon.

In my view academic feminists don't seem sufficiently concerned about the problem of how to gain access to outlets which will give feminism a voice. We used to be concerned about such issues. We (those of us on the Left) analyzed media, and worried about how we could wrest control of the distribution of information away from those who controlled and profited by their ownership of the means of communication. (I am struck by how quaint this language now sounds.) (*Feminist Studies* 2001)

Feminist scholars, perhaps not surprisingly, have been absorbed into the vanity-envy culture of higher education—the pursuit of careers, competitive individualism, star systems, and hierarchies of privilege. On balance, some of us have come to wonder, How much have feminists changed the academy, and how much has it changed us? (*Signs* 2000)

As in my rant, the nature of space as shared and compromised is disavowed in the above excerpts, but nevertheless makes itself visible textually. To take the first extract: "academic feminists" are the object in the initial sentence, but a collective subject—"we" (academic feminists)—authors the second, rendering the relationship between subject and object uncertain. That "we" is rescued for the loss narrative by "the Left" in the third sentence, whose actions are all in the past tense; but the parenthetical present tense of the last sentence is again active, if wistful. The movements between tenses and grammatical subjects and objects in this extract exceed their formal chronological containment. The extract demonstrates uncertainty about the narrator's role as an academic feminist, as much as it expresses critique of those academic feminists she tries—unsuccessfully, in my view—to keep a distance from. The second extract also begins with the blaming of others—"feminist scholars"—for their self-interest and privilege, but the subsequent sentence complicates the initial certainty that the narrator (and the others she identifies with, the we who "come to wonder") is not one of those invested in the "hierarchies of privilege" critiqued. The passive framing of the second part of the first sentence, too, takes

blame away from the feminist scholars implicated, and the final question—
"how much has it changed us?"—unites both ends of the fragment, under-
lining the possibility that the political and depoliticized may be one and
the same subject of the extract. My readings of temporal breakdown here
suggest that while generational difference is central to how loss narratives
work, it fails as a technique because of the contradiction inherent in a
writing subject so actively and ambivalently describing their time as past.

It is easier for narrators of feminist theory as loss to cast themselves as
anachronistic, and for me to cast myself as institutionally voiceless, than to
think through the ways in which academic feminist space is crowded with
subjects telling stories that represent each other in motivated, power-
imbued ways. The question of tone as I have been thinking it through so
far might thus point back to academic institutions, not as depoliticized
sites, but as politically charged spaces within which feminist claims to
authority are enacted. My interest is not in whether or not spaces are
complex—how could they be otherwise?—but in the narrative techniques
through which that complexity is denied (more or less efficiently). A
modest claim at this point, then, might be to suggest that a generational
mode is one of the narrative techniques Western feminist theorists should
be most wary of, since it brings together affect and temporality to imagine
the subject free of the complicity others necessarily remain mired within.
Subjects of progress and loss narratives insist on their absolute separation
from one another, missing the ways in which they utilize and instantiate a
common historiography, missing the ways in which that historiography
grounds post-, quasi-, or antifeminist claims as well. Generational narrative claims thus place too much emphasis on the capacities of feminist
subjects to safeguard as progressive the politics of the narratives they
author. It is small wonder, then, that Western feminist progress and loss
narratives pay scant attention to the amenability of their rhetoric, since we
remain confined to defensive or assertive, rather than reflective, modes, as
I hope I have begun to show.

DISCIPLINARY RUBRICS

As I have been arguing, generational discourse is mobilized to guard
against the messiness of shared space that would problematize the sharp
division between feminist politics and academic feminism characteristic of

Western feminist loss narratives. Yet appeals to generation alone break down when both heroine and antiheroine are academic feminists, when both occupy the institutional spaces understood as the primary site of feminism's demise. If the time of the subject of loss narratives is past, then what is she doing in the present of writing and teaching? How can she be both present and absent at the same time? Here I explore one common way that this tension between narrative and location is resolved, namely through its deflection onto *disciplinary* differences and allegiances. In this register, academic feminist space is divided by epistemological and methodological commitments, and these distinctions are woven into generational discourse to establish certain disciplinary approaches as more rigorous, but importantly also as more appropriate to feminist inquiry.[8] Thus, that which has been abandoned in Western feminist loss narratives is not only a political project or common ground of experience as women, but also the disciplinary basis of a transformative feminist knowledge project. And this loss is frequently presented as one of the reasons for the demise of academic feminism's capacities more generally. This intellectual historiography may strike many readers as odd, given the range of feminist work that has claimed interdisciplinarity as a more appropriate mode for feminist research than disciplinary entrenchment (see Lykke 2004b; Liinason and Holm 2006; Vasterling, Demény et al. 2006). But, as I explore below, if disciplinary claims and generational laments are to be linked in loss narratives, interdisciplinarity itself must be called into question as part of the reason for feminism's demise.

In my discussion of Western feminist progress narratives in the last chapter, I described how momentum is underpinned by binary comparison, where we move from singularity → multiplicity, sameness → difference and so on, and where this move is understood in positive terms. Those shifts are also represented by related moves such as experience → text, which often also have a more direct epistemological or methodological inflection of a shift from empirical inquiry → deconstruction, from what is known to what is critiqued. In loss narratives, as I have explored through this chapter so far, the movement charted is the same as in progress examples, but is negatively inflected. It is but a short step for the struggles for recognition in the Western feminist present to be represented as mutually exclusive disciplinary ones, where (disciplinary) social science rigour and certainty is contrasted to (interdisciplinary) humanities fluidity and openness. To return to an extract discussed earlier, we can see how broad shifts in feminist theory are mapped onto these disciplinary ones:

Since the mid-1980s, women's studies programs have been sites of frictions between faculty from the humanities, especially those invested in postmodernist
critiques, and more empirically oriented feminists from the social sciences. (*Signs* 2000)

In this excerpt, friction is caused by these differences, but note too that the humanities here and elsewhere in loss narratives are closely associated with "postmodernist critiques," which are also to blame for a more general move from politics→institutionalization as we know. While "women's studies programs have been sites of friction" then, these are not equal contests between neutral disciplinary differences, but spaces in which the dominance of "postmodernist critique" over a more empirical orientation is enacted.

The following extract continues the familiar tack of locating the source of Western feminist political amnesia within the academy (the text here is part of a larger parody of this view). But, as above, citation of that amnesia as following disciplinary allegiance divides up the academy into good and bad locations:

1. The institutionalization of women's studies at some visible colleges and universities has made scholars forget the founding tenets of women's studies as they
   slavishly attempt to recreate it in the image of the traditional disciplines.
2. Where once feminist sociology was deeply engaged with issues that women
   confront on the job and in the economy, there is a retreat into the realm of
   discourse.
3. Students today "know how to deconstruct anything" but do not know about
   real relations historically and now between activist movements and feminist
   scholarship is too "internal to the academy." (*Feminist Theory* 2001)

There is a further irony in this extract, which is that those responsible for "the institutionalization of women's studies" are castigated for trying to insist on the field's disciplinary status, while "feminist sociology" emerges apparently politically (and disciplinarily) unscathed. We know too that the "slavish attempts" to mainstream academic feminism have been successful over feminist sociology's deep engagement by the fact that students "do not know about real relations." They can "deconstruct anything," but—and indeed because of this—are unable to generate real insights about the social world. In loss narratives, then, discussions of disciplinary differences tell a story of how the social sciences and empirical inquiry have been forced from popularity by approaches that privilege text and context over world and experience. Through its association with poststructuralist approaches, this shift away from the social sciences and towards the interdisciplinary humanities is often named "the cultural turn," a turn to representation and abstraction over social meaning, as discussed earlier in this chapter. The social sciences are thus forever sidelined, with individual as well as institutional effects:

The "cultural turn" still predominates in feminist scholarship—at least if my social scientist colleagues are justified in their complaints. (*Australian Feminist Studies* 2002)

Such transformations are described as leaving feminist social scientists isolated and marginal within the academy, and in this way the generational lament combines with disciplinary difference to establish certain feminists as the academic "other." The cultural turn is dominant, social science is marginal, and thus the tone of complaint that suffuses loss narratives is given further, this time institutional, validation.

But for the dissent not to appear the result of individual or collective sour grapes, more work is needed to justify this opposition between disciplinary boundaries and approaches. The call back to the social sciences is further legitimated by the assertion of a closed relationship between object and method of feminist inquiry. Thus the social world can only be understood through empirical inquiry, and "deconstruction" is represented as a method that belongs to the humanities alone. Interrogations of social meaning are thus self-evidently presented as accessible through one set of approaches more than any other, as the following extract makes plain:

The project of reclaiming the social also involves rethinking the relations between the theoretical and the empirical. Much feminist attention goes into deconstructing the canon, explaining how the social is constituted within theory. . . . By and large this kind of feminist theory has had an arm's length relationship with empirical research. (*Feminist Theory* 2005)

The social, the empirical, and research are linked in this passage, forming an exclusive chain that belies the "by and large" that would indicate a more open set of possibilities. "[T]his kind of feminist theory" circumnavigates the social, hovers around its edges, explaining its constitution, but is not itself a direct engagement with or transformation of the social sphere. Only through empirical research could attention to real people and real situations be reintroduced into feminist scholarship.

The category of experience thus belongs not only to a Western feminist theory now lost, but also explicitly to the social sciences. This claim works in several ways for loss narratives. First, it identifies certain theorists as continuing to do important feminist political work, even within the more generally demonized academy. This allows subjects of loss narratives to negotiate the otherwise problematic fact of their own location within the very site of that loss. Second, challenges to the view that experience can be directly accessed or politically mobilized as the ground zero of feminism can be represented as disciplinary challenges. In this way, differences of theoretical and political opinion can be overwritten and to some extent neutralized as disciplinary differences first and foremost. One can occupy a political high ground, but represent that as a question of approach rather than ontology. Third, if one endorses a loss narrative that sees the transformation of feminist inquiry as a bad thing, further claims for change can be made as disciplinary rather than only political claims, as in the following excerpt:

A materialist perspective is necessarily a sociologically informed one; hence, in reasserting the importance of the material and the social, I am also seeking to reclaim some fundamental sociological insights. (*Women's Studies International Forum* 2001)

And a statement such as this one—

I believe that if feminist criticism is to continue to matter in the new century, it must be grounded in the real life experiences of human beings. (*Signs* 2000)

—thus becomes both a call for a restitution of experience as the ground of feminist criticism, but also, through the chains of association I have been tracing in this chapter thus far, a call for empirical inquiry over poststructuralist, humanities-based, or interdisciplinary inquiry, which are blamed for both the loss of feminist politics and for the marginalization of feminism within the academy itself.

What these stark distinctions between experience → text and social sciences → humanities in Western feminist loss narrative result in is not, then, a call for a more inclusive interdisciplinarity across the social sciences and the humanities, as one might perhaps expect. This is because to do so would challenge the privileged status of experience and empirical inquiry so central to the development of loss narratives as a whole. More importantly, I think, interdisciplinarity is foreclosed because these disciplinary insistences work to ensure certain subjects and not others can remain part of academic feminism without losing their heroic political status. Instead, interdisciplinarity is fused with poststructuralist or postmodern academic feminist theory and approaches in order to constitute all these terms as interruptions to appropriate feminist engagement with the social world.

Under its interdisciplinary umbrella, the feminist scholarly enterprise has made a significant impact on epistemologies and methodologies. But its intellectual validity has suffered from the intensity of constant theoretical fragmentation and, more particularly, from recent claims that it is both anti-intellectual and anachronistic. (*Feminist Theory* 2003)

In this excerpt interdisciplinarity is no longer a valid position because of its familiar association with "theoretical fragmentation." But here interdisciplinarity is also "anti-intellectual and anachronistic," a claim that only makes sense within the temporality of the Western feminist stories I have been tracing thus far. Interdisciplinarity is anachronistic because it interrupts concerns with the social world represented by "the cultural turn," and it is anti-intellectual insofar as it does not demonstrate a recognizable disciplinary theoretical history or methodological rigour.[9]

In their quest to retain an intellectual and political advantage, Western feminist loss narratives develop a political grammar that has a resonance beyond its immediate aims. Casting interdisciplinarity as "anti-intellectual and anachronistic" chimes disconcertingly with scientific discourses that would see any and all feminist inquiry as biased and, in an era of postfeminism, no longer necessary in a Western academic context. Interdisciplinary feminist inquiry is thus positioned rather worryingly in terms immediately recognizable to institutions that have always been ambivalent about the "rigour" of feminist work. This move is necessary, of course, to separate out subjects of loss narratives from the "feminist" academic subjects that carry the burden of theory's demise, but this collateral damage comes at a potentially very high cost and provides a particularly stark example of the amenability of these stories' political grammar.

Characterizing feminist contests over the nature of the social, political, and subjective as disciplinary differences allows loss narratives to chart the downward turn of Western feminist theory while remaining within its orbit. To condense this theme: empirical engagement with the social world, underpinned by experience as the basis for knowledge production (in both object and subject) has thus been displaced by interdisciplinary humanities approaches that prioritize postmodern deconstruction and culture as method and object respectively. In the process, what is lost is a feminist theory and politics with a disciplinary, materialist ground, as well as the clarity and integrity of its subjects. The result of this set of unfortunate developments is the loss of feminist theory's ability in the present to attend to the large questions of our day: social and economic justice, violence and conflict, and global transformations in power relations affecting people's daily lives. Yet loss narratives still struggle to negotiate the claims of exclusion leveled against them, particularly those arising from interrogations of "earlier feminist" racist or heterosexist exclusions. As we saw earlier in this chapter, displacement of these charges involves a range of techniques, including use of euphemism, the linking of the 1970s and 1980s as equally political, and primarily through locating "blame" for feminist theory's demise in the academy. Such a move can only go so far, though, as we have seen. It also requires the instantiation of absolute generational and disciplinary differences to make sense of which academic subjects one is able to endorse and which one can legitimately demonize.

In the last section of this chapter I want to come full circle by highlighting ways in which anxieties about the status of racially and sexually marked subjects and theories in loss narratives are mediated by over-associating the latter with contemporary academic ills, leaving the former ripe for reclamation in the return narratives that I chart in the next chapter. As I explored in relation to progress narratives, the place of lesbian feminism and the lesbian subject is already somewhat ambivalent. On the one hand, it operates as critique of 1970s feminism's heterosexism; on the other, its own racism is exposed by 1980s black feminism. Whichever line is taken, lesbian feminism, like black feminism, is understood to give way to a more general poststructuralist turn to difference in the 1990s and beyond. In both progress and loss narratives, it is queer theory—in the former, coupled with postcolonial theory, in the latter, out on a limb on its own—that displaces feminist theory and whose subjects emerge most clearly in the 1990s. For loss narratives, queer theory comes to represent, and its subjects to embody, the worst excesses of abstract postmodernism and poststructuralism, of myopic academic attachments, and of interdisciplinary humanities play over social scientific (or other pure disciplinary) seriousness. As one passage ironically suggests:

You know the scenarios: queer theory, feminism typically laments, faces the left's exhaustion at the real challenge of revolutionary change by throwing a party. It invites and cultivates gender dissidence; dresses up individualism to simulate political commitment; celebrates the feminine through drag; and always leaves time at the end of the night for some gay-male-only canonical fun. Feminist theory, the queer theorist says with a sigh, is so indebted to sexual subordination that her masochism requires the repetition that masochism always loves. Every act of theoretical or activist engagement returns her to original sin: gender hierarchy, sexual oppression, material inequality. (*Feminist Theory* 2007)

Queer theory is pitted against feminism in both progress and loss narratives, as delineated here, through a series of oppositions that are by now very familiar: real challenges are counterposed to simulations of "political commitment"; sexual subordination contrasted with celebrations of "the feminine"; gender masochism displaced by "dressing up." Thus poststructuralism, queer theory, abstraction and antifeminism are chain-linked not only through their critique of feminism but through the assertion that what has happened is a *substitution* of queer for feminist concerns.[10]

The staging of oppositions between queer and feminist theory, and the tying of these to oppositions between postmodern or poststructuralist and materialist approaches, has broader implications for how sexuality is conceived of as an area of academic inquiry:

While gender has been considered a structural phenomenon, implicitly at least, in past feminist debates on patriarchy and explicitly in recent materialist feminist analyses (e.g. Delphy, 1993; Ingraham, 1996), sexuality and heterosexuality are more rarely approached from this angle. . . . The rarity of such analyses reflects the displacement of the concept of social structure by postmodern scepticism and the recent sociological emphasis on the fluidity of the social (see Adkins, 2002). (*Feminist Theory* 2007)

In the above excerpt, gender equals structure, and sexuality is fused with "postmodern scepticism." This reading goes some way, I think, toward explaining the otherwise rather curious ways in which calls to reject "the cultural turn" are frequently phrased as calls to reject the dominance of sexual over economic needs. Further, and as indicated in previous discussions so far, not all aspects of the signifying chain need to be present in order to be discursively resonant. Take the following passage:

Pitting "essentialists" against "anti-essentialists," these disputes usefully served to reveal hidden exclusionary premises of earlier theories, and they opened women's studies to many new voices. Even at their best, however, they tended to remain in the terrain of recognition, where subordination was construed as a problem of culture and dissociated from political economy. (*Signs* 2004)

The extract begins with the by now familiar muted acknowledgement of the importance of identity critiques, set against a supposedly parallel dissatisfaction with the limits of current epistemological options. Yet this gloss works at another level, too, identifying current problems as to do with the prioritization of the "cultural" over "political," which is also to say the sexual over the economic, suggested not just discursively but by the mention of "the terrain of recognition," the site theorized as that of sexual rights claims most notably by Nancy Fraser (1996; 1997; 2005). Thus, when Western feminist loss narratives call for disciplinary returns to empirical, material realities, they are also making calls for feminists to resist (queer) cultural seductions and return to a (heterosexualized) pragmatics. These moves are only possible, I want to argue, because of the ambivalent position of lesbian feminism in the first place.

As one might expect, Judith Butler is a key figure in this respect once again, representing and embodying both the success of a queer critique of feminism and the institutional privileging of culture over social life and experience. The following extract is typical in its weaving together of Butler, queer theory, postmodernism, and culture:

Butler, like a number of postmodernists, particularly valorizes these, often "less serious" spaces—of play, masquerade, carnival—because it is here that cultural constructions become visible as such and therefore open to challenge. . . . (*Feminist Theory* 2000)

In its emphasis on "play, masquerade, [and] carnival" (theorized rather differently in Butler than in loss narratives' representations of these concepts, of course), queer theory is consistently characterized as "less se-rious" than approaches that are deemed to interrogate social and political structure directly. That these are disciplinary differences is underscored in the following account of an interview with Butler, in which deconstruction is characterized as anti-empirical:

When pressed by [her interviewer, Butler] states that *"subversiveness is not some-thing that can be gauged or calculated. In fact, what I mean by subversion are those effects that are incalculable"* (Butler, 1992: 84, emphasis added). In order to under-stand this striking anti-empiricism, we must take stock of the way in which Butler's theory of subversion is grounded in discourse. (*Feminist Review* 2000)

What is striking to me in turn about the above quotation is that Butler's response that we may not know what constitutes "subversiveness"—that it might not be quantitatively or directly available and that this non-knowing may not always be a dreadful thing—is immediately interpreted as "striking anti-empiricism" and rendered as the effect of a discursive approach. The possibility that such a position might lend itself to empiri-cal inquiry (as it has for many feminist theorists) is precluded in loss narratives that see only opposition between discourse and empiricism. Indeed, it is likely to be because of her anticipation of what is a consistent conflation that results in Butler's initial resistance to elaborating on the nature of "subversiveness," an elaboration she is "pressed" for.

The overlaying of disciplinary difference onto Western feminist loss narratives serves two functions, then: it allows for social science to "own" materiality, leaving "culture" to the humanities, and discursively links "cul-ture" with play (rather than politics) through its over-association with queer theory and its methods. As a result, and as I discuss further in the next chapter, the "cultural turn" becomes not only a prioritization of discourse and language over real politics, but also an epistemology and era saturated with sexual over other forms of intersubjective and social mean-ing. The designation of queer theory as less serious and as interested in play over politics and abstract understandings of subversion does some familiar straightforward work, of course. It separates past from present, political from textual, rigour from dabbling, disciplinary attention from interdisciplinary eclecticism and so on. And loss narratives thereby also find an appropriate subject to mark out as particularly antifeminist in this regard. But these characterizations also have a particular tone that is significant for my analysis here. In the insistence on deconstruction as apolitical the "parodies" of Butler are stripped of their political content, reframed as mere play, and stripped of their history within a particular subcultural milieu. Instead, camp is reclaimed for a heteronormative discourse that trades in stereotypes of the shallow, decadent queer, interested only in "the arts" and interior design, vicious and self-serving (likely to turn, and easily turned), the very opposite of feminist solidarity. It is intriguingly effeminate (rather than feminist) despite Butler's key role in articulating queer concerns. And in generational terms, despite (or perhaps because of) its superficiality, queer theory is also actively seductive, turning young feminist heads away from material inequalities,[11] seducing those (not) old and wise enough to know better.

R E T U R N

3 As part of her now well-known debate with Nancy Fraser over the best way to theorize and redress sexual inequality, Judith Butler makes the following remarks:

Poststructuralism has thwarted Marxism, and . . . any ability to offer systematic accounts of social life . . . is now seriously hampered by theory that has entered the field of cultural politics, where that poststructuralism is construed as destructive, relativistic, and politically paralyzing. (1997a: 265–66)

Her comment here is ironic, its tone parodic; it is an overly simplistic Marxist critique that is left with egg on its proverbial face. At the time of writing, Butler caustically adds that in rejecting the "merely cultural," associating it with those social movements positioned as "derivative and secondary" to the Marxist analysis they are blamed for fragmenting, social theorists can embrace "an anachronistic materialism as the banner for a new orthodoxy" (1997a: 266). Butler writes from within the twilight of poststructuralism's heyday, and so frames attachment to materialism as nostalgic, as does Wendy Brown in her own subsequent dismissal of what she characterizes as an outdated attachment to "the material" that "refuses the importance of the subject, the subjective, the question of style, and the problematic of language" (1999: 24). Further, for Brown, backwards turns instil "traditionalism in the very heart of praxis, in the place where commitment to risk and upheaval belongs" (1999: 25). There are perhaps clues about the direction of social theory in the possibility Butler signals of that "anachronistic materialism" becoming "a new orthodoxy," but in both influential theorists' accounts, materialism still imaginatively belongs to the past, and the techniques and politics represented by poststructuralist emphasis on language and the subject belong to the present. Yet what is striking to me about the first quote from Butler, above, is how easily it may now be read straight, as a description both of the relationship between these protagonists and as an account of the recent theoretical past.

By the late 2000s, indeed, it is hard to read Butler's comment as *anything other* than descriptive. Few social theorists would dispute that we currently occupy ground beyond the cultural turn, or that materialism warrants another look, investigated as either "the social," or "the embodied," or both. So when Antoinette Burton writes five years after Butler's intervention above that "it would seem that the pathologization of culture and the concomitant embrace of the social-as-savior is at work in a variety of professional venues" (2001: 65), there is no textual irony in evidence. Whatever we may think about that "pathologization of culture," we are by this point firmly post–cultural turn. Despite arguments back and forth between Butler, Fraser, and commentators in the late 1990s about the relationship of poststructuralism to politics (Fraser 1997; Butler 1999a; Fraser 1999; Adkins 2002), despite the strength of international opposition to Martha Nussbaum's public and infamous tirade against Butler (Nussbaum 1999; Kapur 2001; Bell 2002), it appears that we (social and cultural theorists) can now agree that cultural theory did indeed go too far in the direction of the textual. With hindsight one might say, along with Mandy Merck, that in the argument between Butler and Fraser introduced above, Fraser carried the day (Merck 2004). Not only can we agree that the cultural turn is over, we can also agree on what should be claiming our attention instead, what should be happening now or next: namely, that renewed attention to materialism Butler warned us about. Thus, in the feminist literature I am primarily concerned with, and as indicated in the last chapter, we are exhorted to return to a focus on everyday lived experience and to material or embodied realities instead of remaining mired in a conceptual realm deemed to have no value outside of the academy (McNay 2000; Walby 2000; Sedgwick 2003). This is a more general trend within social theory, too, of course. Recent special issues of *New Formations* and *Boundary 2* simultaneously herald the demise of the cultural turn, and debate the significance of "the material," a concept whose current time is never doubted. Similarly, *Theory, Culture and Society*'s guest issue on "Cultural Theory and Its Futures" reflects on the strands of the "material turn" via the body, affect, biotechnology, and lives, and what is announced as a resurgent interest in political economy (Venn 2007).

Wary of Butler and Brown's combined scepticism perhaps, such claims for a return to the material are never framed as a simple recovery operation. The renewed interest in materialism is consistently represented as a knowing return, full of futurity rather than nostalgia. Thus we can be said to agree on a few more things. We can agree that identity and social movement critiques of The Left, or feminism, were important as a way of highlighting the exclusions generated by a unified approach to politics; and we can agree that postmodern and poststructuralist critiques of essentialist or determinist exclusions allowed us to value difference at the epistemological as well as the ontological level. We can also agree that these approaches went unnecessarily to the other extreme, evacuating progressive critique of any political certainties and contributing to the demise of The Left, or feminism; and that poststructuralism's attention to complexity of meaning and interpretation distracted us from more substantive concerns with inequality, experience, political economy, and justice, undercutting any real basis for political transformation. In short, then, we can agree that the last thirty to forty years have not been all bad, that there were some important political and intellectual lessons to be learned about difference and exclusion, but that it is now time to pull back from the deconstructive abyss—which has become its own orthodoxy anyway—and move beyond critique. We can no longer do so as innocents, but if we do not combine analysis and experience, deconstruction and material attention, if we do not return to something that we can really grasp, then we remain powerless to alter the pernicious power relations our poststructuralist tactics can cleverly identify but spectacularly fail to transform. We need a new direction that is neither nostalgic nor taken in by what is quite often rendered as the sheer silliness of postmodern and poststructuralist seductions. In the cold light of day, we know better.

As with progress and loss narratives, return narratives reassure us that we can all share a single perspective of what we think has happened in Western feminist theory in the last few decades. But the tone of certainty is stronger in return narratives because of their role in bringing together different feminist subjects in the present. In the last chapter I suggested that academic feminist space is shared by subjects of both progress and loss narratives and that the tension between these is resolved in several ways: by creating authentic and inauthentic subjects of that space; or when this fails, by marking irreconcilable differences in generational and disciplinary, rather than strictly political, terms. Return narratives, in contrast, offer the opportunity for real synthesis. Subjects of both progress and loss narratives can both become subjects of return narratives if they concede a little ground. I was too stubborn, I see that now, says the former subject of a loss narrative; I was too concerned with critique and didn't listen to your warnings, says the former subject of a progress narrative. And in affective terms, the subject of loss can acknowledge the dangers of bitterness and nostalgia, while the subject of progress can concede to an excess of enthusiasm, inattentive to its own exclusions. Both loss and progress can thus be understood as right in principle if not in execution or care.

This reconciliation is facilitated both historigraphically and affectively, as the rest of this chapter will detail. In historiographic terms, the synthesis is enabled by a shared understanding of what has happened in previous decades in Western feminist theory. As the previous two chapters have explored, progress and loss narratives produce a common understanding of what the past contains, even as they value its markers differently. Return narratives can thus affirm a common present by affirming a shared past. Affect is key here because for this positive reinforcement to make sense, a desire to relinquish misery or enthusiasm for a common pragmatism must be generated in a return narrative's feminist subject. In addition, a return narrative resolves anxieties about who is more co-opted or political by asking its subjects to "take stock" and focus on justice over infighting.

This chapter maps in detail these return narratives in Western feminist storytelling, highlighting central features of their construction and broader textual and political effects. As in the two previous chapters on progress and loss narratives, I foreground the techniques through which one strand of the story of Western feminist theory is told, secured, and rendered as self-evident rather than contested. Many of the themes developed in the previous two chapters recur and are extended here, namely the association of particular methods and disciplines with "the social" and "the textual," the pitting of the political and the subjective against one another, and the discursive management of sexuality and race.[1] As my introduction thus far already suggests, Western feminist return narratives tend to occur in later work than progress or loss narratives, and thus operate as a synthesis. As will be evident in this mapping, the vast majority of return narratives take place after 2000, when progress and loss narratives can both be understood to require amelioration, and when the ills of a postcultural turn can be framed as universally acknowledged. Yet this straightforward chronology is not entirely accurate, in two respects. First, as indicated in the last chapter on loss narratives, absolute differences between narrative forms and tones are not always easily identified. Thus loss narratives may contain an element of a desire for a return, and progress narratives may contain ambivalence that undercuts an otherwise positive account. Second, the call for a return within Western feminist theory may also be found earlier than 2000 even in its purest form, particularly outside of the journal set I am primarily concerned with. As early as 1996, for example, Teresa Ebert insists that feminist theory has substituted a "politics of representation for radical social transformation" (1996: 3) and suggests that we should return to earlier political certainties. Thus, although by the mid-2000s feminist calls for a return, along with those from other social theorists, have certainly consolidated the importance of a postcultural turn, Western feminist progress, loss, and return narratives should also be thought of as overlapping, rather than straightforwardly sequential, even while they rely on a common historiography.

IMMATERIAL INTERRUPTIONS

One of the central ways in which Western feminist stories of progress and loss are brought together in return narratives is through placing critiques of the 1970s as a temporary interruption to ongoing feminist engagement with the real world, as indicated in the following two extracts:

Until the early 1980s the dominant perspectives within feminist theory derived from the social sciences and were generally informed by, or formulated in dialogue with, Marxism. It was these perspectives that were displaced by the cultural turn and subsequently brushed aside or dismissed as a source of past errors. (*Women's Studies International Forum* 2001)

Compared to that of today, the feminist theory of that era had a breathtaking ambition and directness that reflected the worldwide explosion of revolutionary activism from which it drew its energies. We know, of course, that not all aspects of this theorizing have stood up well to subsequent scrutiny, but that is not the point I want to stress here. (*Signs* 2004)

We can read several features familiar from our experience of loss narratives in these excerpts. Both glosses frame a past feminist theory as actively engaged, responsive, and clear. What comes after is in contrast dismissive and reactive, focused on problems rather than solutions. We know from the temporality of both progress and loss narratives that what comes before "that era . . . [of] breathtaking ambition" that needs to be returned to ends at the close of the 1970s. And further, we also know that it is the critique of this "explosion of revolutionary activism" that is responsible for theory's loss of political purchase. As in loss narratives it is abstract critique, "the cultural turn" in the first extract, that is responsible for this dismissal and not identity critiques or their subjects. This certainty is undercut by ambivalence in both extracts, however. In the first, the "errors" are alluded to even as they are "displaced" (both by "the cultural turn" and by the historiography of a loss narrative); in the second, the problems identified by "subsequent scrutiny" are flagged even as they are deflected through the insistence on an alternative focus. What both excerpts share is a concern with returning to that more passionate set of perspectives, but in contrast to the apocalyptic tone of loss narratives, return narratives propose that we advance through a recuperation of what remains valuable. Importantly, "we know, of course, that not all aspects of this theorizing have stood up well," and thus a current return will need to be cleansed of the problems of its first incarnation.

What Western feminist theory has lost through the disturbance of cultural theory is more particular than a general enthusiasm or capacity for dialogue, however. It is a focus on *materiality* in its various forms, as both of the following extracts make plain:

Institutional change . . . must be informed by the debates and theories that 30 years of women's and men's work on gender in the academy have produced but, at the same time, these theories and debates will need increasingly to familiarize themselves with the economic ideologies, the institutional and political struggles, and the very real social constraints and inequities once again facing women and men. (*Australian Feminist Studies* 2000)

Language has been granted too much power. The linguistic turn, the semiotic turn, the interpretative turn, the cultural turn: it seems that at every turn lately every "thing"—even materiality—is turned into a matter of language or some other form of cultural representation. . . .

Language matters. Discourse matters. Culture matters. There is an important sense in which the only thing that does not seem to matter anymore is matter. (*Signs* 2003)[2]

Here, once more, while the insights of the various turns may need to be validated, these approaches have nonetheless been accorded "too much power" institutionally. Importantly, as in the latter extract, "language" is frequently synonymous with postmodernism or poststructuralism in return narratives, ensuring its distance from "matter" by establishing an opposition between language and reality.[3] What *matters*—the economy, constraint, inequity, "things"—has been sidelined in favour of one turn or another. In the first extract above, the reluctant feminist theorist is given a catalogue of instructions for how to combine critique and effective intervention. These instructions work for advocates of both progress and loss narratives, since the latter are compelled to take "debates and theories" seriously, and the former to address "the very real constraints" they have surely forgotten. Indeed, the demise of the cultural turn is performative in many of the extracts I am concerned with, by which I mean that it is produced through the chiding of its advocates and an insistence that we are all on the same page. In the second example a feminist theorist who might disagree with the first statement is convincingly mocked for her attachment to the sequential fashions of the second sentence. By the end of the extract she must identify matter as separate from these turns in order to be a subject for whom matter does in fact matter. The future is clear, then: to retain the relevance of social and cultural theory, the focus needs to shift from words to things.

A change in emphasis, a mutual appreciation alone, will not enable the necessary transformation, however. Poststructuralism has to be abandoned by its previous or current supporters if this is to happen. Again, affect plays an important role in this respect, as the aforementioned chiding of loss narratives' future subjects indicates. In both extracts above it is the *ineffectual* nature of cultural theory that is emphasized in contrast to the urgent tasks at hand. In the first excerpt the "very real social constraints ... facing women and men" should serve as sufficient reason to abandon the frivolity of theory; we need to turn to more sober pursuits. Yet in case playful fluidity remains appealing to a critical renegade irrespective of its political failures, the second excerpt throws a bucket of cold water over cultural theory's dubious pleasures. Instead of subverting meaning, "language has been granted too much power," it has become dominant rather than subversive. Further, and perhaps worse, for those invested in creativity and play, it has become routine, rote, as indicated by the seemingly ridiculous proliferation of "turns" that underscores the "too much" of the extract's first statement. Attachment to cultural theory is thus represented as either frustrating or saturated with an ennui-producing predictability. We can be encouraged to turn away from culture, in other words, precisely because we had already started to grow tired of it.

Should these appeals or chidings not be persuasive, Western feminist return narratives employ a range of textual devices that will be familiar to readers from previous chapters to ensure that the abandonment of language for reality be a *return* to what comes before the interruption. Primary among these is the textual establishment of an absolute distinction between postmodernism and materiality, as suggested by the following extract:

As Rosenau points out, materialist approaches are an anathema to many forms of postmodernism. Postmodernists of various persuasions (both the nihilist "sceptics" and the more moderate "affirmatives") reject those versions of modern social science that claim a materialist reality. This leads them to embrace idealist and relativist approaches to knowledge. (*Gender and Society* 1997)

Postmodernism is "idealist and relativist," while materialist approaches foreground the realities "modern social science" is equipped to identify and analyze.[4] "Modern social science," importantly, does not include any of its postmodern variants. As discussed more fully in the previous chapter, rendering postmodernism and materialism mutually exclusive relies heavily on a reassertion of disciplinary as well as political boundaries. The interruption of feminist concerns with the social world postmodernism represents in this extract is thus also an interdisciplinary interruption of disciplinary rigour and proper objects. In the above excerpt and in the one that follows, postmodern or poststructuralist approaches are fully associated with the interdisciplinary humanities, and materialism with the disciplinary social sciences.[5] And indeed, in return narratives, the call is frequently to both:

A materialist perspective is necessarily a sociologically informed one; hence, in reasserting the importance of the material and the social, I am also seeking to reclaim some fundamental sociological insights. (*Women's Studies International Forum* 2001)[6]

Thus the cultural turn can be said to be anachronistic in two senses: in terms of its interest in language over social reality and in terms of its methodologies, particularly deconstruction and textual analysis. In this sense, in return narratives, postmodern or poststructuralist interdisciplinarity emerges as evidence not only of critique (of disciplines and institutions) but also of lack (of rigour, training, or commitment). Woven into both modes are affective encouragements to leave behind that which one had already grown tired of in any case. In this respect return narratives are an invitation to inhabit several different kinds of knowledge: materialist, disciplinary, and experiential.

One might then suggest that return narratives' construction of the opposition between materialism and the cultural turn is less a question of temporal and hierarchical *relation*, and more the establishment of the two as incommensurable: one cannot be both poststructuralist and materialist. In this respect, the claims that return narratives can fuse the two "periods" are in fact textually unsustainable. Take this passage from *Feminist Review*, where the opposition between social reality and representation is directly critiqued, for example:

We aim to reinvigorate materialist feminist debate . . . grounded in the socio-economic realities of women's lives. We do not intend to construct or support an opposition between the representational and the material. Instead we hope for a step beyond—a shift in focus towards the material but one nevertheless informed by insights and perspectives yielded by feminist work on representation. (*Feminist Review* 2000)

While on one level, this extract makes the case for combining "the representational and the material" rather than prioritizing one over the other, the terms themselves remain separate, discrete in more than their naming. True to the reflexive character of the return narrative, the passage emphasizes the importance of the "insights . . . yielded by feminist work on representation" but only insofar as they "reinvigorate materialist feminist debate."[7] Materialist feminism may indeed need to demonstrate new cognizance of its historical omissions; in contrast, however, poststructuralism offers insights, but is not itself the subject or object of "reinvigoration." Materialism is ever located in the future—is "one step beyond"—while representation defines the past, a past it is time to move on from, all the while one from which we have learned valuable lessons. The return narrative is predicated upon, indeed enacts, a temporality in which the cultural turn is, or must be, left behind. The narrative persuades through its eminently sensible pragmatism. Who could be churlish enough to disagree?

MATERIAL FEELINGS

The incommensurability of the cultural turn and materialism produced in return narratives retells the story of more than Western feminist theory. It also creates a vision of the changing history of a feminist political landscape and its subjects, as I have suggested in previous chapters. In return narratives there are two primary political motivations for a revised materialist approach that necessitate the abandonment of a focus on representation. The first is that cultural theory has failed to change, or in some accounts has actively contributed to, women's disenfranchisement. In this vein, the following passage from *Feminist Theory* is preceded by a recognizable gloss praising poststructuralism's emphasis on multiplicity, fluidity, and critique of essentialism, and continues with the following query:

> Yet if women as a group are still poorer, less in control of their bodies and sexualities, more susceptible to humiliating sexual violence and more subject to performing the lion's share of emotional and janitorial labour without . . . recognition or remuneration, it would seem that little we do to performatively resignify gender affects these conditions. (*Feminist Theory* 2003)

The failures of theory are evidenced by women's continued inequality, their experiences of violence and exploitation.[8] One might perhaps object that a theory's efficacy cannot reasonably be judged by its transformative effects alone; on that basis, since "women as a group are still poorer," all theory to date might be understood as of no value. But here it is not all theory, but performative theory alone, with its obligatory nod to Judith Butler's work, which is judged to have fallen short of the transformative mark.

The second political motivation is rather different, expressed here in the extract from *Australian Feminist Studies* discussed previously, namely, that within feminism:

Theories and debates will need increasingly to familiarize themselves with the economic ideologies, the institutional and political struggles, and the very real social constraints and inequities once again facing women and men. (*Australian Feminist Studies* 2000)

In this excerpt "social constraint and inequities" make their reappearance in the present and are portrayed as resurgent rather than continuous. Playful or deconstructive cultural approaches may have been all very well while inequalities were ameliorated, the argument goes, but now that they are "once again facing women and men" more robust theories are sorely need. In both strands of political argument for a materialist return, theory and social conditions (or their transformation) are fused. In the first, performative theory has failed to achieve social transformation, implying that without the interruption of such theoretical approaches social conditions might perhaps have improved. In the second, the political interruption that cultural "theories and debates" represent can no longer be justified in the face of *re-emergent* inequalities. Either way, cultural theory now has scant political purchase. Holding particular theoretical approaches or methodologies responsible for continued or resurgent social inequality enables return narratives to justify the particular synthesis between subject, object, and mode of analysis that they insist upon. This gesture provides a political rationale for the suturing of material conditions, materialist analysis, and a materialist feminist subject as the basis of political viability. It is through such modes of political discourse that return narratives harness the doubled ennui introduced above, namely that "resignify[ing] gender" is both useless and, through that incapacity, tiresome rather than engaging.

As discussed in the previous chapter, the desire to be an appropriate feminist subject of politics that underwrites most feminist theory has considerable historiographic power in Western feminist storytelling. In loss narratives this desire is staged as a contest for political authority; in return narratives this desire can be shared. This is, indeed, part of the considerable affective pull of return narratives: that they offer a way forward for all feminist theorists, as long as they are prepared to take the small step of finally relinquishing what has already become an unwanted critical and political burden. So while initially reliant on the recognition of inertia, return narratives offer the affective gift of relief once that that small step has been taken. This politically validated relief combines with the textual fusions of subject, object, and analysis—discussed above as technical and political necessities in return narratives—to produce a newly engaged feminist heroine. Unlike the subject of progress narratives, this positive heroine is not blinded to real-world inequalities by the pleasures of abstraction; unlike the subject of loss narratives, she is not nostalgic or hostile. Anyone can be the subject of a return narrative, provided they demonstrate the appropriate affect as well as commitment. This subject, like the narrative she authorizes, is democratic as well as pragmatic.

The framing of the subject of Western feminist return narratives as suffused with positivity is stronger still in the set of approaches where materialism is understood as emphasizing "living and non-living matter, rather than the perhaps more familiar definition of materialism as the social and economic relations between women and men" (Hird 2004: 231). In these, what we might call biomaterial perspectives, materialism and representation are similarly understood as inimical. As with return narratives that prioritize social materiality, biomaterialist approaches insist that *matter* has been actively sidelined as a result of recent cultural theoretical preoccupations and that it is this that needs reintegrating into feminist theory in order to move forward. Thus:

[I want] to illustrate why notions such as matter, ontology and substance have come to be somewhat neglected in Anglo-American feminist work and, second, in the light of that illustration, to highlight what is at stake in the efforts of those who choose to "return" to these difficult issues. (*Economy and Society* 2002)

And to repeat part of the extract from *Signs* included above in a context of its biomaterial plea:

Language matters. Discourse matters. Culture matters. There is an important sense in which the only thing that does not seem to matter anymore is matter. (*Signs* 2003)

Such approaches emphasize the stuff of life in preference to its representation. Often in discussion with or as part of the sociology of science and technology, these approaches home in on life's multiplicity, irreducibility, and unpredictability.[9] In a feminist context, biomaterialist work draws substantially on Rosi Braidotti's explorations, particularly in her last two books, of a nonhuman(ist) ethics focused on transformation and transition over the static power structures reinforced in some versions of postmodern thought (2002; 2006). For Braidotti as for others, a focus on matter keeps alive the possibility that the body has a different temporality to social life, one that disrupts social formations and opens up transformative futures.[10] It is shared interest in Gilles Deleuze that links new materialists to theorists of affect, who explore meaning as it is lived at the bodily level, and in terms of the alternative model of circuits of investment and desire thus revealed (Buchanan and Colebrook 2000; Massumi 2002; Sedgwick 2003).

It is in the emphasis on circuits that we can identify some dissonance between these two uses of "materialism" in return narratives. As in the sociological call for a return to materialism, the biomaterialist call knows the importance of acknowledging that it has learned its difference lessons properly, all the while insisting that it is transformed by, rather than bound to, cultural theory. But its proposition for the future is not to return to prior approaches with a new epistemological and ontological stance, but to suture different theoretical strands in new form. In this respect a biomaterialist approach, true to its biotechnological allegiances, proposes a nonlinear methodology that transforms the past rather than relinquishing or returning to it. Let me give a recent example of the language typical of this approach:

The new generation of feminist epistemologists *assesses* rather than construes (new) paradoxes. Third-wave feminist epistemologists do not work according to a framework of diversity thinking nor does their move beyond the postmodern entail a return to modernist identity politics or equality projects. (*Australian Feminist Studies* 2008)

A fusion of sorts is being proposed in biomaterialist accounts, one that expects paradoxes rather than seeking to resolve these. As in the extract from *Economy and Society* above, then, biomaterialist approaches propose a "return" that is placed explicitly or implicitly in inverted commas. It is a "return" that emphasizes *transposition*, in Braidotti's words (2006), a splicing or recombining over temporal or intellectual recuperation. In this respect, biomaterialist invocations do not prioritize one set of disciplinary methodologies over another, but seek to combine these in a range of new ways. The movement of this form of return is more emphatically forward-looking, then, and might also be considered less hostile to cultural theoretical approaches than the social or sociologically informed returns discussed thus far. Indeed, Braidotti's own biomaterialist sympathies tend to be articulated in terms of an appreciation of poststructuralism rather than its demonization (e.g., 2000).

Yet this epistemological openness belies the historiographic and affective momentum that these biomaterialist return narratives otherwise inaugurate. As with the socially inflected return narratives, biomaterialist approaches appear to value the cultural theory approaches they learn from but do ultimately frame them as anachronistic, unlike the sexual difference theories brought forward into a reinvigorated present. The primary mechanism through which this is achieved is textual affirmation. As the above excerpt from *Australian Feminist Studies* suggests, the emphasis in what is often also termed "new materialist" thinking is on enthusiasm and capacity over the constraint and power identified with both Marxist/socialist and poststructuralist feminisms. In this respect, materiality and representation remain temporally opposed despite the rhetoric of splicing, firmly associating positive affect with the former and negative affect with the latter. As with the aligning of passion and politics in return narratives that privilege a social materialism—"its breathtaking ambition and directness" (*Signs* 2004)—bio- or new materialist accounts prioritize the passion of theory and practice that the linguistic or cultural turn is understood to have lost. Thus, and in this vein:

In order for feminists to develop a fuller account of agency, I argue that the negative paradigm of subjectification needs to be supplemented by a more *generative* theoretical framework. (*Feminist Theory* 2003)

This extract demonstrates both the central desire in biomaterialism to focus on life over death, capacity over structure, and asks for a shift from the epistemological to the ontological within social and feminist theory. As I argue elsewhere, biomaterialist narratives thus tend to pick over "the bones" of a poststructuralism imaginatively laid out on a cold slab, consolidating our sense that its time has passed, in contrast to a wholesale reclamation of sexual difference or biotechnology as the fleshy substance of transposition (Hemmings 2009). Through an emphasis on embodied agency over abstract power relations, the above excerpt links both aspects of new materialist narrative, since agency might be defined as the capacities of subjects to negotiate, engage, resist, or remain in excess of the social circumstances in which they find themselves. In the process, the cultural turn is historiographically rendered as sterile instead of generative, as the opposite of creativity and transformation. This is a particularly interesting aspect of return narratives, in my view. While loss narratives are at pains to highlight the inappropriate playfulness of cultural approaches in contrast to a serious emphasis on oppression, return narratives insist that even this "play" is mythic, masking a routine investment in power as constraining and transformation as foreclosed.

When combined, these socially inflected and biomaterial returns pull the rug from under the feet of poststructuralist advocates, who are variously apolitical and overly concerned with power-structures; over-concerned with the pleasures of interpretation, and yet predictable rather than creative. Despite clear differences, the dual approaches of Western feminist return narratives allow the affective arc described to be one that moves from incapacity to proactive ability, from frustration to generation. In this respect, both materialist accounts utilize similar affects of neglect and disenchantment to secure a theoretical teleology in which the abandoned is cast as the abandoner. Wounded but brave, feminist materialists of both strands can thus emerge triumphant to greet the new dawn. As we know from previous chapters, poststructuralism first has to be stripped of the desired object—this time feeling and creativity, as well as political judgment—in order that these can be found anew in the present. And this has particular impact on what Western feminist theory can think it has inherited and what it imagines it must find now or in the future.[11]

INVOKING MATERIALITY

If the argument needed to be made that we are in a theoretical time and place post the cultural turn, one might reasonably expect to see Western feminist return narratives engage with approaches deemed to typify past obsessions with representation over the current moment of materiality.

Even in narrative glosses one could expect to see direct reference or cursory engagement with concepts. But, as suggested above, the importance of materiality is textually asserted as much to *effect* the move away from poststructuralism and postmodernism as to describe it. The performative nature of return narratives is compelling precisely because it both assumes we all agree that cultural obsessions have gone too far and elicits that agreement in the present of reading. In part, return narratives work, as indicated above, through a series of affective mobilizations designed to prompt an appropriate feminist attitude in the reader: to remain attached to cultural theory is to be left behind, to be both apolitical and uncreative. But if this common position is not argued for, and alternative approaches engaged even in order to be dismissed, how is it secured? How do Western feminist theorists come to concur about what is needed for a rich feminist future? Or to put the question another way, how is it that despite the varied positions that feminists take on questions of representation and materiality, we can accept that they are opposed concepts and approaches? Why are the affective pulls I have described thus far in this chapter successful?

In this section, I begin to focus more particularly on the political grammar of Western feminist return narratives, on the textual techniques through which claims for a material return are made. Specifically, I emphasize ways in which the reader is both persuaded of the need to respond to the call to the material and is made active in constituting its opposite—the cultural turn—as already over. Paradoxically, perhaps, the first technique I want to discuss here is absence. As indicated in my mapping of progress and loss narratives thus far, citation is key in securing a particular historical and theoretical trajectory for Western feminist theory. In return narratives citation remains a central historiographic technique, and as in progress narratives, lack of citation is often more significant than what is included. If we recall, in progress narratives citation lack enables the instantiation of poststructuralist or postmodern approaches as inaugurating attention to multiplicity in Western feminist theory. In these stories the 1970s is rarely directly cited (as a decade or through its theorists), and while the 1980s is more often referenced it frequently functions as a catch-all for early critiques of essentialism, to be surpassed by a more sophisticated—and always later—set of approaches. Similarly, loss narratives tend to indict poststructuralist or postmodern theories as representative of feminist mainstreaming within the academy, rather than as a body of work in their own right. Where key concepts or authors (primarily Butler) are directly cited this is in order to reproduce the sense of a downward trajectory for Western feminist theory. Similarly, the 1970s remains vague, bolstering its status as a mythic era we have abandoned, rather than a decade containing diverse approaches. Return narratives continue in this vein, but take lack of citation to a new level, in most cases entirely removing citation from the frame.

If we cast an eye back over the excerpts included in the chapter thus far, no examples (general or particular) are given in order to make the claim that the cultural turn was inattentive to questions of social and economic inequality or prioritized subjectivation over material possibility. Citations are not needed, indeed, to convince us that the tense I have just used here, the past tense, is appropriate. The cultural turn is over (though often still powerful), and the return to materiality is current (though still marginal). There are two exceptions in the extracts I have introduced thus far, ones that do include some direct referencing, and these are:

Until the early 1980s the dominant perspectives within feminist theory derived from the social sciences and were generally informed by, or formulated in dialogue with, Marxism. It was these perspectives that were displaced by the cultural turn and subsequently brushed aside or dismissed as a source of past errors. (*Women's Studies International Forum* 2001)

As Rosenau points out, materialist approaches are an anathema to many forms of postmodernism. Postmodernists of various persuasions (both the nihilist "sceptics" and the more moderate "affirmatives") reject those versions of modern social science that claim a materialist reality. This leads them to embrace idealist and relativist approaches to knowledge. (*Gender and Society* 1997)

The first references a decade, the 1980s, as a way of ensuring that the materialist perspectives returned to will remain Marxist-informed ones. As discussed when I first highlighted the extract, this general periodization is directly contrasted to "the cultural turn," squeezing identity politics out of the picture without having to discuss this omission further. The second extract is unusual in that it directly references a theorist—Rosenau—potentially leaving open the possibility of dissent, in that we may not agree with Rosenau, or we may not like this particular interpretation of her work. But note that the reference is to a secondary commentator rather than to the objects of critique, "postmodernists of various persuasions," themselves. In this context, the reference to Rosenau provides a deflected authority to the subsequent assertions about "nihilist 'sceptics' and the more moderate 'affirmatives' and what they are said to reject and embrace. The need to reference other critics at all is interesting here, since it is so rare, and may be a reflection of the date of the extract—(1997)—when we are not yet self-evidently in the moment of the postcultural turn even for return narratives.

The otherwise striking lack of even general citation in return narratives is, I believe, a reflection of their need, and power, to unite the opposed progress and loss narratives of Western feminist theory. As delineated in the first two chapters of the book, progress and loss narratives have a similar authorial tone that brooks no argument, but they do, nevertheless, have different presumed audiences, different heroines and *bêtes noires*. If, as I have been suggesting, return narratives allow these political and theoretical accounts to coexist, indeed require this coexistence, then their differences must all-the-time be both allowed for and deflected. We know, then, from previous chapters, that while the trajectory of Western feminist theory is contested in terms of politics, value, and affect, its decade markers are not. We share what has happened, irrespective of what we think about it, and thus a common history can be appealed to in order to produce its proper feminist subject in the present. The general story of a return resonates across progress and loss contingents, then, but only if it remains *absolutely general*. To begin to specify that history would be to raise the spectre of significant rather than superficial interpretative differences. How much more, then, the danger of introducing reference to particular theorists, the meaning of whose work is most certainly not shared or whose representative status is contested? Circumventing the dangers of direct citation, then, common agreement is produced through the dulcet tones of pragmatism. Each side is appealed to and is required to concede some ground: yes, advances were made; yes, important things were lost. What is retained is the common historiography. In effect, then, the absence of direct citation in return narratives is precisely what allows a more elusive citation practice to permeate the glosses. What is cited is that common historiography, and its citation—precise in its vagueness—both references and produces reflective agreement.

If Western feminist subjects of return narratives occupy a place in the present with a shared history we can agree we need to relinquish, then it is no surprise that the dominant tone of these narratives is one of im-

patience. Let us not look back at the past too closely, return narratives
insist, since we can agree there were problems on both sides. But let us
instead turn to the tasks at hand, ones that crowd in on the present, and
take action now to secure a better future. The present is a time of material
concern, then, but this concern must always be presented as emergent, as a
forever new development that requires attention. Thus, despite return
narratives spanning at least a decade as discussed in the introduction to
this chapter, their call to recover materiality is consistently phrased as
revelatory and entirely of the moment. The two following extracts are
typical of this mode:

Our starting point is a co-incidence of ideas, a moment when feminist theorists
are rethinking gender and identity in the context of the "social" and/or the
"material." (*Feminist Theory* 2005)

To many, despite this new attention to materiality, feminist theory has moved
farther away from the economic, and related issues of justice, than ever before.
(*Australian Feminist Studies* 2002)

So strong is this commitment to materialist approaches being absolutely
current that even the second extract, which situates this call in relation to a
broader "attention," must reaffirm its continued neglect. While return
narratives frequently frame this emergent interest as already happening,
then, the "event" of the call to a material return is confined to the present
and can never be resolved. Materiality must thus be represented as crucial,
as needing immediate attention and recuperation, but as—oddly enough
—not having a recent history in its own right. Even the fact of feminist
theory's sustained call for attention to materiality cannot alter our failure
truly to grasp its nature. Materiality has been consistently absent from
feminist debate (despite its continuous presence), and now is the time to
begin to return to it:

This is an urgent research problem. (*Australian Feminist Studies* 2000)

I am excited by the prospect of new materialist debates and new materialist praxis
in the years to come—debates and praxis with many hard tasks awaiting them in
the real world. (*Feminist Review* 2000)

Here material returns are framed as an urgent problem in the present that
can only be addressed in the future. While materialist attention is a current
preoccupation, then, its time is also deferred, its resolution longed for but

always absent. In temporal terms what is striking is that these repeated calls are made as if from a moment of unique insight, a controversial reading of the historical record, and certainly not one that references the myriad similar calls from colleagues within the last decade in any meaningful way. Thus, notwithstanding what I would describe as the persistent, repetitive, perhaps even *mundane,* call to return to the material in Western feminist return narratives, each individual call is positioned as a problem of the present, a new concern: one under-recognized by feminist theory to date and requiring earnest attention now.

How do we make sense of this repeated call to the "elusive material" in Western feminist storytelling? Certainly one effect of its repetition is to make of materiality a trope, a concept invoked, still to be embraced or fully mobilized, in short paradoxically immaterial: a floating signifier, perhaps, or more generously a metaphor. In this context, an otherwise open comment on "precisely the unsettling and unsettled nature of matter" (*Economy and Society* 2002) seems to reaffirm rather than challenge its abstraction. But to point to this paradox of materiality's lack of substance is perhaps to miss the importance of its rhetorical invocation to how Western feminist return narratives work. To return to the opposition between representation and materiality: as discussed above, this opposition situates a contemporary feminist subject as already beyond the cultural turn, yet still needing to repudiate its continued dominance in the moment of "becoming materialist." In this respect, return narratives have to replay precisely this scene of opposition in order to produce the (new) materialist feminist subject in the moment of reading. Ironically, then, the continued power of the cultural turn must be affirmed even as it is undone. The material turn is always to be advocated for, but never achieved, since its necessity remains predicated on its absence.

This need for postmodernism and poststructuralism to continue to be imaginatively dominant in return narratives suggests another important aspect of their temporality. If cultural theory is still the demon to be exorcised from the scene of Western feminist theory, the ideal subject of a material return can still be positioned as marginal in the narrative present. As discussed at some length in relation to loss narratives in the last chapter, the subject of Western feminist theory consistently construes herself as marginal in order to retain feminist authority. Thus considerable time and effort must be spent in constructing materialist approaches as current yet deferred, anachronistic yet pertinent, in order that the subject of these approaches can be figured as appropriately heroic yet undervalued in the present. The following excerpts are typical of the tone of return narratives in this respect:

The questions I pose reflect my bias for a kind of feminist criticism that has become unfashionable in the academy. (*Signs* 2000)

Debate about how feminists should understand and deploy "the material" also brings back into view these often-neglected and unresolved questions of class and power. (*Australian Feminist Studies* 2002)

[I want] to illustrate why notions such as matter, ontology and substance have come to be somewhat neglected in Anglo-American feminist work and, second, in the light of that illustration, to highlight what is at stake in the efforts of those who choose to "return" to these difficult issues. (*Economy and Society* 2002)

The proposed theoretical approach is "unfashionable," "neglected," and "difficult," and those who undertake the task heroic, in that they have the courage to return to what remains sidelined within feminist theory. These brave few dare to be marginal, prioritizing "difficult issues" and "unresolved questions" over academic fashion. Note here that "neglect" is an important term in underscoring poststructuralist and postmodern approaches as interruption. We know that it is this set of approaches without them needing to be named because of the emphasis on "ontology" and "matter" or "the material," but also because of the persistent iteration of those positions as peripheral, of course. The repeated understanding of materialist feminism and feminists as abandoned does more than constitute a center and a margin, although this is an important discursive feature. It also affirms that position as morally and politically superior within a feminist archive brimful of the attempt to hierarchize or relativize harms and identities.[12] As indicated in the previous chapter, no one wants to own centrality in Western feminist theory, and the reiteration of materiality as neglected provides further reader investment in abandoning representation for common sense.

This emphasis on bravery in the face of neglect cannot result in the subject of Western feminist return narratives being placed at the center of feminist theory, however, because this would result in the loss of the marginal position. This is one reason why the moment of materialism's return must be endlessly deferred, despite its urgency. As I detail below, however, the insistence on harm as the basis of subjective authority in return narratives resurfaces in the choice of appropriate objects for materialist analysis. The call to return to the material is one that implies a mirroring of subject and object of analysis, and the centering of the latter as the *raison d'être* of an ethico-political Western feminist theory. If this call is to be persuasive, it needs to have an object in the world, a someone or something that is more marginal than the neglected Western feminist theorist. Casting the return to what is neglected as heroic has implications for other subjects in our material scene, too. While I have argued that this interpellation unites Western feminist progress and loss narratives in the present, it can only do so if the call is heeded. The antagonist who refuses to see sense is thus often rendered as dangerous rather than simply misguided, as taking inappropriate objects for, as well as theoretical approaches to, analysis. The affective aspect of return narratives' political grammar—the pull to occupy a feminist subject position resonant with positive affect—is always intersubjective, because there always needs to be someone who is dominant, someone who is actively and inappropriately producing the conditions of material neglect. Thus, if we consider Martha Nussbaum's diatribe against Judith Butler in the late 1990s, Butler's cultural attachments are not simply deemed politically inappropriate, but further framed as actively preventing the spread of global social justice (1999).[13] Invariably, then, some inequalities emerge as more in need of material attention than others.

MATERIAL FANTASIES

Thus far, I have been looking at ways in which the case for a feminist return to materiality has been made, focusing on how the delayed urgency of return narratives secures a materiality/culture split in order to bring together progress and loss narratives to share a vision of what needs to happen now in Western feminist theory. Further, I have been arguing that this vision of the future mobilizes affective investments to represent itself as both necessary and shared. In the rest of this chapter, I explore the narrative consolidation of the material return by focusing on related oppositions that the relationship between materiality and culture produces and relies on. In the last chapter, I highlighted the association of materiality with the social sciences and culture with the humanities and this division's reliance on a theorization of sexuality as insubstantial "play." This complex of associations is further consolidated in these Western feminist return narratives, where the invocation to leave behind the overblown abstractions of cultural theory is often also one to relinquish queer play for feminist seriousness and the interdisciplinary humanities for disciplinary rigour. I extend that analysis here, highlighting how sexuality can only become understood in material terms in return narratives when figured in terms of harm rather than pleasure. In this respect, and as I begin to explore below, return narratives set up an antagonism between sexuality as "merely cultural" (in Butler's words), and sexuality as "culture bound." Only in the latter context is sexuality marked as worthy of material attention.[14] These opposed meanings of "culture" in Western feminist theory also have implications for how return narratives position "race." If sexuality is ambivalently positioned as between different meanings of culture, racial inequalities are always understood as material and worthy of attention. To phrase this otherwise, we might say that culture sticks to sexuality—and particularly queer theory—as the "opposite" of feminism, while materiality sticks to race.[15] But particularly when understood in transnational terms, as I elaborate below, the analysis of particular harm and "non-Western cultures" can become (con)fused, leading to intellectual and political dead-ends within Western feminist storytelling.

If we recall, many of the extracts discussed in previous sections of this chapter situate material returns as precipitated by the ongoing inequalities that feminism needs urgently to address. Because "women as a group are still poorer . . . [and] more subject to performing the lion's share of emotional and janitorial labour" (*Feminist Theory* 2003), because of "the very real social constraints and inequities once again facing women and men . . ." (*Australian Feminist Studies* 2000), feminist theorists must return to considerations of "unresolved questions of class and power" (*Australian Feminist Studies* 2002), with a concomitant renewal of attention to materialist "debates and praxis . . . in the real world" (*Feminist Review* 2000). The attention to materiality is essential if feminist theory is to be attentive to "economic, and related issues of justice" (*Australian Feminist Studies* 2002) and is to remain relevant and in tune with conditions of social inequality that are nationally and internationally pervasive. Yet, again as delineated throughout this chapter so far, the call to material attention is not enough; something has to be left behind, namely the cultural turn that has proved inadequate to the task of analyzing, let alone transforming, the social world.

Just as the disciplinary oppositions explored in the last two chapters are key to maintaining the separation between theories of representation and that social world that needs urgent attention, so too is the over-association of sexuality with cultural theory, both in terms of theoretical frameworks and the perceived nature of sexual injustice. These epistemological and political strands come together most explicitly in the characterization of queer theory as the quintessential opposite of a material return. A materialist feminism may thus be assumed directly to challenge

the recent dominance of Judith Butler and queer theory within anglophone feminist thinking (*Feminist Review* 2000)

such that the move back to what is, and was, most politically pertinent in feminist theory is co-extensive with relinquishing the frivolities of a queer approach as anathema to a materialist approach. As one commentator astutely notes:

In some versions of the story, this struggle solidifies into a battle between warring camps, where sexuality, queerness, performativity, and aesthetic play line up on one side of the divide against gender, feminism, narrative, and moral norms on the other. (*Differences* 2001)

Even in glosses such as this last one, where the problem of a queer/feminist opposition is illuminated, it is seen as resulting from ontological and epistemological differences that precede the antagonism. In my reading, these juxtapositions are central to the shared historiography necessary for a reader to "see sense" in her own right.

Here is a reminder of two of the examples I introduced towards the end of the last chapter—one ironic, one "straight"—both of which serve to emphasize queer theory's *active* superficiality in relation to feminist materialism:

You know the scenarios: queer theory, feminism typically laments, faces the left's exhaustion at the real challenge of revolutionary change by throwing a party. It invites and cultivates gender dissidence; dresses up individualism to simulate political commitment; celebrates the feminine through drag; and always leaves time at the end of the night for some gay-male-only canonical fun. (*Feminist Theory* 2007)

Butler, like a number of postmodernists, particularly valorizes these, often "less serious" spaces—of play, masquerade, carnival—because it is here that cultural constructions become visible as such and therefore open to challenge. (*Feminist Theory* 2000)

From a materialist feminist perspective, then, and in a language typical of that emphasis on individualized pleasure over political commitment,

Queer theory might be able to produce interesting cakes, but it uses the same ingredients every time. (*Feminist Theory* 2000)

It is not only cultural theory in general that Western feminist return narratives invite their reader to relinquish, then. It is a cultural theory suffused with queer pleasures rather than feminist commitments. In this last extract in particular, the assumption that we have already started to grow tired of using the "same ingredients every time" allows the casting aside of queer theory to feel like part of a feminist theoretical maturity.

This fundamental association of queer theory with frivolity is achieved in several ways in the broader literature too. First, queer theory (quite often in the person of Butler) is routinely critiqued for being inattentive to issues of social transformation (Seidman 1996; McNay 1999; Nussbaum 1999) or for conflating cultural and social transformation (Hennessy 1993; Fraser 1997). In work on the biomaterialist creativities of affect, as we have seen, queer theory might alternatively be blamed for being too focused on structural constraint and not focused enough on the capacities of feeling. The substance of the critique remains similar, however: that queer theory's individualistic and overdetermined play reproduces, rather than challenges, the status quo (particularly Massumi 2002; Sedgwick 2003; Hsieh 2008). We need more not less feeling in order to do the right thing. Second, feminist and queer theory are consistently counterposed, usually with an emphasis on the former's untrendy focus on oppression and the latter's seductive emphasis on individual "performance" (Martin 1994; Weed and Schor 1997; Jackson 2007). Third, and I will return to this part of the argument below, queer theory is situated as a uniquely Western concern (in terms of both subject and analytic object), while feminist new materialist approaches are deemed more mobile. In all three modes of association, Western feminist materialist approaches occupy an ethico-political high ground independent from queer concerns, while refusing a dominant position for themselves within the literature, a framing consistent with the journal accounts I have been examining thus far.

Queer preoccupations are not only framed as frivolous, however, but also as culpable, as suggested by the attacks on Butler I have included in this and in the previous chapter. If queer theory distracts feminist attention away from real politics, its aims and approaches are not merely a lesser alternative, but a constitutive reason for the loss of feminist theoretical and political rigour. Queer theory actively leads both feminism and feminists astray, as suggested at the close of the last chapter, and more directly substitutes for feminist concerns. To be a queer theorist—and people who recognize themselves in such a designation will also know this anecdotally—is thus often to be cast as necessarily inattentive to broader social and political concerns. In the return narratives of Western feminist theory, a focus on sexuality through cultural theory (with queer theory as exemplary of this relationship) is not only inappropriate for feminist theory as politics, but it can also be *the cause* of the turn away from politics, the exemplar of the narcissistic concerns of the superficial over the fundamental, the Western over the global.[16] For Melissa Deem, these slippages mean that a critical focus on sexuality can be understood, implicitly or explicitly, as directly mitigating against the radical promise of political democracy feminism represents (2003). In terms of Western feminist storytelling, the problems feminism faces with respect to the urgent need to return to neglected material realities concern both the critique of sexuality's dominance and a move to disentangle oneself from its (apparently fatal) seductions. In Western feminist return narratives, queer theory is an anachronistic interruption, then; we must move on from it if we are to regain feminist disciplinary respect and political credibility.

Yet even though a queer "emphasis on . . . erotic pleasure and play" (Hennessy 1993: 965) is consistently opposed to the constraints of materiality, or to real pleasure with the capacity to transform the social, this should not be taken to suggest that sexuality only ever appears as frivolous culture in return narratives. It is, after all, a particular kind of thinking about sexuality—as pleasure, individuality, and fluidity—that is marked as problematic and exemplified by the excesses of queer theory. To return to the point I flagged in the introduction to this section, the place of sexuality in relation to culture is more ambivalent than my discussion of queer theory in this section might suggest. An emphasis on sexuality is given an opportunity to redeem itself, to figure itself anew as "sexual politics," if, and only if, the object of analysis is transformed from sexual play to sexual constraint. To offset the characterization of sexuality studies as "merely cultural," in other words, we must take instances of sexuality as "culture bound" in order to demonstrate our commitment to a material return. To return to an extract mentioned earlier, we are given some indication as to how sexuality might be reframed as an appropriate object of materialist feminist analysis:

Yet if women as a group are still poorer, less in control of their bodies and sexualities, more susceptible to humiliating sexual violence and more subject to performing the lion's share of emotional and janitorial labour without . . . recognition or remuneration, it would seem that little we do to performatively resignify gender affects these conditions. (*Feminist Theory* 2003)

Here "performative resignification" is set against women's ongoing inequality in ways familiar for a return narrative, but the primary tension is between particular objects of analysis—loss of control of sexuality, sexual violence—and the mismatched performative approach that we know is associated with queer approaches to sexuality. Queer theory, then, is inadequate to the task of analyzing and transforming inequality generally, and, indeed, also to the task of understanding sexuality itself as anything other than Western play. Importantly for Western feminist return narratives, sexuality can be considered an appropriate area of concern only when it is detached from the cultural turn it is said to typify and reattached to framings of sexuality as tied to the worst examples of patriarchal cultural norms and practices. Given its dubious role as that which hinders appropriate development of a renewed materialist feminism, sexuality counts as evidence of material inequality only in its most violent forms, only when it is most clearly constrained, most clearly straightforward evidence of social inequality: the "humiliating sexual violence" of the excerpt is emblematic here. Thus, when we come across a passage such as this one from *Feminist Theory*—

A feminist politics must needs identify possibilities of intervention to effect social transformation, but an effective politics is one which recognizes the tightness of the constraints which bind women into the social circumstances in which they find themselves (*Feminist Theory* 2000)

—we understand that for sexuality to make the transition from frivolity to "effective politics" in return narratives, that "tightness" is everything.

The mutually exclusive relationship between cultural theory and the material turn in Western feminist return narratives squeezes sexuality into one genre or another. From an affective viewpoint, the concern with heteronorms makes queer transgression a fantasy with no lasting value. If framed in queer terms, it can only be read as pleasure seeking and unconcerned with broader sexual constraint, a somewhat paradoxical representation of the theoretical development that gave us the social and political critiques of heteronormativity. If framed in materialist terms, sexuality can only be represented as fully controlled or violently enforced. Sexuality as an object of inquiry can thus only be pleasure or violence, freedom or constraint, and never both (or neither). My sense is that this opposition between cultural play and cultural binding in understanding sexuality is dominant in how we think about sexuality and one of the broader pernicious effects of the political grammar of return narratives. Two domains where this tension plays out very clearly come to mind: global sexual rights and sexual trafficking of women. The field of sexual rights was initially framed as a concern for women's sexual and reproductive rights in relation to control of fertility and disease (Corrêa and Petchesky 1994) and has more recently been broadened to include global lesbian, gay, bisexual, and transsexual or transgender (LGBT) rights (Petchesky 2000; Miller and Vance 2004). Yet despite this inclusion, there is little attention to the overlaps between the "separate" arenas; the former tends to remain the preserve of feminists and the latter of LGBT activists, in ways that resonate with the return narratives I have been tracking here. LGBT rights are thus for recognition or freedom to sexual expression; reproductive rights concern survival or freedom from coercion. That they may overlap, and not only when homophobia is at its most violent, is rarely acknowledged in the literature.[17] The problem is not simply mutual exclusion with regard to opposed concerns, however; it is a problem of how these concerns are understood as of a radically different order from the start.

Debates about how to theorize or intervene in international sex trafficking of women are similarly polarized. Women who are trafficked for sex are largely held up as the epitome of victimization, in ways that make their own labour struggles, for example, difficult to conceptualize or engage with adequately. In this regard, Rutvica Andrijasevic writes persuasively about the erasure of trafficked sex workers from debates about citizenship (2003), Julia O'Connell Davidson about the lack of attention to "demand" for women trafficked for sex (2006a), and Almas Sayeed about the problematic adoption of anti-trafficking agendas as part of international U.S. control (2006). Yet, in my view rather oddly, the presence of agency within trafficking domains is also often theorized as straightforward evidence of freedom from constraint, as if the one mitigated against the presence of the other. In both rights and trafficking debates, it seems to me that the available languages for thinking about global sexual meaning, the ways in which power operates in complex ways and through multiplication rather than simplification of discourses, remain impoverished. They tend, implicitly or explicitly, to take us back to the debates between Fraser and Butler I began this chapter with, where recognition or redistribution are modes attached to static identity positions. Or they ask us to adjudicate between pleasures and harms in ways that always assume we know in advance which practices and identities go with which, and further assume that a given practice could not be both.[18] Most often, too, "sexual freedom" and "sexual harm" are interpreted through a Western/non-Western binary, where the introduction of the former involves a geographical or conceptual transformation in line with norms of Western sexual liberation.

As we have seen, the exclusive relationship between the cultural and material turns leaves sexuality stranded, forced to be one or the other thing: pleasure or violence, freedom or constraint. But it is not simply that sexuality as an object of inquiry is polarized; so too are its theorists. To choose, or be understood to choose, pleasure/freedom over violence/constraint, also locates the sexual *theorist* as Western or Westernized. In return narratives, unless sexuality is theorized as violence/constraint, it figures as the opposite of "globality," as a limited concern with sexual identity, either in terms of its pleasures and transgressive capacities or in terms of the need for political recognition. One of the effects of this is to assume that the growth of sexual movements globally and their use of "Western" terminology to describe sexual subjectivity—lesbian, gay, bisexual, but also homophobia, closeting, and so forth—are irredeemably "Westernized" and simple impositions (Boyce 2006; Hemmings 2007b). Oddly enough, while such understandings valorize non-Western knowledges and sites, they tend to do so in ahistorical ways that ignore flows of meaning through, for example, colonialism, which means that both the "Western" and "non-Western" inform one another in complex ways. As Judith Butler has recently explored, understanding the sexual constraints of "pre-modern others" in opposition to the sexual freedoms of Western subjects turns acceptance of sexual freedom into a litmus test for citizen-ship for "global others," particularly Muslim others (2008b).[19]

In many cases, Western feminist return narratives make this spatial distinction explicit, contrasting the ineffective myopia of (Western) cultural approaches with the importance of social theory's global capacities:

> I believe it is our responsibility as social theorists to demystify a "fluidity" that has been produced at the expense of so many people in the US and throughout the world. When we settle for merely celebrating prevailing social conditions, we miss an opportunity to work on developing authentic forms of political resistance. (*Feminist Review* 2000)

A theoretical and political focus on fluidity is here cast as familiarly complicit with, or even productive of, social inequalities to the point that it can only be understood as celebrating the status quo. In my analysis, too, this excerpt only makes sense when we know that this celebration of "prevailing social conditions" and embrace of "fluidity" refers to queer theory as emblematic of cultural theory more generally. It is marginal Western sexual subjects more than any other who are framed as invested in deconstructing identity (fluidity) and transgressing social norms—particularly of gender—from within those norms. Thus, in return narratives, parody slips into praise. Instead, "authentic . . . political resistance" can be located both via those excluded in the United States and "throughout the world," marking "fluidity" as absolutely "local" (and limited even in that respect) and materiality (coded in the extract via "social conditions" and "authentic . . . resistance") as global. Somewhat ironically, if sexuality can only be imagined as an appropriate object in Western feminist return narratives when it appears as abjection, political transformation relies more than ever on a history of progress in which constraining conditions will be replaced by the very pleasures return narratives otherwise demonize. In this respect, the message of return narratives might more properly be that queer sexual play is inappropriate only all the while there are "others" who cannot enjoy its privileges.

MATERIAL CONCLUSIONS

Western feminist return narratives consistently harness the overarching opposition between representation and materiality to these spatial oppositions, highlighting ways in which their political grammar feeds into the temporality of Western modernity that has been so widely critiqued. "The West" is the domain of poststructuralism and postmodernism, "the world" the domain of the material. Thus:

The focus on representation has led to a relative neglect of socio-economic concerns. The recognition of the complexity of global issues (sadly, not reflected in this issue) means there is much work for feminists to do. We are left with the question of what new kinds of alliance might be possible in a post-unitary feminist landscape. (*Feminist Review* 1999)

One of the problems with the whole anti-essentialist movement now is that it tends to eradicate commonalities among women. I just recently spent a month in India and I do feel that despite cultural and geographic and economic differences I have more in common with a lot of the women in India than I do with a lot of the men in my own country. (*European Journal of Women's Studies* 2002)

The first extract above reiterates the tension between "representation" and neglected "socio-economic concerns," locating the need for a return to "alliance" over "post-unitary" approaches in the "recognition of the complexity of global issues." While perhaps there is scope for deconstruction in contexts of privilege, both extracts imply, an emphasis on "commonalities among women" remains essential for global solidarity and the capacity to transform social relations. The "anti-essentialist movement" (though what this might be remains obscure) is all very well, but not in the face of those complex global issues or as a way of bridging differences with Indian women. That this renewed commitment to shared feminist aims will be "much work"—a phrase recalling one discussed earlier warning eager materialists of the "many hard tasks awaiting them in the real world" (*Feminist Review* 2000)—should come as no surprise, given the bond between materiality and oppression established in return narratives. But in locating the greatest necessity for a Western theoretical and political "return" to materiality in "the global," in finding the worst examples of that oppression "elsewhere," a temporal as well as spatial dynamic between "the West" and "the rest" is enacted. We return to a Western past, by geographically turning to another present (Wiegman 1999/2000: 118). Thus Western feminist return narratives have a double movement in this context. The return is both to a Western theoretical moment before the interruptions of poststructuralism, on the one hand, and to a space of greater (usually patriarchal and cultural) oppression, on the other. It is the turn to "the global" that necessitates this responsible Western feminist theoretical turn, bringing the Western past and the non-Western present together as ideal companions.

The Western feminist desire for "global others" to carry the burden of displaced anxiety about the nature of the political has a long history of critique, of course. Thus Kapur notes wryly that the investment in the "Third World Woman" as particularly oppressed ignores that same subject's individual and political desires: she needs to be rescued or fed, she never needs sex or intimacy (2001). Nirmal Puwar similarly challenges the fetishization necessary for Western feminist theory to imagine that rescuing "others" will deliver it from its own travails: "The future is seen to lie with the refugee or the subaltern woman who act as crystal balls to the theoretical future. In these visions: For whom are we expecting teleological deliverance? Whose fantasies are projected in this telos?" (2005: 18). Importantly, critics of "the Western feminist gaze" focus on the role of representation, not as opposed to material conditions of global inequality, but as central in establishing and maintaining global power relations. For theorists such as Gayatri Spivak (1988) and Chandra Mohanty (2003 [1988]), most famously, racialized and gendered representation is a formative mode of Western "othering" and key to how Western subjects become themselves in the world. For Spivak, in particular, Western subjects imagine themselves "free" through imagining others as needing liberation (social, economic, or sexual): through representation, and not in advance of the same (1999a).

For Western feminist return narratives to juxtapose the "real" of the global with "the abstraction" of the cultural turn is thus, perversely indeed, to erase postcolonial critiques of representation as one of the primary means through which global inequalities and fantasies of the "culture-bound" are perpetuated (Trinh 1989; Suleri 1992; Chow 1994; Ang 2001). In particular, while arguing for the importance of prioritizing material accounts of economic and global justice, return narratives leapfrog back and forth across literature focusing on the legacies of colonialism in Western feminist theory. As Antoinette Burton notes, those who insist that feminist theory move beyond the cultural turn frequently "rehabilitate 'the social' . . . without significant reference to either the fact of colonialism or the historical impact of decolonization on the social sciences from the

1960s onwards" (2001: 64). In casting cultural approaches to meaning as an interruption to concerns with the social world, return narratives evacuate Western feminist theory of its history of critical race work in order to claim an ethical high ground in the present. In the process, postcolonial subjects (of critique) are transformed into postcolonial objects (of importance), with direct implications for who is able to occupy the subject position of Western feminist.

The vilification of the cultural turn in return narratives, with little attention to its political history, allows a vision of "the lost political" to be lamented and recuperated through a specific temporality. As I hope I have shown, a repeated rhetorical insistence that anti-essentialist lessons have been learned (and thus no longer need to be attended to) enables Western feminist theory's lost material object to be reintroduced as material harm within "the global," with little attention to the legacy of either colonialism or its critiques. The separation of poststructuralism and postmodernism from feminism in these return narratives produces an "innocent" feminist emphasis on global social justice without any attention to the racialized fantasies that underpin this temporal and spatial relation. As I have argued throughout this chapter, much of the textual work necessary to this displacement is achieved by positioning "sexuality" ambivalently in relation to two opposed understandings of "culture"; thus, the cultural turn can be abandoned willingly in favour of more laudable endeavours to free others of their cultural bindings. If Western feminist theorists do not want to be accused of being "merely cultural," then they most certainly do not want to be accused of being "merely Western." In agreeing that we have had enough cultural theory, then, we enact a common historiography whose sexual and racial pivots we might otherwise not wish to be called upon to endorse. When we say "yes" to a Western feminist call to return to "the material" we should be aware what else we might be saying "yes" to.

PART TWO

AMENABILITY

4 The work of this book so far has been concerned with how stories about Western feminist theory's recent past are told and with some of the implications of these stories both for feminist theory itself and for its connections with broader social stories about gender and feminism. There are several points of engagement that have emerged from this inquiry, namely the narrative and grammatical form of the stories told and what I have been arguing is the particular amenability of these forms for other stories. My interest throughout has been on how a range of feminist stories connect with one another, over and above the ways in which they might be different from one another, when one attends to the form of storytelling. In this segue, I want to reflect on what this approach has facilitated, both in terms of the internal dynamics of Western feminist theory's accounts of its past and present and in terms of the implications of these dynamics for related areas of inquiry. In particular,

my focus here is on the ways that a feminist desire to distance ourselves from uses of gender or feminism within which we do not recognize ourselves over-relies on the capacities of a feminist subject to carry the burden of that difference, and in so doing is likely to miss important points of overlap that link a range of narratives about the feminist past and present.

RESONANCES

As I hope I have shown through previous chapters, the three dominant narratives that account for shifts over time in Western feminist theory—those of progress, loss, and return—intersect with and inform one another, despite the claims to difference each narrative makes. These narratives are partial and motivated, speak directly and indirectly to one another, and seek to displace one another as the primary account of what has happened in feminist theory's recent past, as well as what needs to happen next. They occupy overlapping times and spaces, sometimes jostling for position within a single account, sometimes directly challenging each other's logic and the status of the feminist subject of a particular strand. Thus, as we have seen, feminist loss narratives implicate the subjects of feminist progress narratives as misguided and as variously apolitical, myopic, or self-serving; while feminist progress narratives construe the subjects of loss narratives as inappropriately nostalgic and previous "generations" of feminist theory as beset by problems of essentialism and exclusion. Return narratives draw on both these strands, asking the feminist subject of the present to renew her political commitment to the best aspects of feminist politics while remaining sceptical of universal claims that we now know to have damaging consequences. Return narratives ask us to circle back in two senses, then: to what remains valuable before a cultural turn seduced us into the abstractions and proliferations progress narratives erroneously celebrate; and to a more productive political and intellectual frame of mind than loss narratives represent. All three narratives are connected at the level of content, then, in terms of what they agree with, refuse, and advocate, and aspects of each narrative can be found across and within individual accounts. Together, they make up the "presumed" of Western feminist stories, and together they make it hard to think about telling these stories in other ways.

One reason for the success of these conversations across the dominant strands of Western feminist storytelling is that they make sense at a range of levels. While each narrative ascribes different value to what has happened in feminist theory over the last forty or so years, the shifts thus described do remain largely consistent. As I have mapped throughout part 1 of the book, the similarities of narrative form include the common endorsement of decade markers and transitions, shared concepts and binaries, hierarchical ordering of value, and a mobilization of tropes such as "generation" or "the political" in order to secure appropriate affective responses in the reader as well as the writer. These narrative techniques form the backbone of Western feminist storytelling and are what allow for easy movement across strands and the establishment of these particular narratives as self-evident, as held in common within the field. Their persuasiveness is facilitated by these overlaps. This is particularly important for return narratives, as we know, which often endorse elements of progress or loss narratives but require a reflexive transition as part of their momentum. The shared terms and chronology underpinning these narratives allow for contests over feminist value to be resolved without having to revisit what we think has happened in Western feminist theory in the recent past: we are required only to value those shifts differently, not to abandon them altogether.

These internal resonances across narratives are also what enable a strong affective relationship to feminist storytelling in the moment of reading or writing. We (writers and readers of feminist theory) do not hover above the narratives we are engaged with, do not evaluate them from a third point external to that dynamic process. As I hope I have shown thus far, we are in fact partly constructed as Western feminist subjects in and through our participation in the narratives I have been analyzing. We agree or disagree with the narrative strand we encounter partly through how it constructs us, what kind of subject it promotes to the status of "feminist subject," and what that means for our own claims so to become. Sometimes we are explicitly marked as successful or as failed subjects of feminism in terms of loss narratives' indictment of professionalized feminists, for example; sometimes this is more implicit, as when return narratives cajole us into a more pragmatic frame of mind. But in both modes, a feminist reader of these narratives is called to and located, and her acceptance of or resistance to that call positions her as an appropriate or inappropriate subject of feminist theory in the present of reading and as a participant in Western feminist historiography. Should she refuse the terms of that interpellation altogether, refuse the framing of available options, she cannot be understood as a participant in the "common sense" of Western feminist theory, and will remain peripheral at best. The feminist reader is thus highly motivated to remain staked in these narratives. And as I highlighted in chapter 2, in relation to my own stakes in refusing the terms of loss narratives, knowing how these narratives work does not necessarily precipitate their transformation.

It is this shared nature of Western feminist storytelling—narrative and affective—that has led me to use the citation tactics that I have throughout part 1. Rather than seeing these understandings of what has happened in feminist theory as individual, I have attempted instead to flag that commonality. Citing journal place and time rather than author, I have situated these narratives not only as shared by a group of individuals, but also as *institutionally* resonant. They are located through peer review, journal history and practice, and by subsequent citation in other journals and so forth. Particular narratives are more or less popular or unpopular in certain spaces and at certain times, and pressure to frame one's work by invoking a particular past comes and goes, as many of us know from experience. The consequences of not getting this right are often brutal in contexts where publishing in the right venues determines one's academic status and research income for institutions.[1] I discuss my citation tactics more fully in the introduction, but here my point is that our reading and writing of Western feminist stories locates us institutionally rather than only in relation to individual others, or in a more abstract political sense, and that this is rarely given sustained attention. By "institutionally," here, I mean that the meanings of these narratives cannot be fully understood through attention to authorial intent, but require a focus on the resonances between these narratives and others, the loose web of connections that make up the spaces of "feminist theory."[2]

There is a further implication that arises from my citation of place and time over author here: these resonances across and between narratives situate us as feminist subjects in ways we are not fully in control of. I have already suggested this means that our choices as to what kind of feminist subject we might (wish to) become are limited, but there is another point I want to make too, concerning the relationship between these narratives and broader practices. Narratives of progress, loss, and return are enacted not only in journal, editorial, and textual spaces, but are produced and reproduced in sites that we routinely (or occasionally) inhabit. They certainly shape what it means to work as a feminist theorist within the academy, but they also produce a relationship to related areas of knowledge production, such as activist, nongovernmental, and policy spaces. This is the case whether or not these spaces are directly claimed or inhabited by a particular feminist theorist. I do not mean here that the Western feminist stories I have been mapping act somehow hypodermically to give other spaces meaning, but that they operate both as ways of understanding those spaces and as responses to spaces that impact Western feminist stories in turn.

To represent these narratives in this *impersonal* way through my citation tactics, then, is already to be concerned with the overlaps between story and space, memory and practice, across a range of sites. The field of Western feminist theory is always wider than its context of production and its utterances. This is most visibly the case in terms of activism, often a clear structuring presence in feminist theory irrespective of whether a feminist theorist is, or considers herself, so engaged, but it is also true for arenas that may not be named though draw on similar debates, utterances, and concerns. To restate this important point here, whether or not one writes directly about gender or feminism in terms of their activist or mainstreamed mobilizations and manifestations, to write feminist theory is always to be positioned within a broader field. For the Western feminist stories I have been tracing, indeed, questions of political change and activism are embedded in the structure of the narratives. They often underwrite the affective pull of endorsing one narrative thread over another, a pull that is central to the ways in which these stories are felt (individually and intersubjectively) as personal. They may describe aspects of individual experience, of course, otherwise we would remain unconvinced of their truth, but the repetition and modes through which they are articulated are held in common, as I have suggested throughout. Thus the issue of transformation, of what the broader relevance of theory might be, is, one might say, part of the DNA of feminist theory. To be a good feminist theorist is to be able to account for this broader resonance and relevance: it is hard to imagine feminist theory otherwise. But it is precisely this affective pull that allows these narratives to represent their crux as struggles between good or failed feminist subjects, that overstates the difference a feminist subject position will necessarily make to how narratives work, and that allows a feminist eye to be deflected from the politics at work in her own invested construction. In these respects, and as I detail further in the final two chapters of the book, my citation tactics comprise a deliberate attempt to highlight, diffuse, or mobilize the *affective intensity* that I have identified as part of what secures feminist narratives of progress, loss, and return. These citation tactics flag both the importance of "the field" for feminist theory and the ways in which political attention to this field is usually sidelined in favor of battles between individuals or collective investments.[3]

ANACHRONISM

One feature of Western feminist stories that links a range of diverse narratives is the paradoxical positioning of feminism itself as over, or as anachronistic. This might indeed be understood as one of the defining overlaps between the narratives I have been tracing, a central feature of their common political grammar. In the stories I have been tracing, in each narrative vein, feminism is always surpassed. The difference between the narrative strands is partly a question of the affective quality of its passing, certainly, yet it is always surpassed. In progress narratives feminism's plurality and fragmentation is celebrated, and the focus on "other" aspects of difference or coalition claimed as an ethical or political good in contrast to past essentialism. Feminist theories and politics that focus on gender alone (rather than its intersections with "other" vectors of difference) are cast as anachronistic, as belonging to another era, one of irreconcilable error. At points feminism is transcended altogether. In loss narratives unified feminism is understood as having been abandoned for an apolitical emphasis on critique (and more ambivalently, difference or identity, as we have seen), leaving feminist theory incapacitated and its proper subjects stranded in the present. This loss of proper feminist theory and politics is most fully expressed in terms of grief for an era now past, its subject consigned to the fate of anachronism described by progress narratives. In return narratives effective feminism has again been left behind and we can all agree the task is to rescue it from an early grave. We can only do this by acknowledging the damage done and seeking to reinvigorate the past through present concerns; without this attention and commitment, feminism will continue to occupy the past rather than the present. Feminism's loss is common to all three stories, yet feminism is no less strong an object for its chimera-like status. A significant paradox is that this attachment to feminism's demise appears to be a precondition for the take-up of feminist subject status in the present, a precondition that provides key momentum for all three narratives. Whatever else they hold in common, progress, loss, and return narratives recognize the importance of a link between feminist theory and politics and see this as the primary way of evaluating theory as feminist or otherwise. The demise of feminism is thus struggled with from positions that value feminism—however defined—in one way or another and that seek to reinstate it in recognizable form. It is lost, but the commitment of a feminist subject (theorist *or* activist) can precipitate its return. This is one reason why so much time is spent on chiding or persuading those perceived as lacking in that commitment into a more productive frame of mind. But in my view the narrative connections between feminist and other stories about gender politics are too consistent and too embedded for a feminist subject alone to carry the burden of responsibility for political alignment. And as I elaborate more fully in the final chapter of the book, the desire for a feminist subject to do this work leads to epistemological and political dead ends that are impossible to negotiate without thinking through the stakes of this desire.

Part of my argument for the moment is that it is not only these interlocking Western feminist stories and their contested subjects who have "lost feminism," and this in itself may be reason enough to remain sceptical of feminist repetition of such loss. As I have indicated throughout, that demise, whether inflected as success or failure, is a narrative precondition for a range of other stories that do not presume a feminist subject in the present, nor have any interest in restoring her to her former glory. Quite the opposite. The postfeminist discourses that Angela McRobbie critiques, for example, make central a subject who disavows or repudiates a feminism whose gains she inherits (2008). She makes little sense except through her repeated difference from feminism, a difference marked by its success (Scharff 2009): thus, we no longer need feminism because its achievements have made it redundant. This kind of postfeminist discourse is most prevalent in Western media representations of gender equality, and indeed that equality is consistently enacted through assertions of young women's and girls' independence and freedom from feminism. But this is not any old freedom. It is the freedom to be feminine, to be sexually attractive—and available—to men (Gill 2007).

Thus postfeminist discourse, as I highlighted in the introduction to the book, requires the rejection of feminism through the repudiation of particular figures—angry man-haters, lesbians, castrating mothers—and so constructs a strange yet powerful vision of both feminism's successes and its psychopathologies. The successes are always understood as reproductive (the pill) or economic (inclusion in the workforce) and the failures as individual or collective excesses, whereby the pleasures of femininity are abandoned and men are precipitated into repeated crises.[4] While understandable back then, the story goes, the inheritors of feminism's gains today need not pay the same price. Indeed, heterosexual femininity itself can constitute evidence of liberation in postfeminist discourse, where within feminism it is often understood to signify the opposite. While feminist theorists of a range of intellectual and political positions may wish to distance themselves from such postfeminist claims, and understandably enough, we should be wary of jumping to instantiate this difference so hastily. It seems important, first, to address the ways in which postfeminist accounts such as these do in fact resonate directly with progress narrative characterizations of the 1970s as essentialist and uniform, as well as with loss and return narratives whose nostalgia is frequently for an equally imagined feminist past. Without this attention we risk reproducing these narrative similarities in the same moment as insisting on their incommensurability.

At a transnational level, we know from work in feminist political economy that the fantasy of Western gender equality as already achieved is essential for the linked fantasy that a particular model of economic development will give rise to the universal good life, including women's empowerment and opportunity (Peterson 2003; Zalewski 2007). We also know from feminist work in critical development studies that this coupling must of necessity ignore any decrease in quality of life that "gender agendas" have wrought in developing countries, as well as any directly detrimental impact on the lives of women that free market models produce (Bhavnani, Foran et al. 2003; Kašić 2004). We may also be critical of cynical agendas of warmongers whose perverse and unsustained interest in gender equality masks these economic interests (Treacher, Pai et al.

2008). Further we may want to point to the ways in which the fetishization of particular female figures as "the most oppressed" by Western powers with little real interest in sustainable gender equality works against local and transnational feminist efforts to critique and intervene to transform power relations detrimental to women (Braidotti and al 1994; Cornwall, Harrison et al. 2007). As a consequence, we may want to complain about the harnessing of feminist concerns to nonfeminist, indeed often anti-feminist, aims, and distance ourselves from their agendas (Grewal and Kaplan 1994; Duggan 2003), pointing to the co-optation of those concerns and the absolute difference between these and feminist perspectives. In short, we usually want to insist on the difference a feminist subject as well as a feminist approach makes in such endeavors. The difference between good and bad "gender agendas" might thus be understood as directly related to the presence or absence of a feminist subject respectively.

I do not believe that this absolute distinction between feminist and nonfeminist mobilizations of gender discourse can or should be sustained, however. Indeed this scepticism on my part is a primary motivation for the arguments in the book as a whole. If we insist on the self-evident differ-ence a feminist subject makes, the points of co-extensiveness of Western feminist narratives and the institutional sites in which gender is mobilized (both with or without a feminist subject) are more likely to be missed. The Western feminist narratives of progress, loss, and return that I am concerned with participate in these institutional scenes at least to the extent that they share both the same lost object (however inflected), the same chronology, and (in return narratives) the same sites of imagined repudiation or renewal. Insisting that the difference between feminist narratives of progress and loss and the gendered temporality of global governance is the presence of a feminist subject who remains critical is to miss the relationship between the *structure and techniques* of Western feminist stories and their broader institutional life. This is bound to have the effect of reducing rather than increasing accountability for these reso-nances, overstating, I think, the distinction between narrative and subject.

How to detach, even if we wanted to, this transcendent subject from the problematic epistemologies that I have been tracking and that she is a subject of? Further, how might we begin to resolve the contests over who occupies that privileged position of feminist subject? Clearly, given the competing narratives I have been tracing, not all such subjects self-declared would be recognized by others. Who decides which subjects count? If, as suggested in the last chapter, part of the work return narratives do is to produce agreement about the past, present, and future of Western feminist theory, does this suggest that only materialist feminist subjects can take up this position of distinction? And what then to do with the formative exclusions—of queer and postcolonial perspectives, for example—that underpin this agreement? We might want to point to the irony here of an ideal feminist subject whose difference from "compromised gender agendas" is dependent on her own erasures of feminist historical complexity, her own generation of a singular teleology for Western feminist theory.

Centring the feminist subject in order to rescue the political project of feminism from its gender equality cousins does other kinds of work too. Not only does her position as boundary marker between "good" and "bad" uses of gender discourse protect both feminism and feminist subjects from scrutiny, but it also encourages blanket judgments about what falls outside the charmed circle. So gender mainstreaming projects are easily characterized as entirely devoid of feminism, entirely co-opted by Western reconstruction agendas, or on the flip side, as wholly pragmatic and thus beyond critical judgement about epistemological impact. Thus feminist theory is easily reduced to a kind of luxury, a prior engagement to be abandoned in the face of necessity, rather than an ongoing project of understanding the world with transformation in mind. Or, to take another familiar contemporary example, Muslim women's agency is often either fetishized in a "secular" Western feminist desire not to be culturally insensitive or ignored altogether and such subjects sutured to patriarchal traditions in reductive ways. Which boundary markers are erected depends largely on who has won the competition to occupy the political border in the first place, on who is understood to be able to make a judgment that means something in the site under consideration. Insisting that the difference will always be the presence or absence of a feminist subject misses ways in which institutional manifestations of a range of (post)feminist discourses are themselves contested sites in which subjects are complexly staked and identified. I want to suggest, then, that while it is clear that discourses of "the demise of feminism" operate differently depending on who is articulating them, where, and to what ends, and that one important variable in those operations is whether the subject claims or rejects a feminist subject position, the political *resolution* to these differences cannot simply be to reinsert a feminist subject, appealing though that may be to those already so invested.

SEXUAL FRAMINGS

It is not gender equality on its own that is given a specific temporality both within and outside feminism. Gender discourse is fully imbricated with sexual discourse in its postfeminist modes, too, as suggested above in the figure of the liberated young Western woman, in whom femininity and heterosexuality are fused. The characterization of sexual and gendered freedom as part of Western modernity has a fuller discursive life than this somewhat isolated figure might initially suggest, however. As I explored in chapter 3, when framed as "merely cultural" (Butler 1997; Fraser 1997), intellectual and political concern with sexuality is also framed as Western or Westernized. As discussed more fully in that chapter, in loss or return narratives, sexual freedoms or identities are constituted as privileged objects of inquiry, as apolitical preoccupations when compared to global harms and the need for redistributive justice. In feminist return narratives in particular, sexual freedom and its theorization are consistently pitted against "other"—and I have argued, frequently racialized—human rights in a global frame. In short, as in both progress and loss narratives, claims for sexual freedom will always be trumped by claims for attention to racialized harm, except where sexual harm can be theorized as the result of patriarchal culture or global racial inequalities (as in the examples of trafficking or sexual violence). More recently, claims for sexual rights are understood as needing to be balanced against the claims to citizenship that those imagined to be hostile to sexual rights, or to conceive of them differently, may make. Thus sexuality is pivotal in Western feminist historiography, its rising sign marking a turning point between eras pre- and postcultural turn. In loss and return narratives, our postfeminist heroine can provide the perfect alibi in terms of evidence of how damaging this emphasis on sexual freedom can be, indeed. But it is precisely the fact that this ring fencing of sexuality—and particularly identities associated with sexual freedom—as Western is not a position claimed by feminist or other progressive political theorists alone that should raise alarm bells.

Those postfeminist accounts of sexually saturated gender equality in

Western media and popular culture resonate with these more directly transnational concerns with sexual rights in formative ways. When claimed as a clearly good thing, sexual freedom (whether heterosexual or homosexual) also tends to mark the superiority of Western, and particularly secularized, contexts, over those understood as less modern, more patriarchal and religion-bound. As Joan Scott's recent work on what have become known as "the headscarf debates" in France shows, the understanding of sexual liberation as Western can also be easily harnessed to a conflation of sexual liberation and gender equality, which consistently reduces the latter to the freedom to exercise (hetero)sexual independence (2007). In Scott's analysis, Muslim "veiled women" can thus be positioned as self-evidently unequal on the basis that they do not make themselves available to an outside (implicitly male) gaze. Importantly, within this frame, women's equality or inequality more generally can be directly read off their visual self-representation: covered equals sexual constraint equals gender inequality; uncovered equals sexual assertiveness equals gender equality. It is also partly through rendering gender equality as sexual equality that the *temporal distinction* between Western democratic and "other" states or cultures is secured. The latter will become the former when gender (which is also to say sexual) equality has been achieved, and this entry into modernity will also be readable through the freedom (which is to say relative uncovering) of women's bodies. In my reading here, there is a direct relationship between postfeminist media representations of feminism as anachronistic and repressive and representations of Muslim women as patriarchal dupes. The links are secured in the figure of the sexually liberated young Western woman (who does not have to be white as long as her embodiment can be clearly read as "Western"). As with the sense of feminism itself as lost, the sense of sexuality as a Western concern, prerogative, or problem is a widespread position, one that gains fuel from the assumption of sexual equality's absolute difference from other political agendas.

We can begin to see how the relationships between sexual and gendered freedom and repression map transnationally as well as temporally, then. And in this geopolitical context, it is no real surprise that contemporary homosexual identities, understood as Western, are also claimed as part of what makes Western states and subjects more advanced than other states and subjects (particularly Muslim and/or Middle-Eastern and/or

African). As is now well documented, and as I flagged towards the end of chapter 3, the introduction, or attempted introduction, of "citizenship tests" that gauge responses to images of "gay couples"[5] embracing or holding hands in a range of European contexts as a precondition for suitability of entry to Western democracies for would-be migrants, singles out Muslims for particular surveillance (Massad 2007; Butler 2008b; Haritaworn, Tauqir et al. 2008). Such tests mark Muslim subjects as more likely to be homophobic, and predictably enough pay scant attention to the ways in which these imagined havens for sexual minorities are themselves contested sites of sexual meaning and safety (see Cruz-Malave and Manalansan IV 2002; Luibhéid and Cantú Jr 2005; Puar 2005; Luibhéid 2008).

As the work on the sexual torture of prisoners at Abu Ghraib has also indicated, acts culturally associated with homosexuality (such as sodomy) have also been taken up as tools for transgressing the supposed incommensurabilities between Muslim and secularized positions, with the aim of breaking down Muslim subjectivity as part of a violent sovereign project (Tétreault 2006; Puar 2007). The use of sexuality as a temporal and geographical marker of modernity, then, needs to be contextualized as ethnically and religiously marked, and also as reinforcing gendered oppositions. While men's patriarchal homophobia must be left behind as anachronistic in these framings, women are compelled to leave behind outdated attachments to both patriarchal heterosexual modes and segregationist attachments to women (in familial, intimate, or political manifestations). It is unsurprising, then, that in the harnessing of sexuality and gender discourse to transnational regulation, lesbian desire is undertheorized and consistently invisible.[6]

It is tempting in such a discursive complex to want to distance oneself from a focus on sexual identities and freedoms altogether, given the highly problematic mobilizations of these as *de facto* Western, as I have been discussing. Sexuality might perhaps be said to be the new "gender" in terms of the weight it carries in discourses of coercive modernity. I might well want to ensure that I come down firmly on the side of the Muslim migrant thus abused or denied citizenship, or the veiled woman whose face must be seen to be visible within a Western heteronormative sphere if she is to be granted self-determination. One can see the appeal of abandoning sexuality as a relevant epistemic or ontological starting point for political analysis on the basis of these current manifestations, turning instead to the material harms its invocation inaugurates. Or indeed, one might want to point to the various ways in which sexuality as freedom or constraint is constructed in different spaces and places, as I have attempted to do in previous work (Hemmings 2007b), and to challenge the consistent privileging of Western sexual identities (including the kinds of exclusions they enact) in such analytics and practices. One might even want to challenge the value of using Western sexual identity categories at all on the basis of both inaccuracy and potential for regulatory control, as well as in order to establish a more open sexual epistemology.

Such approaches constitute direct ways of pointing to the co-optation of a progressive sexual agenda for conservative ends and of insisting that queer theorists and activists must be vigilant to ensure that a fight for sexual freedom does not reinforce power relations that govern global flows of people and commodities (Hennessy 2000). They also constitute good analytic and political arguments for the importance of an intersectional approach that foregrounds the relationship among and across vectors of power over the privileging of the single axis. But against the persuasiveness of these positions, I have lingering doubts about the longer-term epistemological and political transformations they are likely to effect. One doubt concerns the question I have already raised about the dangers of reproducing the oppositions between sexuality and "other" political vectors of power. In the desire to free oneself from the use of sexual equality in Western discourse—as signalling the end of gender discrimination, or as the "ur" sign of modernity—one risks reproducing the false temporal and geographical separations that the reification of sexuality as a manifestly different site of power actually facilitates. To restate what I think is an important point, in Western feminist return narratives sexual freedom emerges as a uniquely cultural concern, less serious and more superficial than the real issues of global injustice framed as more appropriate objects of inquiry and intervention. In terms of sexuality's a-feminist resonance, we might also say that the links between discourses of sexual liberation, gender equality, and global regulation (in terms of migration and war) only confirm this sense of sexual freedom as a "red herring" in political terms.

Yet for these overlaps to chime effectively, one has already to have accepted that sexual freedom or sexual identities do indeed map temporally and geographically in these ways, and only in these ways, or, that when they do not, the terms themselves must of necessity be abandoned. An acceptance of the sexuality/materiality opposition leaves us ill equipped to deal with the ways in which "materiality" here is racialized and spatialized in Western feminist historiography already. This opposition, ironically enough, prevents us doing the real intersectional work required for a more complex analysis of the mobilization of "sexuality" in relation to "race" and "gender" that is frequently called for in accounts that read sexual discourse for the truth of "sexual freedom." "Sexuality" and "race" can be brought together, perhaps, but have already to be understood as independent terms of analysis and ontological referents. A second doubt about the value of leaving behind an emphasis on sexual freedom because it is perniciously Western, then, concerns the ways in which this leaves such proclamations (that sexual freedom has been attained) curiously unchallenged. Whatever postfeminist discourse proclaims, young Western women *do not* occupy self-evident positions of increased sexual agency, competency, or control, either compared to their own mothers or compared to non-Western women. This is not to say that young Western women never evidence sexual agency either, of course, but to say that this is not a de facto characteristic of this subject. Neither, of course, do Muslim women straightforwardly evidence a rejection or acceptance of secular sexual mores in direct relation to covering or uncovering, as is often presumed.[7] And neither, indeed, does it seem sufficient to imply that because gay freedoms are being mobilized against Muslims (and others) in Western citizenship tests that the concept of "gay freedom" is de facto anti-Muslim.

Let me be careful to be clear here. I am not suggesting that theorists who critique uses of Western sexual identity categories as part of global regulation make the direct claim of the previous sentence. But when critiques ask only how sexual discourse is mobilized in such contexts, who it belongs to and implicates, and what work it does in opposition to migrant subjects or detainees, they run the risk of reproducing the very opposition (between sexuality and "real politics") that grounds the temporality otherwise abhorred. When such arguments either stop at the critique or anticipate that there is a clear "side" to be taken in such debates, and that once taken, the politics of a given position will be secure, sexuality is once more reified as different from—opposed to—a politics of migration, or antiwar politics. There are several consequences of this reification, not least the difficulty of being able to conceive of "identity combinations" that do not assume internal antagonism—e.g., gay Muslim. Further, the "antisexuality" position assumes that non-Western religious, cultural, or political movements cannot be accused of homophobia without that being understood as the imposition of a Western imperialism. It seems urgent to untangle these threads and resist such opposed understanding of political spheres, both in order to challenge the exclusions of sexual discourse and to continue to have something meaningful to say about homophobia in local and transnational contexts. This is particularly important in light of the ways in which women are often absent from debates about sexual asylum or homophobic violence, which, as I have argued, is partly to do with the ways in which gender and sexual discourses are epistemologically and temporally linked. As Jacqui Alexander, Jyoti Puri, and Ratna Kapur among others have argued, sexual identity as Western freedom or preoccupation can easily slip into sexual identity as Western decadence in postcolonial nation-building discourses that seek to control the sexuality of women in particular (Alexander 1994; Puri 2002; Kapur 2005). At the very least, then, an account of the damage done to political analysis by imagining sexuality as cultural, and thus in Western feminist historiography, as Western, seems timely—at least as timely as accounts that emphasize the racialized exclusions of sexual identity when reified as border marker. Here, in particular, I would want to advocate for the importance of attention to overlaps across positions often thought of as distinct, over and above articulations of oppositional political positions imagined to be free from Western taint.

GENERATIONS

The shared attachment to feminism's demise in Western feminist storytelling resonates with a much broader range of understandings of gender and feminist positions, as I have been suggesting, including those understandings Western feminists are heavily invested in disidentifying themselves from. My argument has been that a too singular focus on marking the distinctions between politically progressive and politically conservative uses of gender discourse fails to attend sufficiently to the narrative continuities across those uses, and that this is likely to reproduce rather than alleviate the problems identified. Here, I want to explore a further aspect of the linear temporalities I have been critiquing within Western feminist storytelling, namely that of generational discourse. My interest in so doing is both to extend the discussion of the impact of narratives of progress, loss, and return on what academic feminism can imagine as its present and future and to explore one dominant way in which the independent status of the Western feminist heroine is secured, against the complexities of time and space that mark the field of inquiry. I have reflected on the question of generation in the telling of Western feminist stories at different moments in the book so far, but most particularly in chapter 2, where I sought to unpick its function as a way of glossing over political and theoretical tensions otherwise less easily displaced. Here I carry forward these reflections to consider its role as a universal trope in managing spatial, geographical, and temporal difference within feminist theory.[8]

Western feminist stories of progress and loss use generation as a way of making sense of the shifts feminist theory is presumed to have made. If, as I have suggested, these stories rely on a decade-by-decade approach, it is also the case that these different periods house different authors, of different ages. The present is always occupied by the authors who press on or look back in ways that reflect their own theoretical and political investments. For example, in loss narratives the author positions herself as part of a previous generation: she can look back and appreciate what was lost or what can be reclaimed. The past, when she was young, was brighter and more political; the present and future are doomed, or indeed hopeful, to the extent that she is listened to and her theoretical and political position reinvigorated. Loss of political and theoretical integrity thus occurs both outside of her control and (implicitly or explicitly) outside of her age group, as the professionalized who come after and the even younger who come now are frequently cast as irredeemably self-serving, ahistorical, or apolitical. Attachment to the certainty that feminism is either over or entirely compromised must in this context be seen as one way of ensuring that the subject of feminism remains the same, indeed remains co-extensive with the author of loss narratives. In progress narratives, in contrast, an older generation's errors are moved away from, and the naïve attachments of the then young are replaced by dynamic investments in multiplicity and coalition of the *now* young. Previous generations of feminists do not understand contemporary political or theoretical concerns; indeed, that lack of understanding remains crucial for a new generation's sense of itself as progressing, as leaving older issues (and subjects) behind. In these narratives, the intellectual convictions and political will of young, old, or in between are assumed to be radically different and our lives fully differentiated from one another's. It is rare indeed that these narratives represent or imagine common attachments or interests across the decades.[9] In return narratives, feminist generations can (finally) come together to embrace the future, but what must be relinquished—epistemologically and ontologically—remains generationally distinct.

Generational logic more generally has already been critiqued within feminist theory for a range of compelling reasons that I would endorse, namely that it represents the past and present through generational struggles within a *family drama*, as inevitable and bound to be reproduced with each successive "generation" (Roof 1997; Probyn 1998; McMahon 2005). Feminism is thus locked into a psychoanalytic dynamic of vigorous supersession (by the younger) and melancholic nostalgia (of the older), and figures both mothers and daughters as themselves always bound in antagonistic relation. In this respect, generational narratives are heteronormative and homosocial, as they assume women's cross-generational relationships with one another can only be hostile. Luce Irigaray and Judith Roof have both cautioned further that such hostility has at its root the assumption that both mother and daughter want the father/phallus/power, and thus intergenerational competition is always about sameness masquerading as difference (Irigaray 1985a; Irigaray 1985b; Roof 1996). And it is Julia Kristeva who most famously theorizes generation geographically as well as temporally, insisting that "consideration of generations of women can only be conceived of in [such a] global way as a succession, as a progression in the accomplishment of the initial programme mapped out by its founders" (1981: 194).

There are other related reasons to be wary about the use of generational discourse. It is, in my view, deeply ageist within this heteronormative frame. Even where hostility is replaced with mentoring and encouragement, on the one hand, and recognition and respect, on the other, the assumption remains that feminist theory cannot but be passed on to the "next generation," as though only the young, or young-ish, could carry its flags and burdens. I have before me an image of a relay race where the baton is either carried forward or dropped, the moment of touch a singular one of transmission. The baton passer drops back once the burden has been passed, watching proud or critical from the sidelines. One cannot be both passer and inheritor at once, of course, and inheritors must also pass on the baton or else run round and round the same ground until they collapse. For those selfish daughters who refuse to be mothers, their barren inheritance is redundancy and exhaustion. Believing themselves forever young, convinced of their own regenerative capacities, they just do not know when to step aside. Such visions are heterosexist insofar as they assume the failure to age gracefully can only be narcissistic and irresponsible and have at the centre of the feminist scene a critical daughter tutting at her mother's embarrassing performances. In generational narratives, creative, political, intellectual feminist space is never shared beyond brief moments of encounter, transitional moments for the young who are the only real subjects of linear narratives (the rest of us are dead or dying). Impossible here to grasp the possibility of feminist spaces of friendship, desire, affiliation, and productivity that produce variegated historical accounts whose subjects (of any age) shuttle back and forth between their own and others' memories, representations, and fantasies of past, present, and future.

To return to Kristeva, generational narratives of feminist history are invariably spatially and temporally universalizing, insofar as they presume a uniformity of "progression" and a singular subject passing on that history to a successor subject who is recognizable and recognizes *that* history. The model is *de facto* developmental, assuming a common object and end across geography, though in fact imposing a singular, dominant story as shared.[10] As discussed throughout the book thus far, a shared global feminist future requires the fantasy of a shared oppressive past, already moved beyond in the West, but culturally present for the South and East. The Western feminist progress, loss, and return narratives with which I am concerned reproduce geographical as well as sexual power-relations, in that they privilege an abstract generational discourse over located historical or geographical specificity. They make little if any reference to context, despite the fact that we know, for example, that institutionalization of feminist thought is extremely uneven across time and space. Within Europe alone, feminist theorists teach and conduct research and publish in radically different circumstances and with varied degrees of financial and intellectual support.[11] A loss narrative that critiques feminism for its increasing professionalization and abstraction thus takes one particular exception as the model, and then blames feminism in general for this development; a progress narrative that critiques feminism for its continued adherence to identity categories now that "woman" has been thoroughly deconstructed does the same. Or to ask the question a different way, since the majority of feminist theorists globally work in constrained conditions, in and out of the academy, with or without funding, often for little or no remuneration, who are we talking about when we assume feminism as a knowledge project has lost or transcended its (identity) politics?

Generational framing of Western feminist stories sees others as more or less invested in feminism by prioritizing time over context. There are individual as well as political reasons for the use of generation as explanation for shifts in Western feminist theory too. Even where differences of generation within feminism are positively viewed, it is the differences between cohorts of feminists, rather than similarities across time and space, that are emphasized and that are understood to mark generation as such (O'Barr 2000; Thorne 2000; Calloni 2003). Thus, as discussed in chapter 2, generational accounts reproduce the assumption of a linear progression of Western feminism and feminist theory, one in which those positioned as passing on their inheritance may have achieved much, but they must also be "left behind": they are ontologically as well as theoretically or politically anachronistic. Those posing as inheritors are ceded a legacy and a debt, both of which have to be honored, and be seen to be honored (Wiegman 1999a; Adkins 2004), if the brutal transfer of relevance is to be mediated. For Western feminist stories what this means is that the affect infusing feminism's demise is always also one of personal loss or liberation, but never accountability. "Generation" is in fact precisely what allows affective investment in the feminist subject to remain positive at the individual level. To retain relevance if passed over, those inheriting may be marked as unworthy or ungrateful; to refuse duty, those passing on can be disrespected or forgotten. If feminism has been lost, or if it remains as anachronism, then this is always someone else's fault. A previous generation clung too long to outdated modes of political unity; a current generation of feminist academics lacks political vision; a presumptive generation of young women has abandoned feminism entirely. The young or old are superior or inferior, their concerns unrecognizable, their perspectives myopic and narcissistic (Sherry 2000). Generation allows loss without

responsibility and progress without obligation. The tension is familial in
the worst ways. It reinforces the violent Oedipalization of "inheritance"
(Kristeva 1981; Roof 1997) and underscores its heteronormative dynamics.

Considerable work has to be done to retain the temporality of Western
feminist storytelling as generational, partly in order to mediate the stark
empirical inaccuracy of what is represented. Different generations, we
presume, are different ages, with the old being those "left behind" and the
young being the beholden or else the carelessly forgetful. When does a
generation begin and another one end when we are describing communities of practice? When do I become a different generation from my
students, for example? When our distance in age is sufficient for me to
have birthed them? When their interests look too different from mine to
be recognized? When I sludge my way to the bathroom in the morning,
rather than leap up with enthusiasm to meet the new day? Or simply by
virtue of having students in the first place? In fact, of course, the young
and old, and ages we can only presume lie in between, are subjective,
overlapping positions, even in flat empirical mode. Rosalind Gill expresses
similar doubts about the empirical accuracy of generational claims in
feminist theory in her review of Natasha Walter's *The New Feminism*,
noting, "Even though I am almost the same age as [Walter], I felt . . . old,
unreconstructed and cynical" (2000: 140–41). Because Walter represents
her own position as "new" and her cohort as "young," Gill's differences in
perspective work to place her "before" Walter historiographically. Generation thus carries the weight of what might better be characterized as
theoretical or political differences of opinion manifest in the present,
rather than across time. In effect, generation is performative: reading
Walter makes Gill feel old, and this makes sense because the political and
affective conditions for understanding certain feminist attachments as
anachronistic are already in place. Generational discourse thus not only
substitutes change over time for contest or concurrence in the present, but
further, acts as a mechanism for obscuring these contests or concurrences,
deflecting these onto (naturalized) ontological differences.

INSTITUTIONAL MAPS

The theoretical and affective deflection of contest onto generation marked
in Gill's discourse, above, can also be traced in debates about the proper

name of the field of inquiry. As I have explored elsewhere, arguments over whether we should call the field "women's studies" or "gender studies" in particular tend to instantiate a chronology as well as a theoretical or political intervention (Hemmings 2006). Those in favor of the designation "gender studies" often locate it as a necessary shift within a Western feminist progress narrative. In this context gender studies is consistently understood to represent the expansion of the field to include masculinity studies, transgender studies, queer studies, and postcolonial studies, a set of linked interests beyond "women" as a unified or isolated category (e.g., Fernández-Kelly 2000; Gillis, Howie, et al. 2004). Gender studies may also be claimed as an appropriate term for interventions within social policy, development studies, or international relations, where the focus is articulated as on gender *relations* over women's interests per se. In this sense gender studies is positively claimed to describe shifts in perspective both within and outside the academy. In the process women's studies is frequently represented as both politically and intellectually anachronistic, and importantly as part of an earlier generation of institutionalization (see Threadgold 2000). The claiming of gender studies as a theoretical and political advance is thus often a constitutive part of Western feminist progress narratives and directly links these with both Third Wave political formations and gender mainstreaming endeavors.[12]

In contrast, and rather unsurprisingly, the claim that "women's studies" best designates the field tends to inflect this same history as one of depoliticization, represented through the attempted neutralization of women's studies' transformative capacities (e.g., Klein 1991). Within loss narratives in particular, "gender studies" becomes a sign of the desire for institutional acceptance and evidence of the loosening of ties between academic feminism and a broader transformative agenda (Evans 1991; Demoor and Heene 2002). Or it is cited as evidence of the increasing instrumentalization of the field in the context of mainstreaming agendas (Kašić 2004), signaling precisely the loss of a feminist agenda in ways I have indicated above. Alternatively, claims for women's studies over gender studies may emphasize the importance of that history as central to what the field means (Wiegman 2003) or as a site that appropriately houses (rather than prevents) debates over the meaning of "woman" that characterize the international, institutional life of this diffuse project (Griffin and Braidotti 2002). These last efforts, in particular, situate the refusals of "gender studies" as historically informed and resolutely European respectively. They also mark the belief that no single designation could finally and accurately represent the field.

What remains common to many of the debates I have had to simplify above is the *temporal* separation of women's and gender studies. Women's studies is consistently represented as coming first, subsequently to be displaced or contested by gender studies. Thus Diane Richardson and Victoria Robinson ask of gender studies, "Should we welcome [them] ... or should we be critical?" (1994: 11), as if participants in both the field and the naming debates all occupied the same questioning location at the outset, namely women's studies. Since this is clearly not the case—hence the debate—the question serves to reproduce the teleology of inheritance that marks these arguments as generational. Women's studies is marked as original, with gender studies as the (young) upstart whose behaviour remains subject to parental correction. This generational portrayal of women's studies and gender studies emphasizes the two as entirely separate projects with distinct subjects and objects. It detracts from any analysis of the complex interactions and overlaps among projects thus named, always knowing in advance who and what constitute a properly political feminist project. To this extent, gender studies advocates are likely to miss the ways in which whatever we call the field, gender tends to (re)attach to women whether we like it or not. And women's studies advocates are likely to miss the different histories and locations within gender studies, some of which may indeed be resolutely apolitical, some of which most assuredly are not. Further, similarities across the institutional life of the field, whatever it is called, overlaps across curricula, and pedagogic approaches, for example, are likely to be overlooked when the name itself is understood to signal radical differentiation across time and space. Even in an institutional context in which the move from women's to gender studies *is* an accurate description of historical shifts, in other words, this does not in itself tell us very much about the different ways in which that position may be occupied.[13]

In a U.K. graduate context such as the one I teach in, named the Gender Institute for many of the reasons articulated above but mainly because of institutional constraint, teacher and student attachment to "gender studies" as the descriptive term for the field may be shared or contested but often for quite different reasons.[14] Thus, one participant in this space may endorse gender studies because of their interest in and commitment to intersectionality or deconstruction; another may find it a useful term because of its broader institutional recognition in policy and development studies, but prefer the term "women" in rights contexts; yet another may have hoped that a space so named would have attracted more men into it and worry about the slip of gender into women's studies the scarcity of male graduate students is understood to represent. And by the end of a given year, each of these positions may have shifted on the basis of experience and debate. Faculty may similarly embrace or resist the designation of our working site, as suggested by the range of titles we have individually adopted, or been encouraged to adopt. We occupy the space of the Gender Institute and teach its Masters and PhD Programmes in Gender under the following designations: Reader in Feminist Theory; Lecturer in Gender, Development and Globalisation; Lecturer in Gender Theory, Culture and the Media; Professor of Gender and Political Theory; Lecturer in Transnational Gender Studies; Lecturer in Gender and Social Science; Professor of Economic Geography and Gender Studies; Visiting Professor of Sociology and Gender. In addition to the clear marking of disciplinary positions within what is an interdisciplinary institute, these differences also mark a range of inflections within the field, and reflect upon one another when seen in context. I chose my own title, Reader in Feminist Theory, out of a desire to mark my intellectual and political attachments within gender studies, but I realize here that it also marks a dissonance or discomfort with "gender studies" (a discomfort I would also have with "women's studies"), or a potential framing of the other titles as somehow not feminist. Naming here does considerably more than mark a linear history, and it raises many of the same concerns pertinent to spaces named "women's studies" in a range of other institutional contexts. A linear account of loss or progress in relation to women's or gender studies always fails to get at the texture of struggles over meaning and practice, and a generational view of transition must always displace engagement with the mirroring across different positions in favour of their antagonisms.

But this chronology—from women's to gender studies—is inaccurate from another perspective too. Not only does it ignore the animated negotiation of these terms that characterizes the life of the field, it also proposes a located set of shifts as universal, as already indicated. Women's studies may be the term originally chosen for the entry into the academy of a feminist knowledge project, but this point of origin is not common to all contemporary manifestations of that project. While the United States, the United Kingdom, the Netherlands, Australia, and others may share that trajectory, this is not true for academic institutionalization across most of Scandinavia, India, Central and Eastern Europe, Italy, or France, to name just a few examples. In these and other contexts gender studies is as likely as women's studies to be the name of the initial forays into the academy, or indeed, academic feminism may nestle within disciplinary contexts, un-named as separate from its particular forms of (inter)disciplinary critique and invention. There may be little separation between policy or main-streaming and gender studies in some contexts, and barely any direct relation in others, but what is common is that women's studies is not their point of origin. Indeed, it can only be framed as such if we understand this international institutional unevenness in terms of a time lag, a transhistori-cal developmental narrative that holds those "origin sites" up as everyone's past, even if only imaginatively. The generationalism of debates about the proper name of the field, then, mitigates against analysis of a complex institutional present, and also obscures a sense of the field as genuinely transnational. Indeed, the differences in how people occupy a space like the Gender Institute, which houses mostly non-British students from across Europe, North America, Latin America, East Asia, and parts of Africa, are in part a reflection of that transnational unevenness and the contests over meaning that occur when concepts and debates themselves travel (Bal 2002).

To conclude this section, generational celebrations and laments within Western feminist storytelling prevent attention to contest over precisely the histories they purport to describe. They reinforce the heteronormative dimensions of linear histories, and act counter to international, institu-tional analyses of both the field and its effects. Further, generational accounts turn attention away from epistemological differences within Western feminist theory and frame the recent past in primarily ontological terms. As suggested, a generational account can be used both to explain the absence of a feminist subject of both postfeminism and gender in global governance and to ensure that the responsibility for feminism's demise always remains someone else's. Generational temporality allows for the necessary separation between good and bad uses of "gender" and preserves the space for restitution for the appropriate feminist subject (usually whoever is speaking). While it seems that generational accounts will always have a winner and loser, it is worth remembering that generation always produces a tension. The young may inherit a feminist legacy (whether they want to or not), but they are also expected to learn from their elders, who may turn out to have been right all along. Family dramas may be temporarily resolved, but they are also de facto bound to be replayed. The key here is that generational accounts propose a *dynamic*, and thus always hold the possibility of the "return" of the cast-out family member. The playing out of relational affect—wounding, injury, betrayal (Wiegman 1999a)—is significant, then, because it refigures restitution, both of past perspectives and, importantly, of the neglected subject.

UNRAVELING

Thus far in this chapter I have been interested in flagging ways in which the political grammar of Western feminist stories overlaps with broader discursive meanings and practices of gender and feminism. My point has not been to establish cause and effect, as if the structure and content of feminist narratives of progress, loss, and return could be understood directly to produce postfeminism or the relations between sexuality and gender in a global regulatory framework, or indeed vice versa. Rather, my attention has been drawn to the narrative similarities that allow resonance across accounts rather than to what are often presumed to be disjunctures between them. Thus, across a broad range of accounts of gendered meaning in a contemporary global sphere, *including* Western feminist accounts of the recent past, feminism is left behind, sexual identity is tethered to specific locations, and transformation must needs occur in contexts always already constructed as lagging behind in both gender and sexual equality. These chronologies reinforce understandings of the "non-West" as developmentally lacking and as needing guidance from those inhabiting modernity.

In Western feminist stories the narrative amenability I have been tracking is further secured through use of generational discourse that substitutes change over time for a focus on theoretical and political contest. In reifying generation as a key factor in losses or gains in feminism, the individual subject of Western feminism is privileged over attention to geopolitical or institutional differences across time and space. This is, of course, not entirely surprising, given that feminist theory and practice are always saturated with a sense of political urgency and responsibility, which means that whether or not one takes up an appropriate feminist position is key to how politics is presumed to work. It is paradoxical, perhaps, that it is precisely the individual and collective passions required by feminism that lend themselves to a prioritization of good over bad affect in consideration of what makes feminism different. A good feminist subject must, in these narratives, be both heroic and marginal, conditions that propel generational, often bad-tempered, certainties over consideration of ambivalence or incommensurability.

If, as I have been suggesting, the political grammar of Western feminist stories is thus amenable to temporal and geographical hierarchization in a global frame, particularly when gender and sexuality are at stake, then continued insistence on the difference a feminist subject makes will only compound the difficulties at hand. If, as I would want to insist, these global orders of meaning that mobilize gender and sexual discourse for profoundly inequitable and violent ends are pernicious, then it is important that we consider the fullest possible range of interventions into their expansive logic as well as particular execution. Reflexivity concerning the amenability of feminist storytelling seems a minimum requirement for sustainable transformation under such circumstances. Certainly, ongoing argument over the proper subject and object of feminism *as distinct from* other modes of gender discourse seems misplaced at best, and unlikely to disrupt the narrative amenability I have been discussing. Assumptions about what singular genre of feminist theory, method, and practice can renew lost feminist capacities fall into two related traps, in my analysis. They consolidate understandings of feminism as anachronism, on the one hand, and propose one response as most significant, which is in fact to say one feminist subject, on the other. In this respect I am concerned with prioritizing attention to contest and the terms of resolution of those contests over and above an emphasis on particular subjects as a priori suited to transformative politics.

This approach has clear sympathies with Judith Butler's project in *Gender Trouble* (1990), in which she sought to separate the subject of feminism from its presumed object, and with a range of poststucturalist feminist accounts that call the hidden "I" of political attachment to account.[15] But the diagnosis of the problem is only one part of the politics of this project, and my proposed interventions differ from Butler's emphasis on parody or variant repetition in shifting gendered signification. This project focuses more particularly on the importance of narrative formation, and thus the political potential of renarration itself. By "renarration" here I do not mean the proposing of an alternative history or histories of feminist thinking, since this would similarly instantiate an ideal feminist subject (and object) of that history. Nor am I making an argument for relinquishing feminism because of these pitfalls.[16] As already indicated in my introduction, however, the desire to be entirely free from a corrective account is always bound to fail; the difference is primarily a question of focus. Instead I am interested in experimenting with alternative *ways* of telling feminist stories (rather than telling different feminist stories as such) that start from resonances and meanings that the dominant narratives I have thus far been concerned with act to obscure.

The last two chapters of this book elaborate two attempts to renarrate Western feminist stories in ways that foreground the importance of textual tactics for transformative politics. Chapter 5, "Citation Tactics," returns to the politics and practices of citation I have been teasing out thus far, while chapter 6, "Affective Subjects," explores alternatives to the singular grammar of the Western feminist subject I have been interested in. In both chapters my primary concern is with what lies just out of focus in the Western feminist stories I have been mapping, as I endeavour to fold these obscurities back into dominant accounts. In so doing my aim is both to shine a spotlight on the politics of narrative and to refigure the subjects and objects of feminist narrative to different effect. This aim is clearest in chapter 5, however, where I "recite" Western feminist narratives of progress, loss, and return from the perspective of "citation absence" in contrast to the over-valuation of particular citation traces in dominant accounts. Further, in both chapters my attention is focused on the significance of affect in narrating and renarrating feminist stories, though it is a more sustained area of inquiry in chapter 6, as the title suggests. If, as I have been arguing throughout, affect is central to how narratives of progress, loss, and return work to produce appropriate feminist writing and reading subjects, then renarration will also both utilize and reframe affect in turn. Thus, I focus on the importance of affect as central to how narrative meaning is secured, but also as an ideal critical starting point for renarration. Finally, in both experiments I centre on the question of the politics of history as produced in the present. While both chapters are concerned with renarration of Western feminist history, they do so from the perspective of historiographical imagination in the present, rather than the truth of the past as the primary guide to contemporary politics and theory. This difference is significant in that it highlights the historicity of the present as multiple and open, and thus feminism as amenable not only to conservative mobilizations, but also to the political renarrations I advocate here, or that a reader may also imagine.

CITATION TACTICS

5 The question of citation practice has run
throughout the book thus far and is the
principal focus of this chapter. I have argued
that the citation practices internal to Western feminist narratives of progress, loss, and return are
partly what enable a combined chronology across the
strands, and that these similarities go a long way to
producing a shared vision of both what has happened
in the past and what needs to happen in the future.
Citation practices produce consensus on the difference between eras of feminist theory, however these
are valued, and they allow the narrator to remain
the subject of feminist theory in the present, however hard she must struggle to retain this position.
Citation—direct, or indicated by its absence—is a
central technique through which feminism is marked
out as epistemologically, politically, and temporally
distinct from poststructuralism, and this difference is
key to the sense of the present as one in which we have
turned, or are turning, away from culture.[1]

To recap briefly, Western feminist progress narratives' insistence that feminist theory has moved to a more expansive present, one full of new epistemological innovation and complex objects and analytic frames, relies on a flattened vision of the feminist past. To claim unparalleled vibrancy of a postmodern or poststructuralist project in the present, progress narratives rarely cite the 1970s directly, position the 1980s as the exclusive decade of identity politics, and position the 1990s as the era of intersectional complexity. In citation terms, this carving up of the past into neat decades means that the 1970s comes to carry the singular weight of an essentialism now past, the 1980s becomes overburdened with the citation of black and / or lesbian feminist authors, who rarely make it into the 1990s (except as postcolonial or queer theorists), while the 1990s teems with individual authors whose marked similarity to and difference from one another underlines the comparative intricacy of this period. Loss narratives mark the distinction between decades in a similar fashion, but inflect each period with counter-investments or alternative politics. Here, instead, the 1990s carries the generalized weight of a depoliticized move away from feminism proper, and key theorists are either singularly invoked as emblematic of this move, or noticeably absent, while the 1970s and the 1980s (where extra-institutional) are gestured towards but their interlocutors rarely specified. Indeed, loss and return narratives both suffer from a general citation scarcity. Return narratives' citation practices are similar to those of loss narratives, but more consistently reference the work of key figures (from the 1990s) in order to signal cultural theory's break from a more appropriate concern with materiality. They may also cite the 1970s or 1980s as exceptionally political in comparison to contemporary theoretical preoccupations through individual or decade reference.

As discussed in some depth in part 1, these citation practices do not simply produce a superficial but otherwise more or less accurate history, as is to be expected in any general account. They do not simply gesture towards a more complex past that cannot at that moment be specifically delineated. They are not practices that simply lack depth. They are productive rather than descriptive narratives of the recent past, giving us accounts in which specific contributions to that history—black and lesbian feminist contributions—are by turns erased or fetishized. But Western feminist stories are also ambivalent about these contributions in ways that remain unresolved. Thus, for progress narratives to position the present as more complex and attentive to difference than the past, black feminism figures as important, but primarily as *catalyst*, constrained by its citation as a 1980s critique. It is neither part of the 1970s (which must remain essentialist) nor fully part of the present that has transcended identity. Lesbian feminism, in contrast, is variously located as that which black feminism critiques (i.e., cited as a 1970s phenomenon) or as part of the critique of heteronormativity in the 1980s that ultimately leads to the present of queer theoretical maturity. Black and lesbian feminism are still more ambivalently located in loss and return accounts, which have to tell the story of a progressive depoliticization up to the present moment. In loss narratives this tends to be resolved by citational absence—just not mentioning black or lesbian feminist work at all—or by firmly identifying the difficulty as one of institutional identification over political attachment. In return narratives, queer theory is sutured to "the problem of culture," now fully surpassed, while black or postcolonial feminist theories are evacuated from the historical record in order to be found anew in the present.[2] In each case, citation practices secure the chronology and affect central to narrative momentum, and in each case, these erasures are incomplete or resonant, haunting the present in ways that might usefully be magnified.

I have been arguing, then, that poststructuralism is kept apart from feminism in Western feminist storytelling at a profoundly high cost and that these generalities produce a common sense of the recent past that reduces accountability and fosters amenability in relation to broader mobilizations of gender and feminism, as discussed in the previous chapter. I want to continue this attention to citation practice in the dominant narratives of Western feminist theory here, by homing in more closely on the citation of particular authors as emblematic of the distinction between feminism and poststructuralism, over and above the general citation practices of decades, politics, and epistemologies. More precisely, this chapter examines the role given to Judith Butler and her work (particularly *Gender Trouble* [1990]) in precipitating the shift from (feminist) politics to (queer) culture. As discussed in part 1, Butler is consistently credited in Western feminist stories with being "the first" to challenge the category "woman" as the foundation of feminist inquiry, and she is overwhelmingly cited as representative of the 1990s, whether celebrated or demonized. Here I consider more fully the importance of Butler's cited presence in all three strands of Western feminist storytelling, in terms of the work this does to position sexual critique as antithetical to feminist critique. Further, I examine Butler's role in this respect through her own cited influences in the same narratives. As suggested in chapter 1, Butler is consistently cited as the inheritor of a male theoretical legacy over and above her feminist (or female) influences. Once again my attention will be on what is excluded from this historical record by particular citation practices and on what hovers around citation pushing on its historiographic limits.

This chapter further relies on and develops my own citation practices as a set of tactical responses to the problems of citation in the securing of the dominant narratives I am unpicking. The first tactic will already be familiar from the previous chapters, namely the citation of narrative glosses by journal location and date, rather than by author. While loath to repeat myself too much here, I want to emphasize nevertheless that this tactic has two useful effects that are heightened in this chapter. First, it emphasizes these citation practices as held "in common" rather than being individual practices. This is important in terms of underscoring that my concern is not with individual interpretations of Butler's (or anyone else's) work, but with the centrality of *how she is cited* for the coherence of Western feminist narratives of progress, loss, and return. Second, it emphasizes the narrative construction of hierarchy (star status) as embedded in feminist historiography, rather than as peripheral to it. It has become commonplace to critique "famous" academic feminists for reproducing rather than challenging hierarchies, yet my analysis makes clear that selective citation is essential to how Western feminist stories work. We produce feminist chronologies in which decades (in general) need to be associated with authors (in particular) if our broader claims of progress, loss, and return are to make sense. My de-authorizing citation tactics are thus intended to reveal the problems of citation that themselves authorize the dominant strands of Western feminist storytelling that I am interested in challenging. I use this approach to bring into relief the political grammar at the heart of feminist narrative, to shine a spotlight on its construction and function.

Yet these tactics of de-authorization can only go so far, as I indicated at the end of the last chapter on narrative amenability. Even at their most effective, they can only reveal what is already dominant, which is not where I want to end my analysis. A feminist political renarration, which I would describe as the intervention into dominant feminist narratives with the aim of making them less amenable to global spatial and temporal hierarchization, will need something further. Thus, I extend my citation tactics in this chapter to try and follow the traces of what hovers around the edges of these citations of Butler and her antecedents. In this chapter I develop a citation strategy I am calling feminist *recitation*, in which some of the hauntings of Western feminist stories that matter to me are folded back into the textual heart of narratives of progress, loss, and return. Starting from what my own affect and memory inform me is excluded from a historiography that separates feminism and poststructuralism, I meddle with citation more directly. The recitations that result are intended to open up myriad other histories and to be suggestive of alternative modes of institutional, political engagement in the present.

ODD COUPLES

In chapter 1, I began discussion of the role of key figures in securing Western feminist progress narratives. Depending on the discipline or interdisciplinary area of a given journal, theorists such as Donna Haraway, Gayatri Spivak, and Judith Butler are cited as provoking a shift from one form of feminist analysis to a radically different one, and often away from feminism altogether.[3] Of these, Judith Butler is by far the most commonly invoked of her cohort. Whether for progress, loss, or return narratives, Butler is routinely positioned as forcing feminist theory onwards, beyond itself. The following two excerpts are typical (and probably very familiar) examples of this situating of Butler:[4]

Perhaps more than any other feminist theorist, she [Butler] has systematically elaborated a way of understanding gender identity as deeply entrenched but not immutable and has thereby pushed feminist theory beyond the polarities of the essentialist debate. (*Theory, Culture and Society* 1999)[5]

At least since Judith Butler's seminal book *Gender Trouble*, published in 1990, feminist and gender studies have been concerned with how new conceptions of the body affect and reform disciplinary questions in the humanities, as well as to some extent in the natural and social sciences. (*Nora* 2002)

Butler marks—indeed "pushes"—feminist theory and gender identity into a new era, the impact of which has resonated across disciplinary arenas.

Butler is located as quintessentially poststructuralist, such that it is her interpretation of *this* tradition (and no other) that moves feminist theory "beyond the polarities" of previous accounts of gender relations. Thus,

Judith Butler transformed the study of gender by using Foucault to apply poststructuralist conceptions of the subject to it. (*Australian Feminist Studies* 2000)

We can see already from these few examples, then, that there is a tension between feminist theory, on the one hand, and its transformation via poststructuralism into "something else," on the other. Butler's citation (and the citation of similar figures where relevant) consistently signals the death of one way of thinking and the inception of a newer, entirely different one in progress, loss, and return narratives: it rarely evidences ongoing contests within feminism over the study of gender, women, or feminism. This sense of radical alteration is facilitated in the above excerpts by the textual movement between feminist theory and gender (or gender studies, or identity), which ensures that we are not merely moving between feminist phases, but rather also moving away from feminism itself with these poststructuralist shifts.[6]

The clearest way in which key theorists are textually framed as initiating changes in feminist theory that ultimately lead to its demise or thorough transformation is the situating of those theorists themselves as primarily engaged with, or even dependent upon, the male theorists on whom they draw. And indeed representation of key feminist figures through their male antecedents or contemporaries is the single most important technique through which feminism is separated from the cultural turn said to be its death knell. The following statements are typical of this kind of citation practice:

Haraway must acknowledge a siblingship with Derrida over those central questions of humanism concerning origin, authenticity and universality. (*Body and Society* 1996)

To certify the Derridean assumptions upon which thinkers like Spivak draw. (*Critical Inquiry* 1998)

The Foucauldian critique represented by Butler and others has only recently been introduced into gender studies. (*Nora* 2002)

At one level these citation practices are uncontroversial. It is, after all, quite true that Haraway has an affinity with Derrida, and Spivak all the more so. These theorists do indeed take up Derrida in a range of ways and develop conversations across disciplines and traditions in part through this affinity. And no one who has read Butler could fail to recognize her debt to and development of Foucault in the context of feminist analysis. She engages his work directly in much of hers, and in my view gender studies is much the richer for that dialogue. But what is striking across the journals I have been analyzing is the repeated nature of these citations in common sense glosses, over and above any other ways of locating these theorists. My concern is not, in other words, with the representation of these theorists as engaged with Derrida or Foucault—they are indeed so engaged—but with the uniform representation of that engagement as primary or exclusive.

The citation of key feminist theorists' antecedents as peculiarly male underscores the separation of feminism and poststructuralism that is key to how Western feminist stories work in several ways. On the one hand, it marks this separation in the moment of citation itself, moving the feminist theorist cited out of a feminist tradition. She is not only a critic of feminism or gender studies, but criticizes out of an attachment to her male antecedents. At another level, then, this representation of antecedents signals an attachment to the single male over the history of feminist theory, a point I will come back to below in discussing citation of Butler more fully. This representation of Spivak, Haraway, and Butler as "Derridean" or "Foucauldian" then, might be properly thought of as "hetero-citational," in that it utilizes the opposite sex couple form to mark the shift away from feminism, whether positively or negatively viewed. On another level, these couplings transform what we think of as feminism and poststructuralism too. They mark poststructuralism itself as male and the attachment to these (prior) figures as the application of poststructuralism to a radically distinct arena, feminism. It is feminism that is transformed by the hetero-citational attachment; poststructuralism remains unmoved by the encounter, it seems.

In effect, these hetero-citational practices produce not so much a moment of reflexive reconsideration of feminism and its direction, but the instantiation of a *parallel* theoretical teleology to feminism, one that intersects with it only at this particular moment of critique. In casting her lot with her male antecedents, our feminist heroine does not only take feminism as an object of critique, however. She also operates as a feminist (or postcolonial, or queer) endorsement of that parallel teleology in progress narratives. Her "feminist" nature may need to be in quotes, but it does need to be present. If Spivak, Haraway, or Butler attach to the Derridean or the Foucauldian over the feminist critique, then perhaps these male theorists' attention to difference really is superior. In progress narratives, then, deconstruction, not feminism, is the defender of difference. For example:

> The deconstructive project comes to the defense of difference, in opposition to "the founding of a hysterocentric to counter a phallic discourse." (Spivak, 1983: 184) . . . While nearly all feminist theory at some level opposes binary opposition, the deconstructivists are the most radical in their call for an opposition to sexual dualism itself in the name of "the multiplicity of sexually marked voices," or relationships that "would not be a-sexual, far from it, but would be sexual otherwise: beyond the binary difference that governs the decorum of all codes" (Derrida, 1982: 76). (*Signs* 1991)

Deconstructivist feminist theory carries the day in the above excerpt, and so, one might argue, feminism's critical role remains intact. But this "deconstructive project" is explicitly defined against feminist masquerades in which "sexual dualism" is the pretender to a radical throne. As I suggested in my mapping of progress narratives in chapter 1, citation of Spivak in such a context marks "the founding of a hysterocentric" as not only essentialist and old-fashioned, but as also ethnocentric or racist. This implicit citation of "1970s feminism" is negotiated both through the terms employed, and the citation frame of the 1980s. And this irredeemable radical feminism is further contrasted with the "most radical" deconstructionists, in this case, finally, Derrida. In the hetero-citational suturing of Spivak to Derrida, here as elsewhere, Spivak is the reference that guarantees that the attention to difference remains "feminist." Yet, of course, that attachment concomitantly moves her away from feminism textually and historiographically, a facet of this citation practice not lost on those who adhere to loss or return narratives.

As indicated above, it is Butler who is most continually positioned as the theorist responsible for moving feminist theory away from itself. And to really underline how this "hetero-citation practice" works to keep poststructuralism and feminism separate, it is to citation of her influence on and participation in feminism that I now turn. The excerpts positioning Butler as the first to challenge a sex/gender distinction, or the first to challenge the ontological grounding of feminist epistemology in the cate-

gory "woman," also consistently cite her primary intellectual influence as
Michel Foucault, as the examples from *Nora* and *Australian Feminist Stud-*
ies above suggest. Indeed, Butler's critique of existing feminist theory is
routinely described simply as "Foucauldian." In addition to the above
excerpts, let us consider the following, which serve to highlight some of
the different ways in which Butler and Foucault are conjoined:

Feminists inspired by, among others, Michel Foucault, however, have questioned
this understanding of feminism as critique with reference to Foucault's arguments
for the existence of an immanent relation between power and knowledge. Judith
Butler, for instance, thus understands feminist critique as a theoretical exercise
that is always already implicated in the very relations of power it seeks to adjudicate (Butler 1995b, 139). (*Nora* 2004)

One especially revealing feature of Butler's style is the preponderance of subject-
verb disagreements. I want to speculate that this penchant, by reflecting the
difficulty of sustaining a Foucauldian critique of the singular self and the biological body, reveals the tensions continually at play in efforts to combine poststructuralism with feminism. (*Critical Inquiry* 1998)

Foucault and Butler and the influence of discourses of race have served to make
many scholars wary of the categories man and woman, for fear of the "sin" of
essentialism, of assuming a pre-formed individual identity. (*Australian Feminist
Studies* 2000)

During the recent decade feminist sport studies have, as feminist scholarships in
general, been strongly influenced by post-structural approaches and the social
constructionist paradigm, for example the contributions of Michel Foucault (e.g.
1979, 1990) and Judith Butler (e.g. 1990, 1993). (*Nora* 2006)

At one level, these juxtapositions underpin the primary assertion in such
glosses, namely that Butler is front and centre among feminists in her
challenges to female essentialism. This framing isolates her in ways discussed in relation to other theorists, above, and textually reiterates that she
emerges finally, not from feminism, but from a parallel, male poststructuralist teleology. As acknowledged above, this repeated positioning of Foucault and Butler is entirely appropriate in many ways. Butler does consistently cite Foucault in her writing; Foucault's work does indeed pre-date
Butler's. In these respects there is nothing amiss. But the sheer repetition
of this direct and exclusive influence across progress, loss, and return

narratives that cite Butler asks me to look at little closer at this otherwise self-evident proximity, to ask how this coupling is secured and to explore what it precludes. An initial comment concerns the hierarchies made manifest in this particular hetero-citational relationship. This is not an equal relationship; it is one of inheritance and debt, and is consistently represented as such. Butler's progress, her ability to transform feminism, arises in and through her adoption of the uniquely Foucauldian approach. In the first two examples above, Butler derives her perspective and style, understands or represents things, *because of* Foucault: "Butler's account of agency *relies* on Foucault's idea of 'subjectivation' which denotes the dialectical aspect of identity formation" (*Theory, Culture and Society* 1999; my emphasis), for example. Since this reliance is concomitantly represented as the chief intellectual development in her work, Butler's transformation of feminism itself is rendered derivative.

The latter examples operate slightly differently. In the excerpt from *Australian Feminist Studies*, "the categories man and woman" come under attack from the combined forces of Foucault and Butler and "the influence of discourses of race." Based on my analysis of race in Western feminist narratives of progress, loss, and return in part 1, I read this alliance in part as performing the "rescue" of critical race critique from the accusation of its over-reliance on identity. But if we read outside of this understanding, the extract more straightforwardly pits these combined forces against feminist essentialist sinners. The last excerpt demonstrates, to my mind, some of the routine work achieved by citation of Foucault and Butler together. While frequently cited as mere "examples" of a poststructuralist approach (see also the "among others" and "for instance" of the first excerpt from *Nora*, above), their repeated combined appearance operates to secure their critique as occurring from outside of, rather than from within, feminist scholarship. Indeed, the juxtaposition of Butler-and-Foucault is so common that even where she is not directly cited, it is hard not to read in Butler's textual resonance. For example, in the following extract from *Nora*, only Foucault is referenced in terms of his influence on the field:

During the 1980s and 90s the concepts of patriarchy and feminism gradually disappeared from women's studies and gender research in the Nordic countries. Instead, many researchers took inspiration from discourse theory, especially from the works of Michel Foucault. (*Nora* 2004)

Although Butler is not named in this rather familiar gloss, the repetition of her pairing with Foucault across *Nora* and the range of journals I have been concerned with means that she is intertextually resonant. She lingers in the passively rendered disappearance of the concept of "patriarchy," and in the wholesale shift from feminism to discourse theory whose teleology I have been discussing thus far and for which she is responsible (in choosing Foucault over other partnerships).

Butler's over-association with Foucault does not in itself effect a separation of poststructuralism and feminism, although it certainly exerts considerable influence in that direction. This division is also secured through positioning other feminist theorists in relation to the parallel trajectory I have been delineating in particular ways. One common tactic in progress narratives is the citation of Butler and other feminist theorists as providing the necessary critique of natural "sex," but with Butler retaining her position as "the first" either explicitly or implicitly:

From a Foucauldian perspective, the making of the gendered self, or gender identity, is the product of disciplinary practices of the body that ensure the reproduction of heterosexuality as the norm. The body is seen as material that is enrolled in the production of gender rather than as providing the biological foundation for gender differences (Butler, 1993; Grosz, 1994). (*Body and Society* 2002)

Here, then, Butler and Grosz are both cited, but it is a later Grosz text that is referenced to evidence her own critique of biological foundationalism. Butler thus remains textually identified with forerunner Foucault, the chain of inheritance made safe. In the rather more negative formulation of the same relationships effected in loss narratives, other feminist theorists are often positioned as critics of Butler in her Foucauldian association. To continue with the citation of Grosz, in the following loss narrative gloss from the same journal, Grosz and Butler are antagonists:

Grosz is critical of Butler (1990) precisely because she does attempt to retrieve the concept of gender within the Foucauldian optic. Butler wrenches the body away from a discrete ontology of substance designated by the marker "sex," and reinstates it—together with sex—*within* the category of gender. (*Body and Society* 2000)

Grosz is wary of Butler because of the same association that is celebrated in the slightly later progress narrative from 2002. Instead of providing

needed reflection on the limits of an essentialized ontological foundation in feminism, Butler—applying "the Foucauldian optic"—violently
"wrenches" apart signifier and signified. The tone of the extract is interesting here too: one might say that Butler is cited as male-identified in two
senses. She allies herself with Foucault, as we have already seen, and she
forces sex and the body apart in a violent mode: she "wrenches" rather
than, say, teases the two away from one another. Thus Butler's citation
produces her as male-identified in terms of the company she keeps and in
the way she behaves.

Western feminist loss and return narratives generally endorse this association of Butler with Foucault, frequently blaming her errors of judgement on his bad influence. The following is typical:

Recently there have been a number of constructive critiques of Butler's Foucauldian concept of power. (*Australian Feminist Studies* 2002)

It is not Butler per se who is challenged here, but her "Foucauldian
concept of power." These "constructive critiques" seem mild enough, indeed they identify the problem as ostensibly lying somewhere else, namely
with Foucault, but in the process Butler's work is reduced to this association. As the next two extracts affirm, she is textually cast as easily influenced, as blind to the limits of Foucault's ideas for a feminist analysis, and
thus also often as important but misguided:

Possibly because of its difficult task of dislodging commonly held assumptions,
possibly because of the influence of Foucault and Derrida, recondite abstractions
characterize postmodernist feminist theory in general and Butler's books in particular. (*Critical Inquiry* 1998)

For Butler, on the authority of Foucault and Derrida respectively, the possibility
of resistance is simply inherent in the nature of power or of language (Butler,
1997), but the conditions favourable to the exploitation of these windows of
opportunity for personal and social transformation are never interrogated. (*Feminist Theory* 2000)

While Butler's association with Foucault (and less commonly, in fact,
Derrida) confer authority in Western feminist progress narratives, this
same repeated association positions her as a dependent in loss and return
narratives. Butler's lamentable abstraction and lack of attention to social
conditions are thus understood to derive from familiar male influence. All

three narrative strands reproduce the same vision of Butler's intellectual development, and all frame this development as produced though her proximity to her male antecedents. When positively inflected, this relation propels feminism into a more nuanced era; when negatively inflected, this dependency overwhelms other (feminist) considerations. Whether celebrated, lamented, or derided, hetero-citation of Butler's intellectual debts uncouples feminism from poststructuralism and leaves the former mired in the past or in a future on the other side of poststructuralism, when feminists may be brave enough to think for themselves.

My characterization of the pairing of Butler and Foucault as hetero-citational practice within Western feminist theory is, of course, intended somewhat ironically. Foucault is not a poststructuralist male antecedent like any other,[7] but one so thoroughly associated with queer theory as to be its veritable, venerable daddy.[8] It is not any old poststructuralism that Butler is sutured to in this association, but a poststructuralism that places sexuality at the discursive centre of both modernity and our own contemporary interpretations of the same. The citational repetition of Foucault-and-Butler in Western feminist accounts of progress, loss, and return thus cannot be understood to provide a straightforwardly male poststructuralist history to her work, but importantly, underlines that this is a *queer* poststructuralist history, as the following examples make plain:

First, there emerged a genre of scholarship, inspired by the work of Michel Foucault and Judith Butler, particularly queer theory, which explored new aspects and dimensions of the socially constructed, performative character of gender and sexuality. (*Nora* 2003)

Influenced especially by Foucault's *History of Sexuality*, feminists, along with queer theorists, now deconstructed the sex/gender distinction by arguing that not only is gender socially constituted, but sex is too. (*Australian Feminist Studies* 2000)[9]

Situating Foucault as chief precursor to Butler's new deconstruction of feminist epistemological presumption isolates the latter from feminism in two ways, then. The first, delineated above, is in the instantiation of a male poststructuralist history that runs parallel to the feminism it critically transforms but is not a part of nor turned by. The second, suggested here, concerns the designation of that history as queer and thus also as crucially *not feminist*. As discussed throughout part 1, the dominant narratives of

Western feminist storytelling view Butler's critique of the sex/gender distinction as a contest between discrete investments in sexual politics or feminism, and never as a continuation of debates about the relationship between these fused arenas of inquiry. In progress narratives, Butler's queer critique—via Foucault—allows for an expansion of feminism beyond its myopic essentialist concerns. In loss and return narratives, Butler's queer critique—via Foucault—constitutes a lamentable interruption of a feminist politics, one recuperable only through a subsequent rejection of sexuality and culture as viable critical vantage points. In effect, the citation of Butler's Foucault as the thorn in feminism's critical and political side is also a key technique through which the opposition between sexuality and gender, discussed at some length in the last chapter, too, is chronologically imagined and maintained.

The pairing of Foucault and Butler sticks ontologically as well as epistemologically or historiographically, exceeding textual citation. It sticks to Foucault in ways that are familiar from existing arguments that question the amenability of his theoretical and political accounts of the subject and the social to feminism (e.g., Hartsock 1990; Ramazanoğlu and Holland 1993). In these texts, many of which emerge around the same time as Butler's *Gender Trouble* (1990), Foucault's lack of explicit attention to gender relations is presented as evidence of the limits of his approach to power for feminism overall, whether or not his work is otherwise understood as productive or interesting (see Sawicki 1991; Bordo 1993). In such accounts, it is often Foucault's maleness that is called up in order to explain that lack of direct attention, a process that fuses femaleness and feminism, and interestingly for us here, brackets out any difference Foucault's "queerness" might itself make to our sense of what maleness is or does. In the patterns of citation within Western feminist stories that I am concerned with, citation of Foucault as singular antecedent to Butler underwrites her position as transformative or dismissive of feminism in a doubled sense. Foucault's maleness stands in for "male poststructuralism" more generally, anchoring Butler to the parallel teleology I have been tracing, while Foucault's queerness provides a further layer to Butler's betrayal, re-emphasizing her allegiance to sexuality over feminism. In the process, Foucault's influence can only ever be imagined as disruptive, as a kind of viral incommensurability that precipitates a strangely passive Butler into acting counter to her and feminist theory's own best interests.

The ontological becoming of Butler through this citational process is concomitantly crucial to the separation of queer theory and feminism in Western feminist stories. Both as "the first" to critique feminism and as "the one" to carry the burden for poststructuralist, queer interruption of materialist feminist concerns, Butler's pairing with Foucault forces her out of feminism proper. As I have argued above, this works by drawing a theoretical strand from poststructuralism to queer theory, a strand represented as parallel to or intersecting with, but never fully part of, feminist theory. In both progress and loss narratives Butler's citational association with Foucault propels her beyond feminism, or marks her as nonfeminist. She is, as I have been arguing, textually masculinized, forced to choose Foucault again and again over other potential alliances.[10] Butler's textual masculinity can only be either asexual (moving feminism beyond sexual difference, "wrenching" sex from the body), or gay male (throwing in with the boys). The kind of textual masculinity offered to Butler is not that of Halberstam's female masculinity (1998), and its potential gayness not a version of Sedgwick's female anality (1987), but a closed effect of the limited narrative choice on offer between femaleness and maleness. In this respect, the "odd couple" Foucault and Butler make might better be understood as "hom(m)o-citational" rather than hetero-citational.[11] In its repetition, this hom(m)o-citation may have parodic effects in that it has the potential to expose the heteronormative and generational presumptions at the heart of dominant feminist historiography. But even this playful representation of Butler and Foucault's relationship cannot shift one of the primary exclusions marked by this dominant citation practice. In the citational coincidence of male and queer poststructuralism, representation of Butler as feminist queer, indeed lesbian queer, remains a contradiction in terms.

CITATION TACTICS

One reasonable response to this dulling of Foucault's and Butler's separate or combined significance for Western feminist theory would be to suggest that this kind of flattening is bound to occur with representations of theoretical super-stardom and to advocate a move away from their fetishization altogether. Feminist writers have consistently argued against the instantiation of a "star system" (e.g., Ahmed 2000b), on the grounds that it reproduces rather than challenges institutionalized knowledge production, reducing what counts as feminist theory or practice in the process. The first issue of the interdisciplinary U.K.-based journal *Feminist Theory* included a thematic section devoted to challenging common conceptions of what feminist theory is and who produces or practices it.[12] Further, Liz Stanley and Sue Wise argue that the star system in academic feminism is something that "jobbing academic feminists" (2000: 275) are complicit in. Its reproduction is something that we actively participate and invest in, to problematic effect. Perhaps then, as Rachel Torr suggests in her critical response to my own work on this question, we should disinvest in Butler, Spivak, and Haraway, rather than focusing on them still further, and seek instead to build a more egalitarian history of feminist theory (2007: 11–12).

It might be possible to interpret my citation tactics so far in the book as making a similar point. In citing context over author, I am clearly privileging conditions of production and collective practices over individual argument, success, or failure. I have taken this tack on the basis of histories and fantasies as shared within feminist academic production rather than belonging to particular writers. If we combine this approach with my critique of the citation of key figures in Western feminist stories as part of what enables the separation of feminism and poststructuralism, which in turn instantiates the shared fantasy of feminism as lost and particular individuals as responsible, then we might expect an additional move on my part. We might expect advocacy of citation of the obscure, of the hidden, as central to a history of feminism that can stand as a viable alternative to the privileging of the few, not in the sense of the provision of a singular alternative history that will produce a more faithful and correct feminist account, but as a way of introducing a range of other histories that are currently unavailable. This would be an interesting and provocative approach, but perhaps one that would nevertheless be likely to slip into endorsement of particular authors for future stardom. But still, why focus on representations of Butler, citation of her theoretical influences, and her role in the telling of Western feminist stories? Why not continue to think through Western feminist theory as a set of common practices, secured through particular techniques, best addressed without recourse to fetishistic author designation?

In part, the answer is that this project is driven less by egalitarianism and more by the desire for feminist approaches that are accountable for their narrative amenability. My journal citation tactics are less about diffusing individuality (though this may be one effect, and one I am pleased with in our era of inane citation chasing), and more about the clearest way of getting to the shared politics of narrative form. In this sense, insofar as citation of Butler has emerged as a key critical tactic to ensure narrative coherence within the overlapping strands of Western feminist storytelling, my interest is in *amplifying* the resonances of her citation, rather than downplaying the same. Butler is invoked time and again in passing statements about what has happened in Western feminist theory, whether the history produced is otherwise brimming with positive or negative affect. She serves as the heroine or antiheroine in these chronologies, yet is, as I have indicated in this chapter thus far, also separated out from that history in significant ways. Citation of Butler, as I have elaborated, allows feminism to be anachronistic in all the narratives I have been mapping; her textual presence is pivotal rather than peripheral to this process. Citation of Butler is essential to the culture / materiality divide, to arguments about fragmentation or diversification of feminism, to oppositions between sexual and critical race politics, and to the affective sense of what has gone wrong or right in the last thirty to forty years of academic feminist institutionalization. In short, a focus on representations of Butler seems essential to revealing techniques through which Western feminist theory reproduces its narrative momentum. Attention to her citation may, by virtue of its repetition, offer a way into the fabric of these narratives, may open up the condensed meanings and histories folded into and carried by this textual fixation.[13] And in my discussion of the curious coupling of Butler with Foucault, I hope I have already begun to suggest ways in which such attention might reveal more about Western feminist theory's investments than mere refutation alone might do. Utopian egalitarianism may in the end leave the politics of the present intact.

My interest in Butler's citation also goes beyond the desire to establish what might be happening when she is cited, though it certainly is that. The analysis of her association with Foucault has highlighted how and why Butler is left stranded within a parallel poststructuralist linearity, forced into inheriting a singularly male, queer history, into bearing primary textual responsibility for feminism's demise. But such citation of Butler also has an *ontological impact,* as I began to indicate above. By ontological impact, I do not mean what or how Butler signifies in and of herself, but how her citation restricts where and how she signifies and determines the conditions under which "her person" is cited intertextually and over time. I am not prepared, it turns out, to leave Butler mired in this history, and indeed, I also want to resist Foucault's animation in our narratives as mere liberating or domesticating influence on feminism. This means both that I am not prepared to leave this couple alone and that showcasing and analysing the significance of Butler's citation for Western feminist progress, loss, and return narratives is enough. The identification of hetero-citation or hom(m)o-citation as techniques does not enable either character to signify differently. Instead, I want to propose an approach that starts from what is made impossible, what is obscured in making Butler exceptional in Western feminist storytelling. Which other possible histories and presents are precluded by representing her as breaking with her feminist antecedents? What difference might it make to start from these absences, to start again from this motivated refusal, but without replacing Butler as a central character in narratives of progress, loss, and return?

Or perhaps I should more accurately say, *my refusal*; I should more accurately say that such citation has intersubjective rather than simply ontological impact. I am, once again, not a neutral observer of these histories and citation practices, but someone who has vested interest in challenging them, and these investments are brought to the text rather than only being produced in the moment of reading. I do not want to leave Butler stranded in a history that reduces her theoretical resonance, in part because this reduction does not fit with my own reading of her, my own reading history. When Butler is tied to Foucault in ways I have suggested, what are erased are not only alternative readings of the two of them, including readings of their own association, but other citational threads that move back and forth across Western feminist history. It is not just Butler whose relationship to feminist theory and practice is thus compromised, but my own coming to feminist theory through *Gender Trouble* (1990), which drew together feminist theories of sexuality and gender and linked so well to the radical lesbian feminist or anti-psychoanalytic texts I had otherwise been reading. In my graduate student readings of the early 1990s, Butler creatively developed Monique Wittig's (1980; 1982; 1985)[14] critiques of heterosexuality as the framing condition of sex/gender distinctions, and her reading of Wittig seemed to echo my own disagreement with what I then thought of as Wittig's certainty that the answer to the problem of heteronormativity was lesbianism.[15] And what of Luce Irigaray (1985a; 1985b), the champion of the sceptical reading and of loving attention to the disagreed-with text, and the anxiety about what came to be thought of as her essentialism?[16]

It came as no surprise to me then (or now) that the feminist philosophers Butler strikes up a critical conversation with in *Gender Trouble* are Wittig and Irigaray, and no surprise that she folds Lacan and Foucault into the discussion. What I find utterly discordant is how Wittig and Irigaray remain virtually unremembered in citation of Butler's primary antecedents in the Western feminist narratives of progress, loss, and return I have been interrogating.[17] In the particular glosses I have been concerned with, psychoanalytic tracks are less visible (neither Lacan nor Irigaray are very evident), since this would interrupt the materiality/culture opposition central to Western feminist storytelling in quite a different way.[18] Irigaray haunts narratives of progress, loss, and return in this respect, but as one who has been cast out, only to be recuperated in return narratives that emphasize embodiment over epistemology. But the lack of citation of Wittig as a primary influence on Butler is a forgetting of rather a different order. Given that Butler is cited as providing "the first" feminist critique of sex/gender from a *queer* perspective, the absence of Wittig in this frame looms large in the present. In my reading her deflection is essential to sexuality's and materiality's incommensurability and to the understanding of a queer trajectory as parallel to, rather than overlapping, co-extensive, or emergent in dialogue with, feminism. In other words, citation of Butler's primary affiliate as Foucault both reduces his contributions as suggested and enables the erasure of a particular kind of lesbian history from Western feminist storytelling. In return narratives, too, lack of citation of Wittig (compared to Irigaray) ensures that the materialism advocated remains a socialist or even sexual difference theory, rather than a lesbian materialism.

And so I do not want to leave Butler stranded at, constituting even, the border between poststructuralism and feminism, for rather complicated reasons. I do not want to leave her there because I want her to be able to signify a different history or histories, not one that leaves (lesbian) feminism behind. Neither do I want my own reading history to be erased. But this reading history is not *only* a question of personal motivation. It is frustration that leads me to ask a series of questions about Butler's citation in Western feminist storytelling—frustration at the burden she is given and that, perhaps, I feel implicated into sharing—and joy, or the memory of it, that allows me to piece together another way of tracing Butler's resonance across, rather than tangential to, feminism. These twinned affects are both brought to the text, but they are felt in the process of reading. Starting from such investment seems one useful way of teasing out what might be textually sidelined, yet affectively present, in narratives of progress, loss, and return. In this respect my own reading history—the one I see still writ large in *Gender Trouble*—operates itself as a kind of haunting of the narratives I otherwise participate in. It operates, I want to argue, as a way of renarrating these stories from the starting point of my earlier comment that "[i]n the citational coincidence of male and queer poststructuralism, representation of Butler as feminist queer, indeed lesbian queer, remains a contradiction in terms" (175).

What new ways of telling stories might emerge if we refuse to accept this citational separation, and starting from affect and memory, we recite those traces of the past that echo still in the present? Instead of asking "Where has Wittig gone?," instead of remaining frustrated by her absence, I want to ask what happens when we invite Wittig back, what joys and unremembered sorrows re-surface when we bring her out of the shadows and into the spotlight?

RECITATION

Recitation: reading aloud of something; reciting of something, from memory; revisiting material previously encountered (review); un-forgetting.[19]

Thus far my citation tactics have been concerned to highlight the importance of citation practices in securing the dominant narratives of Western feminist storytelling and to identify potent absences, hauntings in the shadows of these narratives that cannot be consigned fully to the past. The next step is to "recite" these stories starting from the affective investments I approach the text from, and that are activated by my reading process, as suggested above. For this approach not to be a mere prioritization of a different, but nevertheless singular, history, the attention needs to be firmly placed on what happens when we fold what haunts these stories back into them, making visible what is, importantly, *already there*. To fold what is almost-but-not-quite forgotten back in is a process that inquires after obscured dimensions of the present, rather than one that seeks an alternative history to replace those that are dominant now. Haunting, for Avery Gordon, never simply references the death of one possibility, but also a "seething presence" in the present (1997: 8), or as Victoria Hesford interprets Gordon, an "echo of a potentially different social or political experience" (2005: 229). Recitation is partly an adaptation of some of the more familiar literary liberties taken by, among others, Jean Rhys in *The Wide Sargasso Sea* (Rhys 2000 [1966]), J. M. Coetzee in *Foe* (Coetzee 1987), and more recently Joan Anim-Addo in *Imoinda* (Anim-Addo 2003), in which the potent absences or half-presences in the original text become central in their rewriting. Recitation in the context of feminist theory is thus not the telling of a new story, but a renarration of the same story from a different perspective.[20] It operates as a breaking open of the presumed relation between the past and the present, rather than an instantiation of a new, fixed relation between the two. I visualize recitation, then, as an intervention, a mode of engagement that values the past by understanding it affectively and politically rather than in terms of finality.

To begin this experiment in renarration, I want to mobilize "Monique Wittig" as my point of entry in reciting passages that overdetermine the separation of feminism from poststructuralism, and sexuality from materiality. As suggested above, I have chosen Wittig because folding her influence back into Butler's citation follows the tracks opened up by my own frustration at the erasure of the lesbian feminist history of materialist sexual politics. Further, that erasure is a pertinent one, without which the positioning of Butler as "the first" to critique the category "woman" would not make sense. In addition, this choice reflects the ambivalent position of *lesbian feminism* in Western feminist storytelling more generally, an ambivalence I have identified through the mapping that comprises Part I of this book. But my choice of Wittig also raises important questions about accountability. Wittig is a *particular* lesbian feminist and should not be understood to stand in for lesbian feminism in general.[21] My choice of Wittig over Gayle Rubin, Pat(rick) Califia, or Audre Lorde, for example, produces a particular kind of lesbian recitation of Western feminist storytelling. But while acknowledging the ways in which recitation is bound to produce its own exclusions that need attention, I also want to be clear that the choice of Wittig, while certainly partial, is not random. In addition to the reasons suggested above, I have chosen Wittig for this experiment because of her central presence in *Gender Trouble*. Engagement with Wittig occupies Butler for as many pages as her engagement with Foucault in this text, and indeed, she is respectful and critical to both of them (and others). Lorde is not mentioned, however, and Rubin only briefly. To be concerned with the politics of the present (rather than historical absence), recitation must start from potent hauntings, not from arbitrary or more general political juxtaposition. In this respect, Wittig is not one choice among a infinite number.

Let us turn to what recitation in this context can achieve, then. Recitation requires reintroducing the original example in each case, and then reinterpreting it through that substitution. In straightforward terms, what this tactic effects is a disruption of a chronology in which Butler comes before other feminist theorists, a disruption of the framing of Butler as "the first" to offer critiques of the epistemological and ontological grounding of feminism in the category "woman." Let us look again at one of the extracts quoted earlier:

Feminists inspired by, among others, Michel Foucault, however, have questioned this understanding of feminism as critique with reference to Foucault's arguments for the existence of an immanent relation between power and knowledge. Judith Butler, for instance, thus understands feminist critique as a theoretical exercise that is always already implicated in the very relations of power it seeks to adjudicate (Butler 1995b, 139). (*Nora* 2004)[22]

And let us recite this as: "Feminists inspired by, among others, Monique Wittig, however, have questioned this understanding of feminism as critique with reference to her arguments for the existence of an immanent relation between power and knowledge." The first thing to say about this recitation is that it functions as a kind of joke, a rendering of the past as unnatural, an opening up of the original text to allow us briefly to glimpse a different history that emerges in the retelling. But further than that the recitation describes something plausible, provides a different history that resonates with what feminist theorists already know: that Wittig, among others, does indeed highlight the relation between knowledge and power within feminism. Now, in the second sentence of our recitation, Butler takes up a particular strand of feminism to suggest that feminist critique is implicated in the "relations of power" it is caught within. She does this because of Wittig not Foucault, because of prior feminist theory that was concerned with the relationship between power and knowledge. Interestingly, here, the "among others" of Wittig, and the "for instance" of Butler, make more textual sense than in the original because the frames of reference have shifted to concern *varieties* of feminist theory. To think of Butler as not only having male antecedents, then, not only shifts our sense of Butler's history, but also allows us to think of Western feminist theory as more multiple, without having to specify a singular alternative.

Employing these citation tactics to re-read similar glosses reinforces this sense of an opening up of feminist possibility, rather than a closing down of the same. What is challenged is the presumed separation between feminism and poststructuralism that the repeated suturing of Butler to Foucault otherwise effects. We can reorient ourselves to Western feminist theory as having a complex history, one that draws on multiple traditions. Thus, to return to a different extract:

Foucault and Butler and the influence of discourses of race have served to make many scholars wary of the categories man and woman, for fear of the "sin" of essentialism, of assuming a pre-formed individual identity. (*Australian Feminist Studies* 2000)

To recite this as "Wittig and Butler and the influence of discourses of race have served to make many scholars wary of the categories of man and women, for fear of the 'sin' of essentialism, of assuming a pre-formed individual identity" effects a number of changes to the political grammar of Western feminist theory. In the first instance, we see a combined critique of essentialism that runs across feminism and links it to "other" scholars similarly "wary." Butler is no longer the one who breaks with or single-handedly transforms feminism; she is positioned as part of a tradition within and beyond feminism. This mode of recitation allows feminism to hold those who critique it within its terrain; it represents a thoughtful, reflexive feminism that changes incrementally and unevenly rather than though seismic shifts and generational rejections. This is significant because it challenges the representation of feminist theory as a linear history of progress or loss (and so the return) and suggests that feminist theories also act upon other traditions, rather than remaining passively acted upon, as hetero- or hom(m)o-citation practice would have it.

My experiments have also indicated that recitation via Wittig may not only have such affirmative effects. It may not only represent a generous, open vision of a feminist past and present otherwise stultified. In the above example, introducing different protagonists does not alter the implied chastisement of those wary of the "fear of the 'sin' of essentialism." If the extract is read as a lament, it is one that cannot disentangle feminist theory from the burden of this "fear." The "void . . . at the heart of Butler's notion of politics," in Nussbaum's words (1999), is not necessarily filled because of Butler's connection to other possible histories of Western feminist theory; "the void" may simply have a longer feminist history. In particular, in narratives of loss or return that see Butler's attachment and proximity to Foucault as problematic, the negative affect is not necessarily altered because of a reanimation of Wittig's significance. For example, let us consider the following extract introduced earlier:

> For Butler, on the authority of Foucault and Derrida respectively, the possibility of resistance is simply inherent in the nature of power or of language (Butler, 1997), but the conditions favourable to the exploitation of these windows of opportunity for personal and social transformation are never interrogated. (*Feminist Theory* 2000)

To recite with "the authority of Wittig and Irigaray respectively" does not alter the extract's suggestion that Butler fails to interrogate "conditions favourable to the exploitation of these windows of opportunity." Indeed, it extends this failure as a characteristic of feminist theory that Butler inherits, rather than as a problem that can be deflected onto a parallel or interrupting trajectory. This in itself is an interesting effect of my feminist recitation here: it makes it difficult to isolate poststructuralism as that which has prevented or obscured a previous feminist political capacity, and thus challenges narratives of return as well as loss. The situation may be worse than subjects of loss and return narratives believe: there may be no prior materiality untainted by abstraction to return to. Instead, feminist recitation situates the problem of political transformation as a *continued feature* of feminist theory that nostalgia for a unified era is misplaced within.

Thus, in a similar vein, recitation via Wittig alters how Western feminist narratives of progress and loss isolate abstraction as a sign of *increasing* feminist depoliticization. The excerpt below makes this transformation particularly clear:

Possibly because of its difficult task of dislodging commonly held assumptions, possibly because of the influence of Foucault and Derrida, recondite abstractions characterize postmodernist feminist theory in general and Butler's books in particular. (*Critical Inquiry* 1998)[23]

To recite the extract as "possibly because of the influence of Wittig and Irigaray, recondite abstractions characterize postmodern feminist theory in general and Butler's books in particular" provides a pleasing (to me at least) reorientation of our understanding of when and where abstraction in theory belongs. Here then, feminist recitation realigns postmodernism and feminism as abstract allies rather than always at odds. Indeed, one might suggest that this recitation allows for a repositioning of feminist theory at the heart of postmodernism rather than as marginal or opposed to it. This recitation resonates because of what haunts the present that would narrate Western feminist theory otherwise: the importance of abstraction in terms of feminist epistemological development, in the ability to imagine otherwise, as well as in the engagement with the importance of the systemic. Again, despite the tone of lament in the extract, the loss cannot be situated chronologically. Recitation in this vein thus resists a generational approach that safeguards the certainty of the feminist subject in the present.

In this reframing—of Western feminist theory as consistent in its concern with abstraction, with the relations between language, power, and politics, however valued—critique of Butler ceases to be a call for the reinstantiation of an imagined era of feminism before abstraction, but an engagement with ongoing traditions within rather than outside of feminism. To further expand this point, let us recite the following:

Recently there have been a number of constructive critiques of Butler's Foucauldian concept of power. (*Australian Feminist Studies* 2002)

The extract now reads: "Recently there have been a number of constructive critiques of Butler's Wittigian concept of power." This particular recitation propels a number of resonant reconsiderations. At one level, it suggests simply that "constructive critiques" of Butler are also critiques of a model of power she adapts from Wittig: the critique is thus again of a feminist tradition, rather than of Butler's Foucauldian roots. At another level, of course, the presence of Wittig in the text alters the way we read Butler and the nature of the critique that we assume is taking place. Butler may be being assessed for her reliance on Wittigian materialist feminist frames, for example, or Wittig may herself be being revisited as less materialist than we might at first have assumed. In Butler's attachment to Wittig the meaning of both figures is as transformed as is the accepted sense of what has happened in Western feminist theory. The recitation via Wittig in this passage (as in others) relies on plausible resonance, yes, but it also precipitates an uncertainty about what precisely the trajectory is that is being criticized. Feminist recitation thus allows us not only to revalue what haunts the feminist present, but also to rethink how the threads of the past come together. We might not be able to be sure that we have wholly gained or wholly lost something; we might need a politics of contextualization as well as conviction.

As suggested in my discussion about the choice of an alternative to Foucault in this experiment, my playful Wittig-Butler romance brings to the surface a resonant lesbian history to feminist debates about the relationships among sex, gender, and sexuality. Such a history contrasts with those that see critiques of heteronormativity as interruptions to the history of Western feminist theory, and, importantly for me, ones that hold sexual and material analyses forever apart. Let us explore further some of the lesbian feminist resonances that arise when we recite Butler via Wittig. To return to another extract included earlier:

Influenced especially by Foucault's *History of Sexuality*, feminists, along with queer theorists, now deconstructed the sex/gender distinction by arguing that not only is gender socially constituted, but sex is too. (*Australian Feminist Studies* 2000)

This passage now reads as: "Influenced especially by Wittig's *The Straight Mind*, feminists, along with queer theorists, now deconstructed the sex/ gender distinction by arguing that not only is gender socially constituted, but sex is too." As with several feminist recitations above, this renarration makes perfect sense. Both Wittig and Butler (whose presence is implicit intertextually) do indeed make the claim that "sex" is socially constructed, and both theorists foreground the importance of what Butler comes to call "the heterosexual matrix" as the epistemological and political context for that insight. In this sense my feminist recitation resituates sexuality at the heart of a feminist commitment to social constructionist critique. In addition, recitation also emphasizes the relationship between queer theory and this history of feminist critique, reminding us of the contingent nature of sexual politics Wittig is here seen to inaugurate. Queer theory and feminism are thus themselves paired to reinflect a Western feminist history that otherwise frames the former as an abandonment of the latter.

Since Wittig creatively combines lesbian sexual politics with Marxist dialectics in her own work, feminist recitation of her relationship with Butler and feminist/queer poststructuralism more generally refigures the presumed opposition between sexuality (as culture) and materiality (as oppression) so central to Western feminist loss and return narratives.[24] Recitation reinserts a history of materiality into the heart of feminist concerns with sexual identity and politics. Butler's repeated citation as moving away from materiality through a concern with representation and performativity or parody is thus revisited if we insist on the Wittigian influence in her work:

From a Foucauldian perspective, the making of the gendered self, or gender identity, is the product of disciplinary practices of the body that ensure the reproduction of heterosexuality as the norm. The body is seen as material that is enrolled in the production of gender rather than as providing the biological foundation for gender differences (Butler, 1993; Grosz, 1994). (*Body and Society* 2002)

In the recitation—"From a Wittigian perspective, the making of the gendered self, or gender identity, is the product of disciplinary practices of the body that ensure the reproduction of heterosexuality as the norm"— Butler and Grosz, so often antagonists in loss and return narratives, take up the lesbian feminist tradition of investigating the relationship of sexuality to the body, its regulation and relationship to social practices of gendering. Sexual politics thus becomes one way materiality is thought through by feminists, rather than a central reason materiality has been abandoned. I have already spent considerable time in the book pointing out the limits of this separation of sexuality and materiality, and some of its problematic effects. Recitation points here to the importance of insisting on sexual meaning outside of a culture/materiality split as part of what makes feminist theory well positioned to challenge (rather than reproduce) that discursive opposition.

In these experiments with recitation, then, Wittig is repositioned as a precursor to poststructuralist feminist concerns with sex, gender, and sexuality rather than as antithetical to them. The particular haunting I am

tracing not only concerns the materialist history of queer poststructuralism, but also the lesbian character of materialist feminism. Citation of
Butler as not engaged in ongoing feminist materialist debates both rubs
out whole sections of *Gender Trouble* (the book seems to shrink before our
very eyes) and isolates Wittig within a desexualized materialist tradition.
Putting Wittig back into Western feminist storytelling is thus to change
the history of materiality too, to challenge the framing of feminist interest
in materiality as a "return," and to insist that sexuality and materiality may
be linked other than through harm alone.[25] They may be, *they are*, linked
through a history of feminist theory that cannot think properly about
social and political transformation without the inclusion of lesbian figurations and histories.

There are limits to what this practice of feminist recitation can renarrate, of course. Let us take two examples where substituting Wittig for
Foucault does not, in my view, resonate as effectively as the examples
discussed above:

One especially revealing feature of Butler's style is the preponderance of subject-
verb disagreements. I want to speculate that this penchant, by reflecting the
difficulty of sustaining a Foucauldian critique of the singular self and the biological body, reveals the tensions continually at play in efforts to combine poststructuralism with feminism. (*Critical Inquiry* 1998)

During the 1980s and 90s the concepts of patriarchy and feminism gradually
disappeared from women's studies and gender research in the Nordic countries.
Instead, many researchers took inspiration from discourse theory, especially from
the works of Michel Foucault. (*Nora* 2004)

In the first extract a renarration with Butler's "subject-verb disagreements . . . reflecting the difficulty of sustaining a Wittigian critique of
the singular self" does not make sense, since Wittig does not present
such a critique. In the second extract it would be similarly meaningless to
suggest that Wittig's discourse theory influenced researchers, since again
Wittig does not develop discourse theory in her work. It is precisely when
the nature of a particular theoretical tradition (Butler's or Foucault's) is
specified rather than invoked that recitation is put under the most strain.
Indeed, perhaps it is simply not necessary in these cases, because it is a
particular rather than a generic comparison that is being made.

That strain points in another direction too. It highlights the limits of substitution *per se* as the basis of narrative recitation that is the direct replacement of Foucault with Wittig, when Foucault may indeed be an appropriate figure. Let us look at the following extract:

First, there emerged a genre of scholarship, inspired by the work of Michel Foucault and Judith Butler, particularly queer theory, which explored new aspects and dimensions of the socially constructed, performative character of gender and sexuality. (*Nora* 2003)

To read Wittig for Foucault here reconfigures feminism and queer theory as co-operative rather than discrete theoretical traditions, and is thus useful in similar ways to those suggested thus far. But this process of recitation is not intended to excise Foucault from a queer tradition, and this is a danger with my experiment so far. Foucault himself becomes the haunting presence hovering over the privileged coupling of Wittig and Butler, and although a vision of Foucault as displaced "third wheel" to the dominant relation may itself be pleasingly generative of a rather different historiography, it is perhaps a displacement too far. The limit to recitation in these extracts reminds us that the purpose of feminist recitation is not simple substitution, of course. It does not represent the resolution of a competition for primacy between Foucault and Wittig in claiming Butler's attentions, but a laying bare of what is at stake in the critical certainty that Butler's primary affiliate is (always) Foucault. Feminist recitation can produce a temporary break in accepted narratives of Western feminist theory, but it cannot—and should not—be conceived of as settled alternative.[26]

CONCLUSION

These final reflections on the feminist recitation process return me to the question of my choice of Wittig in the retelling of Western feminist stories. I hope I have situated this choice as a motivated one that emerges from my mapping of Western feminist storytelling thus far, and one that seeks to make particular rather than general erasures visible. I hope, too, that my experiment—the recitation of citation practices central to narrative function within these stories, in order to remind myself, and readers, of other resonant histories and interpretations—has struck a chord. The potential permanent erasure of Foucault's presence within Western feminist storytelling has further confirmed for me the importance of recitation as a *reflexive approach,* however, rather than as a proposition for an alternative history in which Wittig herself may become fixed, cast in resin, placed in a museum to be viewed as the more authentic historical antecedent to Butler. As Elizabeth Grosz pertinently notes: "The past is never exhausted in its vitalities, insofar as it is always capable of giving rise to another reading, another context, another framework that will animate it in different ways" (2000: 1020). As a practice, then, feminist recitation starts from affectively invested erasures in order to reveal possibilities for thinking the past and present differently. The process is one that is intended to open up and foreground absence, provide a break in the monotony of the repeated, and suggest other historiographies that are politically and theoretically transparent.

That transparency is the most illusive aspect of recitation in my undertaking; I believe it is also the most important. As discussed, the choice of Wittig in my feminist recitation experiment is not accidental. She represents my interest in folding histories of lesbian feminism back into Western feminist storytelling, histories whose haunting is most tangible in the attempts in progress, loss, and return narratives to reduce sexuality to culture and oppose it to "feminism proper." Recitation of Wittig forces a renarration of materialist feminism with sexuality at its heart and animates accounts of poststructuralism as sutured to, not separate from, feminism. My choice of Wittig allows me to combine a political and theoretical commitment to thinking sexuality and feminist studies together again, and at the same time forces me to locate myself within the narratives I re-read. Starting from my own frustration and remembered pleasure is a process that allows me at once to illuminate and interrupt the potent erasures that I have been tracking and to begin the archaeological work necessary to create a fuller picture of the possible meanings of sexuality within feminist, social, and cultural theory. I think these recitations matter, because they provide a break from the claustrophobic assumption that feminism is anachronistic, has been left behind, is dead and buried. Importantly, they provide a renarration via feminist traces present in these dominant narratives already. They are grounded and fanciful alternatives. They ask us to refresh our memories and allow ourselves to be turned.

AFFECTIVE SUBJECTS

6 The Western feminist stories I have been concerned with require and produce a heroine who is continuous with her past and remains the subject of a familiar present and future feminism. She is the subject of the story told, her trials and tribulations constitute the hurdles overcome. The individual narrative is driven by the extent to which she is characterized as abandoned, successful, betrayed, respected, tenacious, frustrated, or otherwise, and reader engagement is in this sense also saturated with affect: we do or do not identify with the subject of narrative and its objects. As I have suggested throughout part 1, these narratives are contested; they are staged as refutations and resentments of other positions, subjects, and narratives. The arguments circle around subject status, are as much about identifying pretenders to the position of feminist subject, as they are claims to occupy that position. The right to be the heroine, in other words, is one of the main prizes fought over within Western feminist nar-

ratives of progress, loss, and return. Western feminist return narratives are particularly interesting in this respect, insofar as they allow an affective resolution to these contests over history, meaning, and subjectivity. Return narratives allow the feminist present to be shared by subjects with different readings of the same history, with one prerequisite: that each subject acknowledge that her own singular position was previously too emphatic, lacked nuance, and now needs revision.

To restate this argument briefly, return narratives ask subjects of Western feminist progress narratives to admit that they may have been too hasty in rejecting earlier approaches as essentialist and to acknowledge that important feminist political insights have been lost, while they ask subjects of loss narratives to admit that they were too hasty in dismissing important critiques of essentialism's exclusions. Theoretical and political resolution in return narratives relies on agreement that the cultural turn was an abstraction too far, and requires mediation of the twinned affects of hope and despair that characterize progress and loss narratives respectively. In return narratives, then, a broader range of feminist subjects can occupy the Western feminist present, but only on the basis of a shared sense of what has come before. As discussed throughout this book thus far, the affective manifestations of this historiographic investment are a shared sense of loss at feminism's demise and a shared hope that a reinvigorated feminism may be possible in the future. That the subjects of that future feminism will be the same as those concerned with its progress or loss now is never questioned. Indeed, so strong is the attachment to the subject of a Western feminist return narrative being the one to reinvigorate feminist theory and politics that the twinned affects of keen loss and muted hope that underwrite this history are set on textual replay, lest other perceptions of the past and present suggest a different future.

Further, as I argued in chapter 4, "Amenability," the narrative insistence on feminism being over and in need of recovery in the familiar, slightly altered, form that marks return narratives means that the distinction between postfeminist discourses and Western feminist stories about our own recent past comes to rest on the overburdened significance of that feminist subject. If these overlapping narrations of the social world coincide in terms of their historical markers and juxtapositions, the difference must lie in the feminist subject's capacity to reinvigorate rather than abandon what has come before. The difference between a progressive agenda and co-optation is thus the desire for that *return* to feminism. The answer to the problem of loss that Western feminist storytelling relies on is a redoubling of the affective attachment to that lost object and to one's authority to determine where it may be found, with what methods, and by whom. As I have tried to show in this book, there are particular costs to a presumption of shared agreement about the proper subject of the Western feminist present because it produces a common history that she is presumed to inherit. As we have seen, that history is marked by oppositions between materiality and culture, politics and theory, and good and bad feminist subjects, and relies particularly on a separation between poststructuralism and feminism, whether positively or negatively inflected. Such oppositions produce a history of feminist theory caught into decades and pit racial and sexual meanings and identities against one another. In return narratives the damage done to feminism by a poststructuralism over-associated with sexuality can be rectified by a return to the more pressing concerns of a racialized materialism writ in global terms. As discussed at length in previous chapters, Western feminist storytelling thus instantiates similar chronologies and oppositions to those taken up by postfeminist discourses, in which feminism is also over, sexual freedom constitutes gender equality's ambivalent yet transcendent sign, and continued gender inequality exists elsewhere in cultural or geographical arenas that lag behind.

It is not only a question of overlap, however. In my view, it is precisely the extent to which Western feminist storytelling invests in an absolute difference between a feminist and a nonfeminist position that consolidates rather than alleviates its amenability. It is precisely in the construction of a particular heroine through generational, political, and geographical deflection of contest over feminist meaning that the conditions of overlap emerge. It is precisely the endowing of one feminist subject and not another with the capacity to take feminism forward that produces the shared narrative of feminism as over in the first instance. It thus makes little sense for me to propose a proper *feminist subject* to resolve the power dynamics I have been mapping throughout this book, appealing though that pull may be. This would be as likely to instantiate a singular history as the narratives I have been examining and would circumvent an exploration of the political grammar of Western feminist theory that enables the relationship among Western feminist subjectivity, affect, and historiography in the first place. Instead, in this chapter I want to think through what happens when we trouble the relation between subject and object that lies at the heart of Western feminist storytelling. I take this line, not with a view to getting rid of the feminist subject (as if one could), but in order to explore both how to make visible the entanglement of feminist subjectivity, temporality, and exclusion, and in closing, to approach the subject from perspectives that might allow her to signify otherwise, as the subject of an/other political grammar, one of entanglement rather than freedom.

This interest has been present throughout the book, indeed. I have been concerned with exploring and challenging the relations among subject, history, and exclusion in the dominant narratives of Western feminist storytelling in various ways. The tactic of citing journal and time over author constituted a direct attempt to situate repeated claims that might otherwise appear to be individual, shifting analysis away from the subject (who is right or wrong) and onto the political grammar that makes up the narrative strands of feminist stories. This tactic might be thought of as one of diffusion, perhaps, an attempt not to settle disputes but to ask after the terms under which only certain arguments can occur and recur. In chapter 5, I experimented with renarrating feminist storytelling by intervening more directly in the making of the feminist subject of a particular present. Here I "recited" Judith Butler's representation as the theorist both responsible for the transformation of feminism (whether positively or negatively valued) and as primarily reliant on male antecedents, particularly Michel Foucault, for the development of her own critical trajectory. I sought to interrupt the hetero- and hom(m)o-citational practices that provide a separate teleology to feminism outside poststructuralism in order to allow Butler to signify as a different kind of feminist heroine. By suturing her to Monique Wittig instead, I sought to reveal a lesbian materialist history to feminist poststructuralism and to reference a more complex feminist past, present, and future than existing narratives usually allow. In practicing recitation, I hoped to precipitate the imagining of feminist subjects as inheritors of contradictory legacies that cannot be resolved by a return to a fabricated past free of contest.

There are two primary issues that arise from that experiment that I want to take forward to think through Western feminist subjectivity as tethered to temporality and geography in this chapter. The first is the intention to disrupt rather than dismiss the feminist subject. In the last chapter I sought to interrupt the political grammar that produces a recognizable feminist subject in the present, one whose history cannot be tampered with. The process of recitation was instead intended to allow subjects to emerge whose presence disrupts the generationally determined, damaging spatio-temporalities I have been mapping. I proposed a potential set of realignments that do not simply invest these institutionalized histories with alternative affects, but scramble their component parts in ways that, I hope, resonate to allow a shadow life to be glimpsed, one version of the possible. While imagined and temporary, a feminist subject of the recited present emerged as one with a material queer history, or one carrying the burden of a particularly feminist abstraction. Recitation thus reconfigured the relationship between past and present by focusing on what I took to be formative hauntings; in the process a different subject, one who has not "lost" feminism, began to be visible. This is one subject among many possible feminist subjects, not a singular necessity to pin our hopes on. We cannot, of course, abandon subjectivity, but we can call it to account (in ourselves as much as in others) and explore other modes of historical and textual signification.

The second issue to take forward is the motivated nature of both subject construction and its critique. Recitation cannot supply an alternative history to displace narratives of progress, loss, and return, but should be thought of as a way of *recombining* half-submerged narrative traces from the starting point of political exclusions haunting the present. Yet equally important in this respect has been the recognition of that starting point as engaging my own attachments, my own reading history. I have a motivated relationship to the question of both feminist history and subjectivity, and part of my interest in critiquing these dominant narratives has been that my own status as a feminist subject lacks coherence without this recitation. In highlighting what I consider formative exclusions in feminist political grammar, then, I am also highlighting my own stakes in the field of Western feminist theory. But this is not so much an admission as it is a confirmation of my sense that engaging the political grammar of Western feminist storytelling requires relinquishing a fantasy of neutrality.[1] This is part of the paradox of unravelling the conditions under which Western feminist subjectivity comes to signify in the narratives I have been analyzing; the closer one comes to unpacking its emergent force and misplaced presumptions, the more it seems one is brought up against one's own affective attachments.

Starting from these insights, this final chapter continues to explore the paradoxes of subject construction as a central feature of Western feminist storytelling. Instead of starting from and attempting to dislodge the narrative building blocks of Western feminist narratives of progress, loss, and return, this chapter engages the subject/object relation that anchors this historiography more directly. For if, as I have argued, the prioritization of a singular Western feminist subject instantiates a particular version of history, it also produces objects (or even other subjects) in the present, whose histories are simultaneously written in what Sara Ahmed has called the moment of "encounter" (2000a). To reconsider a subject/object relation in the Western feminist present, then, may be to imagine other histories and *intersubjective* relationships that are less routine or overdetermined than those I have been unpicking. As part of this approach, I am interested in pushing at and identifying the *limit* of Western feminist subjectivity in a given context. My aim towards the end of the chapter is to home in on the narrative gaps that one cannot rush to fill in: pauses, if you will, in the grammatical construction of subject. Through this final chapter, my concern is with where the limit to the fusion of space, time, and subject in Western feminist theory might be found.[2]

In the first sections of this chapter I explore two related feminist efforts to transform the subject/object distinction, those that focus on empathy and those that focus on agency. Both conceptual developments reflect existing interest in challenging the priority given to the "one who knows" within feminist theory. While theorists of empathy point to the importance of intersubjectivity (the capacity to feel with/for others), theorists of agency extend our understanding of who counts as a subject in the first instance. Feminist theorists such as Lorraine Code (1995b), Patricia Hill Collins (2000), and Sandra Bartky (2002) have theorized empathy as a technique for challenging the myopic world view of the Western feminist subject. A shared focus on empathy for these authors stresses the importance of the feminist researcher extending her view beyond her own subjective concerns and imagining the world, or knowledge, through the eyes of the other. It contrasts autonomy with intersubjectivity and finds the latter to be both more valuable and more in tune with the collective practices and the epistemological judgments marginalized communities make (see particularly Collins 2000). The shift to an intersubjective epistemology is one I generally support, but in this chapter I explore ways in which the practice of empathy often manages rather than transforms the subject/

object distinction I am identifying as a barrier to telling Western feminist stories otherwise. While empathy encourages the proliferation of feminist subjects in the present, it relies on an extension rather than diminution of the subject's capacities and on recognition of agency in the other who is being empathized with. It is always marked by that which cannot be empathized with and draws that limit as a self-evident boundary for what (and who) can be included in feminism itself.

This chapter is equally interested in what happens when empathy fails, when recognition of agency in the other falters, or when misrecognition prevents the development of intersubjectivity. Here I focus on the importance of affect once more, since failed empathy is often expressed through a resurgence rather than diminution of feeling. I theorize ways in which the breakdown of empathy produces a crisis mediated instead by prioritizing "bodily knowledge." Turning from empathy and agency to horror, I suggest that "the unspeakable," that which produces a ripple of visceral horror in the subject, *frames* rather than exceeds the subject/object relation and allows for the continued coherence of a Western feminist subject's narrative in the face of potential rupture. My inquiry asks after what the unspeakable reveals about subjective investments in what can be included in Western feminist stories and after the role affect plays in the constitution of a Western feminist subject's place and time. In the final pages of this chapter I start from those moments of affective intensity to see if they might shed light on what is obscured when we accept the terms under which the Western feminist subject remains intact. What kind of politics emerges at this limit, and the place of the encounter with what remains unreadable for the feminist subject?

EMPATHY

Western feminist theory has long been concerned with challenging a singular focus on the subject as the one who knows. As indicated in the introduction to this chapter, one way in which feminist theorists have sought to extend the boundaries of the feminist subject has been through theorizing empathy as a mode of linking to others and as promoting intersubjective relations over and above individual status in relation to knowledge and practice. In this respect feminists invest in empathy because of its capacity to move the subject beyond the limits of her own vision. In terms of my critique of the over-investment in the subject of feminism, then, and in the attempt to disrupt the political grammar that produces that subject as one with a singular history, empathy seems worth exploring further as a potentially useful concept.

At its heart, feminist concern with empathy represents an exploration of the best way of developing ethical relations to other people and has been developed particularly strongly in the context of reflections on epistemology and research practice. Thus the question of empathy has been key to feminist perspectives on the production of knowledge, forming a central part of the foundational critiques of objectivity that are understood to lie at the heart of androcentric academic practice (e.g., Alcoff and Potter 1993; Harding 1993). Empathy is understood both as a way of challenging the subject/object distinction that grounds the social sciences for example and as a way of confronting the authority of the speaking or writing subject who represents others (Roof and Wiegman 1995). The empathetic critique is twofold, suggesting the importance of *feeling as knowing* on the one hand, and thus the importance of the researcher or knower as embodied rather than abstracted; and on the other hand, it emphasizes the importance of moving beyond the subject and towards intersubjective practices and modes of knowing (Skaerbaek 2004; Skaerbaek, Duhaček et al. 2006). Ann Oakley's foundational essay on the importance of empathy in interviewing women remains exemplary of both interlocked concerns. For Oakley (1997 [1981]), establishing genuine relationships with her interviewees, getting them to open up to her and share information from a position of trust, forms the core of her critique of the "smash and grab" mode of empirical observation favored by masculinist social science. In Oakley's analysis, it is the ability to feel as and with others that forms the basis of intersubjective trust and that allows for the emergence of a different *quality* of knowledge, as well as its extension to include hitherto marginalized subjects.

The intersubjective dimension of knowledge generation at all stages of the research process is also vital to Sandra Harding's discussion of "strong objectivity" (1993), Nancy Hartsock's development of "standpoint epistemology" (1998), and Lorraine Code's insistence that feminist theorists take "subjectivity into account" (1993). All three theorists emphasize researcher empathy as critical for politicizing knowledge from the margins and for calling into account its own purported neutrality.[3] At the heart of

the critique of objectivity, then, lies not simply an emphasis on subjectivity per se, as is sometimes suggested (Hekman 1990; Hekman 1999), but
on relationality. In this respect a Western feminist knowledge project has
prioritized the ability to appreciate the other, to render them a subject in,
rather than object of, the research process. Patricia Hill Collins puts
empathy still more fully front and centre in *Black Feminist Epistemology*
(2000), echoing Oakley's insistence on the ability to empathize as a condition of being understood as trustworthy. Collins understands empathy as
central to African-American community formation, and real dialogue as
the basis for evaluation of knowledge claims within those communities. In
this she joins other U.S. feminists of color who stress empathy as necessary
for white feminist engagement across cultural, ethnic, and racial privileges
(in particular Lugones 1990), a point I return to below. Importantly for my
argument here, the development of empathy is thus understood as a direct
critique of dominant feminist historiography in that it foregrounds the
relationship between the occupation of a subject position and the exclusion both of other subjects and their histories. Hill Collins makes this
relation explicit in her emphasis on empathy as already central to the
knowledge practices of the marginalized communities she is concerned
with, and thus as demonized as the basis of knowledge in contexts of
privilege.

Despite the importance of developments, there are many persuasive
critiques of feminist empathy in terms of both its emphasis on feeling and
its intersubjective dimensions. It is considered problematic when perceived as deriving from women's natural capacities to feel with or for
others, for example, or as a positive endorsement of their socially instilled
intersubjective capacities. In particular, feminist critics have pointed out
that empathy is frequently assumed to arise from self-evidently common
interests among women, rather than being worked for, and is unable to
account for clear differences of location that require considerable work to
overcome or that may remain blocks to understanding (e.g., Bar On 1993;
Bailey 2000).[4] These assumptions are likely to lead to sentimental attachment to the other, or worse, substitution of one's own interests for those of
the other. Caren Kaplan, for example, argues that declarations of empathy
tend to precede the incorporation of difference, rather than signaling
enduring respect for the same (1994). Thus empathy may be dismissed on
the basis that it extends the self into the other, reinforcing subjective

starting points instead of transforming them, allowing for a gobbling up rather than a genuinely subjective or epistemological movement precipitated by engagement with the other.

Such critiques seem reasonable, certainly, and I share the concern about women's "natural capacities" for feeling. But they have been countered by arguing that these gestures of incorporation are characteristic of *failed empathy*, a "lazy and false empathy in which we take the other's place" (Dean 2003: 96). Such critiques might thus be said to say less about empathy itself and more about the ways in which one may fail to achieve it: a case in point would be "sentimental attachment" as a poor substitute for real empathy. Lorraine Code addresses these concerns directly, insisting that "good empathy" transforms objects of study into living beings and subjects, while "bad empathy" seeks instead to tell someone how they feel (1995a). In bad empathy the subject's needs and expectations are projected onto the other; in good empathy the subject responds to and respects the other as a subject.[5] In Code's view empathy is akin to a feminist "ethic of care" that values intersubjective experience as part of what is and can be known and is an important way of recognizing knowledge as embodied but not static.[6] Bad empathy keeps things as they are; good empathy transforms intersubjective relations. Following Simone de Beauvoir, Code insists that empathy helps to describe and engage particular rather than abstract instances and people, and is thus capable of generating accountable rather than universalizing knowledge. Thus, Code remarks further that "empathy at its best preserves yet seeks to know the 'strangeness,' respects the boundaries between self and other that the 'forbiddenness' affirms" (1995a: 141).[7]

This emphasis on the difficulties attending "good" rather than "bad" empathy is taken up by María C. Lugones in her landmark article "Playfulness, 'World'-Travelling, and Loving Perception" (1990). Lugones argues that if white Western feminists are interested in bridging racial, ethnic, or religious differences (across space or time), they need to accept that this will not be straightforward. She emphasizes the importance of *discomfort* in the process of "travelling towards the other" in her piece, which also stresses that one need not leave home to make this journey. Indeed, for Lugones, lack of discomfort in the genuine attempt to reach out across difference is itself suspect, indicating a potential lack of real transformation on the part of the subject. The presence of discomfort may thus also be a way of judging empathy's integrity, the difference between good and bad modes. Lugones's work has been taken up by theorists endeavouring to speak or think across cultural and geographical differences among feminists (Sylvester 1995), and in particular to speak or think about practices of female genital cutting (FGC), where questions of incommensurable experience are often starkly brought to the fore in Western feminist accounts (Gunning 1992; Davis 2004a; Pedwell 2007). The consistent tone of these engagements with Lugones, despite other differences in approach, is of the inevitability of that discomfort in empathizing with unfamiliar, specifically non-Western, practices. Indeed, the question of empathy for white Western feminists very often arises specifically in relation to cultural or religious practices thought of as pushing against the limit of what might be considered feminist. As a result it features regularly in considerations, not only of FGC, but also of the meanings of Muslim women's covering practices, for example, where concern is with how far these practices are examples of difference as such and how far examples of patriarchal imposition.[8] In these respects empathy is understood as a way of extending not only the Western feminist subject's perspective, but also which subjects and practices are included in a feminist present and past.

To extend the definitions a little further, then, good empathy will emphasize the independent life of the other subject; bad empathy will project itself onto the other who can only become a subject in the empathetic one's image, and always subsequently. Empathy can be the mechanism through which Western feminist subjects transform their own comfort as subjects in order to appreciate and understand the other, and in the process perhaps a different understanding of the temporal and geographical diversity underwriting feminist subjectivity—or feminism *tout court*— may emerge. Thus, for a range of feminist epistemologists, empathy can help mitigate forms of representational violence that shore up existing power relations between and across sites separated by time and space, as well as between individual subjects. This account seems eminently reasonable; it stresses the work that the Western feminist subject must do in order to recognize other subjects and simultaneously refuses to let her off the hook in terms of responsibility for location, history, and feminist myopia. Yet it remains unclear what the motivation for the Western feminist subject to put herself through this discomfort might be. Interestingly, in an earlier co-written piece with Elizabeth Spelman, Lugones speculates on possible reasons for undergoing this disorientation, given that it would be easier, and surely more pleasant, not to do so (Lugones and Spelman 1983). Rejecting altruism as a sufficient or appropriate reason (a potential instance of bad empathy, presumably), one laudable incentive proposed is friendship. Friendship is here understood as a prior or emerging investment in the wellbeing of the other person, one that folds one's own happiness into that of others. In this sense, empathy follows a prior intersubjective investment rather than producing it, and the difference between comfort and discomfort can thus be temporarily as well as temporally resolved.

This identification of friendship as one possible reason among others—love, care, necessity, perhaps—to precipitate empathy in the Western feminist subject raises rather than settles several questions I have about its transformative capacities, however. And these questions also seem resistant to being resolved through the distinctions between good and bad empathy upon which so much feminist work in this vein relies. In the first instance, I remain unconvinced that it is always possible to tell the difference between good and bad modes of empathy, particularly when affective attachments are in play. Friendship is complicated, as we know, and not always innocent of projection; I am often drawn to people who remind me of what I think of as good aspects of my own character, for example. Love is at least as complicated, as is care, since these are dynamics in which each participant may feel variously put upon or cherished, and in which I would hazard once more that one cannot always tell the difference. In this sense, it seems insufficient to separate out good from bad empathy, since the insistence that only the former can produce real, honest, politically appropriate intersubjectivity seems at least ill attuned to the actual nature of intersubjective dynamics. But even if we could, for a moment, imagine the difference as absolute and thus good empathy as a clear way of challenging the singular investments and myopias of the Western feminist subject, there are other difficulties with this model I want to explore below.

First, there is a de facto temporality to this process that remains insistent, and that I want to unpick. It has been suggested that the subject called upon to be empathetic and thus precipitate herself into intersubjective relation with, rather than subjective evaluation of, the other must at some level have a prior attachment to the other in order to recognize her as an other-who-will-become-subject. As Lugones indicates, some affective relation—she focuses on friendship, but does not rule out other attachments—would ideally be in place in order to make the uncomfortable move that will not be reification or projection. And in that respect, as indicated above, attachment usually precedes, rather than being produced by, empathy. If no actual attachment exists, the other that the subject will come to empathize with will need to be transformed in a different way. The relationship is thus a temporally bound one, insofar as it is the other that will become a subject in the eyes of the empathetic one, grammatically speaking, rather than the other way round. It is a relationship between subject and other-subject, then, where I use the term "other-subject" to describe this process of the other's becoming, a process that the empathetic subject has by definition already achieved. The term describes not only a temporal relationship, but also the empathetic subject's viewpoint rather than that of the other-subject in any empirical sense (who may have other ideas about the nature of the relationship in both temporal and hierarchical terms). Empathy does little to challenge the temporal grammar of the Western feminist subject, in other words, even as it suggests ways of expanding the subject's horizons.

Second, although shifts in subject position through empathy are important, they do not really get to the conditions under which (good or bad) empathy can arise or to the conditions under which it is bound to fail. The inclusion of more subjects in the field of knowledge, and a more dynamic relationship to them, is surely a boon for feminist theory, but the conditions of recognition of the other-subject often appear to be entirely in the subject's hands, whether or not an affective attachment already exists. Indeed, rather ironically, good empathy might be said to enhance rather than diminish the powers of the empathetic subject, requiring renewed marshalling of existing reflexive skills and the learning of new ones, in the desire to extend subjective recognition appropriately. Empathy thus in many ways reinforces the *position* of the subject, however the subject herself may have altered, and in this respect preserves the capacities of the subject who can reflect on both self and other.[9]

And there is a further difficulty I want to end this discussion of empathy with, and that is the assumption of reciprocity. The feminist literature on empathy acknowledges that the other-subject may not wish to be so recognized when the empathy is "bad," but it is always assumed that "good" empathy would be appreciated. Indeed, an assumption of reciprocity is what regulates empathetic temporality, since it is key to final mutual recognition of subjects in the present of feminism. But what if the other-subject is not interested in intersubjectivity or refuses the terms of empathetic recognition? To be empathized with could be a horrific prospect, one resulting in the dissolution of self, when the empathetic subject is associated with violence, for example. On this particular point, I have been much influenced by Dasa Duhaček's work on citizenship and intersubjectivity in contemporary Serbia (2006a; 2006b). Drawing on Hannah Arendt, Duhaček highlights the importance of a commitment to generous citizenship without an assumption of reciprocity, since to expect the latter is to ignore the historical and political reasons why this may not be able to be given. Duhaček's development of feminist ethics in this context centres on responsibility over reciprocity in order to mark the historical and political conditions under which certain subjects come to be the ones in a position to extend recognition, while others are not. To expand Duhaček's framework here, even if all the other conditions necessary for good empathy to arise are in place, incommensurabilities of location and perception may well disrupt the subject's ability to transform herself through feeling as/for the other-subject. The other-subject, in other words, may not be interested in sharing.[10] Thus, while I think that existing work on empathy offers a rich starting point for challenging the status of the Western feminist subject as singular heroine of dominant feminist narratives, it cannot be claimed to resolve many of the problems inherent in the subject/object relation I am concerned with here. It is likely to reinforce rather than unpick the position of the empathetic subject, and cannot account for historical or contextual stumbling blocks that frame the possibility of intersubjective relations. I return to the question of what happens when empathy fails later in the chapter, as this lack offers a productive way of thinking about the limit of Western feminist subjectivity; but for the moment, I want to turn to the question of agency and recognition that has implicitly informed the discussion thus far.

AGENCY

The ability to empathize with an other-subject requires a dynamic of recognition that is ultimately, as discussed above, in the hands of the empathetic subject. If good empathy requires an ability to recognize others as subjects with lives not reducible to the political, ethical, or ontological frames of the subject, then we need to inquire after the conditions under which that recognition occurs. If, as Nancy Fraser argues, recognition is one of the conditions of democratic participation (1996; 1997; 2001), there are prior questions to be asked about the basis of that recognition. What, in other words, enables recognition, and what prevents it? I want to suggest here that the primary condition implicitly or explicitly required for recognition of other-subjects in feminist theory is the presence of agency. If empathy concerns the subject's ability to feel outside of their own experience and requires a commitment to the possibility of intersubjectivity as the basis of ethical engagement with the world, agency concerns the ability to act as a subject in the first instance. And, of course, this means that the two are linked, in that subjects must be understood to have some measure of self-possession or autonomy in order that empathetic engagement not be a transfer of the subject's own qualities (and hence bad empathy). What I have been calling the other-subject must first be seen as independent both of the subject and of other others and must fit the criteria for being an agent in the Western feminist subject's eyes. While empathetic engagement necessitates some transformation of self on the part of the subject, the burden of proof remains firmly on the part of the other-subject to display requisite agency before empathy is even possible.

The feminist literature on agency is by now quite vast, and I will not attempt a full overview here.[11] But I do want to point to some ways in which the question of agency is key to the relationship between subject and object in Western feminist theory and to the political grammars of Western feminist storytelling I am concerned with. Even in my brief discussion in this section so far, I have made certain claims about agency that are in fact highly contested. Thus, I have already conflated agency with "self-possession," "independence," and "autonomy" in ways that have been variously critiqued as privileging a Western liberal model of political resistance or as a structuralist analysis of power that is ill adapted to an understanding of its complexities. My statements of fact assume that agency marks and can be read primarily through signs of resistance, and it asserts a version of independence that privileges freedom from rather than attachment to context and other subjects. Such a view also presupposes that an example of agency cannot simultaneously be an example of something else, which enhances a focus on co-optation of a pure politics rather than the amenabilities I have been more interested in unravelling in this project.

Kalpana Wilson provides a useful reminder of why agency as a concept has been so important to feminist theorists (2008), highlighting its history as vexed from a socialist feminist perspective in particular, within which suspicion of agency arises from its focus on individual rather than collective capacities and on an economic model of "individuality" that values only one's ability to enhance (others') capital accumulation. In a rather different vein, Judith Butler's conclusion to *Gender Trouble* also argues for a view of agency detached from individuality on the basis that its over-association with individual capacity ignores both the vagaries of power and the ways in which power acts to make individuals *feel agented* as part of how it operates (1990: 142–49). Despite these well-founded suspicions about agency, both Wilson and Butler note from their different perspectives that one cannot simply jettison the concept of agency because of its potential masking of other social factors. To do so would be to leave subjects in a double bind: subject to power in whatever form and unable to critique it or free oneself from its grasp without raising the spectre of false consciousness or co-optation. Feminism itself—minimally, the belief that gender relations can and should be transformed—has at its centre the assumption that individuals and collectives may act counter to dominant interests while still being subject to their effects, of course. And in this respect agency is bound to remain important, if complex or compromised, within feminist theory.

One of the primary reasons for a continued emphasis on agency concerns this issue of oppressive relations and individual or group capacities, but with a particular focus on challenging discourses of victimization *within* feminism. Such work sees assumptions about where and when women are culturally or socially duped as needing further analysis, and homes in on moments or contexts in which women exercise agency as of primary significance. I am thinking here of Kathy Davis's critical investigations of women's agency in cosmetic surgery (1994; 2003), or the range of writing exploring sex worker agency (O'Connell Davidson 1998; Doezema 2001; Andrijasevic 2003; Agustin 2007). While not ignoring adverse social and political conditions, these theorists advocate taking women's agency seriously precisely in order to understand how power works. Whatever the differences, what these approaches share is a poststructuralist inflection, in terms of understanding power as negotiated rather than fixed and through attention to representation as key to how meanings are made. Thus Julia O'Connell Davidson and Rutvica Andrijasevic are as interested in how subjects are represented as *agency-less* as they are in where instances of agency may be found.[12] In this respect recent work that prioritizes agency is likely to foreground the investments of the researcher or writer in denying agency to particular individuals or communities and in tracking how theoretical perspectives need to change in order to account for complex models of subjectivity and power.

These combined efforts to critique a feminist "victimization thesis" and pay attention to modes of representation often implicitly or explicitly reference Chandra Mohanty's landmark article "Under Western Eyes" (2003 [1988]), in which she locates the question of agency as part of colonialism. Mohanty critiques Western feminist representations of "Third World Women" as devoid of agency, as passive victims of localized patriarchies and global imperialism. In her analysis of development publications, Mohanty explores the ways in which the gaze is central to the framing of non-Western contexts as lagging behind in terms of gender equality. Representations of who has agency and who does not, for Mohanty, are thus key to temporal and spatial hierarchies in Western feminist theory. Following Mohanty, debates about the meaning of agency and its intersubjective dimensions have been critically tied to debates about culture and difference. Thus transnational feminist scholars have interrogated the ways in which the denial of agency to certain (non-Western) subjects is better thought of as a product of a Western imagination rather than the result of analysis of particular practices, histories, and affects. In a similar vein, Uma Narayan has also asked who we are listening to in order to come to the conclusion that women are subsumed under patriarchy; she suggests that we think carefully about who speaks for tradition, and in whose name (1997; 2000). And Nadje Al-Ali responds to the relentless circulation of Western media images of Iraqi women as passive, oppressed shadows by providing intricate histories of Iraqi women's individual and collective resistance (2005; Al-Ali and Pratt 2008). These theorists, and many others, have emphasized women's actual resistance to the conditions that oppress them as a mark of agency and thus of subject status deserving of recognition.

A linked, but slightly different challenge to the limitations of Western feminist ideas of agency has come predominantly from scholars critical not only of the transnational unevenness of requirements to evidence agency, but also of the assumption that this is best demonstrated in resistant mode. Work in this genre emphasizes agency as likely to be formed through attachment rather than resistance to prevailing norms and builds on the critiques of Western political theory's conflation of autonomy and agency. Saba Mahmood's work is instructive here (2005). Via ethnographic work on the Islamic piety movement in Egypt, Mahmood argues that agency should not measured by its distance from norms, but rather at a contextual level through an examination of how norms are practiced and negotiated. In the process of challenging Western feminist assumptions about *where* agency may be identified, Mahmood's work also queries the autonomous foundations of agency as peculiarly Western, suggesting instead that agency may be practiced and experienced as shared or intersubjective.[13] Sumi Madhok takes the critique of Western modes of agency in a slightly different direction by exploring the practices of rights workers in South Asia. Also through an empirical approach, Madhok demonstrates that these workers' conscious negotiations of the norms they cannot directly challenge constitute a form of agency, offering a persuasive critique of what she terms the "action-bias" of current Western theories (2007).

Western feminist failure to see agency in unfamiliar others is characterized as one of two forms of myopia, then: a failure to see resistance in unfamiliar modes and an insistence that independent resistance is agency's primary sign. In many respects this work to expand the meanings of agency has been highly successful, empirically extending the range of practices understood as indicative of agency and critiquing a Western feminist gaze that seeks only to recognize its mirror image. This work goes a long way towards challenging Western feminist presumptions about who needs saving, from what, and by whom. These interventions do more than force a re-evaluation of current transnational dynamics too. They suggest different histories of feminism in which the Western feminist subject of a return narrative is not the only heroine, or in which the other-subject does not require or want recognition in order to thrive. A re-evaluation of agency appears, then, to have the capacity to disrupt the Western feminist political grammar that I have been concerned with.

But before cracking open the champagne, I want to reflect a little more on the limits of a focus on agency, however reconceptualized, for offering an/other political grammar for Western feminist theory. The first lingering doubt I have about the expansion of agency as offering a way out of Western feminist myopia concerns the exceptionally broad take-up of agency as critical trope, particularly in contexts where the object of critique is feminism. Readers will perhaps be familiar with the antifeminist accounts by writers such as Katie Roiphe (1993) and Christina Hoff Sommers (1994; 2000), who insist that second wave feminism created a victim culture that must be wholly jettisoned if women are to be strong, agented figures in the modern world. For Roiphe and Sommers, feminist attachment to misery and victimhood prevents relationships between women and men, and leaves men unable to express desire for women or assert their own needs without being labelled misogynists. In a different vein, Wilson (2008) revisits Mohanty's figure of the oppressed "Third World Woman" to highlight that transnational development agencies have now adopted "agency" as their primary mode of representation of women. For Wilson, institutions like the World Bank rely on characterizations of women as efficient and responsible (in contrast to men) in order to advance their own neoliberal agendas. Women's "reliability" is thus naturalized as part of their investment in economic development, rather than contextualized as a feature of their primary responsibility for childcare, say, and the oppressive conditions under which women are able to exercise limited choices disappear from view. Agency is thus mobilized discursively as the *opposite of inequality* rather than as part of the negotiation of power relations in constrained circumstances. Ironically enough, then, in both contexts, a failure to embrace agency as characteristic of women's position can be marked as indicative of an anachronistic attachment to sexual and economic inequalities that have now been transformed, reinforcing the very colonial temporalities we are interested in disrupting.

There are aspects of this discursive mobilization of agency as inequality's opposite that also inflect some of the feminist reconsiderations discussed thus far. To return to Mahmood's account of women involved in the "politics of piety" movement in Egypt, my second reservation is that there is a sense that evidence of agency will self-evidently mediate against hasty judgment of practices such as veiling. This assumption also constitutes agency in inverse proportion to harm, and in this respect as a self-evidently positive force. Yet this is rather odd, since surely agency in itself does not tell us much about the political or ethical *quality* of practices thus characterized: one can be an agent of violence against others, just as one can be an agent for change. In this respect the presence of agency in individuals or groups does not really tell us much about what one might say next, does not necessarily determine whether or not one might want to advocate for or against a particular practice. In short, the fact that women in the piety movement are clearly agented does not mean a feminist could not strongly advocate for abolishing that movement, though it may (and this remains important) alter the basis on which that case is made.

Indeed, this problem of judgment does continue to haunt debates about veiling practices associated with women's Islamic piety in particular. Thus agency may be identified in the political donning of head coverings as part of regime resistance historically (e.g., Afshar 1993; 1998), or as a form of resistance to the imposition of Western norms in officially secular contexts contemporarily (Özdalga 1998; Scott 2007). Alternatively, agency may be located, as in Mahmood's work, in the active and willing participation in religious practice, rather than in resistance to it, as discussed. And of course there is some overlap among these arguments for a given author. Yet extending definitions of agency to include additional practices may simply defer rather than defuse the moment of feminist judgment. On the one hand, Western feminists may simply not accept arguments that situate veiling in these histories of action and affirmation; on the other, they may accept an extended vision of such practices to include veiling as agented.[14] But even in the latter case, which might be understood as a successful challenge to the limit of Western feminist recognition, it is usual to establish a hierarchy or continuum of covering practices. Thus, Western feminist perspectives tend to mark a distinction between covering of the hair but not the face, or covering of the hair and face but not the full body or the eyes, in terms of acceptability. Or there might be an endorsement of covering for politically resistant reasons, but not when insisted upon by a patriarch, say. Such responses continue to affirm one version of agency over the other on the basis of what can be recognized as such by the empathetic feminist subject.

A hierarchical ordering of which practices count as agented means that the question of judgment is shifted rather than resolved. And this deflection of judgment leads to a third reservation about the usefulness of a focus on agency as the basis for recognition of other-subjects. Agency cannot be endlessly extended to all practices, however resignified, if it is to retain any kind of meaning. It will always operate as a limit to the relationship between the subject and object of inquiry, even if the limit is obscured. If all veiling practices were universally understood as signaling agency in their wearer, for example, a question mark would surely hover over some other practice. Proliferation of which practices may be included does not in itself resolve questions about the basis on which agency is determined, or by whom. Will there not always be others who fail to fit even the most extended definition? In this respect the status of agency as privileged marker of subject status seems misplaced, since it overdetermines the importance of agency in intersubjective relations: for who would claim to exercise continual agency, even within expanding parameters, I wonder? An over-emphasis on agency as the basis for recognition within feminist theory, then, seems to rely on the subject's capacity to extend their horizons to an infinite degree. While flawed, the Western feminist subject need only become *less myopic* about what falls within the range of practices understood as agency in order for recognition to be more democratic. Yet, as suggested, embedded in all the above developments of agency, is the spectre of the limit, both of agency itself (in the self and other-subject) and of the subject's capacity to reach new horizons. In each case, the presence of agency is understood to warrant renewed respect and attention, as though its lack would equally warrant a turn away.[15] In fact, it seems to me that the fetishization of agency within Western feminist theory can often be a way of avoiding the inevitability of judgment, of what happens when agency cannot be the basis of empathetic recognition.

TEMPORALITY

One central way in which the question of agency as the basis for empathetic recognition is mediated, that is, as inevitably raising the spectre of limit, is through a return to the temporalities of the subject I have been exploring throughout. As indicated in this and previous chapters, the Western feminist subject of return narratives becomes a subject of a particular history, one in which feminism has been lost and must be found again. Where it will be found is instructive, since it is through interventions "elsewhere" in contexts assumed (much more broadly than within feminism alone) to lag behind Western feminist equality agendas that a feminist subject will be able to redeem herself. So far in this chapter, I have highlighted how a focus on empathy, while an important way of foregrounding intersubjectivity as key to possible historical and political transformations, instantiates a dynamic between the empathetic subject and the other-subject (who can become a subject only under certain conditions). I have used the term "other-subject" as a way of representing the temporal and hierarchical difference between intersubjective positions in this relationship. My point here is that this is a vision of the one who will be empathized with from the perspective of the subject thus empathizing, not a description of an empirical relationship. Indeed, it is precisely the refusal on the part of real subjects that disrupts this intersubjective dynamic. But the imagined time lag is important, I think, because it describes both a temporal problem of localized empathy, which is always about a relationship in the making, and figures larger problems of temporality in Western feminist storytelling as suggested.

A focus on agency, in contrast, offers the hope of tracing different histories of a range of possible feminist subjects, but as discussed above, leaves a Western feminist subject position largely intact. The relentless search for agency to populate the feminist present shifts the limit of recognition rather than engaging the conditions under which it arises more directly. If agency needs to be present in the other-subject for empathetic recognition not to be a projection of the subject's own needs and expectations, then those who occupy the other side of the limit linger on the outskirts of the feminist scene, threatening to disrupt intersubjectivity if they cannot be made sense of. These others cannot, of course, simply be abandoned within a feminist ethics of intersubjective value: an attempt to fold them back into the precarious present must be made. And in fact, where agency is disputed from a Western feminist position, empathy can still be theorized as central to recognition of the other-subject, if what is recognized is *shared objectification* rather than autonomy. Thus I can put myself in the other's shoes even when their agency is in dispute precisely on the basis of a shared experience of objectification. This is, I think, the basis of arguments such as Leti Volpp's (2001) that compare practices of *un-freedom* across cultural, geographical, and religious sites.[16] Where these comparisons are contemporaneous, they tend, as discussed above, to be hierarchized on the basis of better or worse harms, rankings that are themselves based on Western narratives of progress, loss, or return.[17] More often, the shared objectification approach does not take place contemporaneously, but links two distinct times and places—the Western feminist subject's past and the other woman's present—in order to be able to imagine a common future. In the case of full veiling or FGC, for example, our own patriarchal past becomes the basis for recognition: we recognize in the other the objectification that we once experienced (Gunning 1992). Thus Western feminists can continue to empathize on the basis of their having also experienced *lack of agency* at a point in the past now over. In a slightly different temporal twist, the Western feminist subject recognizes that the disputed practices concerned were imposed through colonialism rather than through choice (e.g., Davis 2004a). Empathy beyond agency, then, involves a Western feminist subject who can reach back into her own past in order to recognize other-subjects in the present. In doing so, not only is her certainty about where agency lies affirmed, so too is her clarity about where Western feminism has got to. Even if ongoing conditions of objectification are identified in the Western feminist present, these temporal tricks allow these to be theorized as anachronisms, as pertinent to a past that Western feminism has now resolved.

In the various modes of empathy discussed so far, discomfort may be allayed by prior investment in the other's wellbeing, by the extension of agency to mean a broader range of practices, or by asserting a temporal difference that empathy can help transform. In each case, the subject remains intact, if altered. Empathy, then, may undo a subject/object relation, replacing it with a subject/subject relation, but those on either side of the slash are not equal; they are held apart by relations of recognition that are temporally as well as spatially managed. I recognize you; you meet *my* criteria for recognition; I arrived here first among eventual equals. To rephrase, in the historiographic terms that have concerned me throughout this book, empathy as the basis of feminist claims to knowledge and an ethics of intersubjective transformation underwrites rather than challenges the linear temporality that produces that knowing feminist subject in the present. Indeed, I want to state more directly that these empathetic moves precisely enable a Western feminist subject to occupy that position in the plural, sophisticated, yet political present. They describe the limit rather than the resolution of a desire for intersubjectivity.

But what of those moments or relations that cannot be so managed, nor put into narrative according to the established grammar of Western feminist stories? What of the stumbling blocks to empathy that cannot be rerouted via imagined histories of "the West'? What about those practices that cannot be recognized as part of agency—present or future—without the concomitant demise of the status of the one who recognizes? What of practices that cannot be recuperated into the subject/object (or subject/subject) relation by overpopulating a present or future with so many unequal subjects? Looking back can only go so far, it seems to me, towards equalizing intersubjective relations, insofar as this approach too will encounter its limit, will encounter practices or other-subjects that cannot be given a history without disrupting the narrative of the Western feminist subject. The subject may be forced, perhaps, to encounter a history in which she is not recognized or not recognized in ways that she may be content to rest with. She is not so much being expected to open herself up to include, recognize, or relate to the other-subject, nor is she being asked to be accountable for the temporal and spatial effects of her othering practices, important though these requirements may be. The Western feminist subject may, instead, be confronted with a far worse scenario: that she may not be the subject of history at all.

In this understanding of the temporal limit of Western feminist subjectivity, I take my cue from Gayatri Spivak (1999b). Writing of a conference that she was involved in organizing on "Europe and its Others" in 1982, Spivak remarks upon the committee's shocked response to her alternative suggestion of the title "Europe as an Other" (1999b: 199). She understands that "shock" as an interruption to the presumption that however roundly critiqued, the European subject remains at the centre of history. I am convinced that Spivak's resultant proposition—that Western feminist theorists need to interrupt their presumptive status as subjects to alter the grammar of the subject—is a sound one. Not in the sense of a simple inversion, in which the subject turns over the opposition, gaining a perverse pleasure from a chosen objectification that remains reliant on dualism, but through a consideration of how one might figure in an other's history. Indeed, this chapter could be thought of as an attempt to extend Spivak's insight in terms of how one might textually approach the importance of imagining oneself other, rather than seeking endlessly to ward off the limit enshrined in the subject/object relation that governs Western feminist storytelling. One possibility I want to explore in the rest of this chapter starts from that "shock" that Spivak highlights, from those "interruptions" to the political grammar of the Western feminist subject that force the limit into view.

Shock turns quickly to horror, and in what follows I explore the role of this particular affect in filling the gaps left open by the grammatical failure to secure the subject. When faced with that which cannot be empathized with, when faced with a history that cannot be absorbed into one's own, when faced with the dissolution of the self, affect rushes in to protect, to secure the subjective limit that allows for continued coherence. In this sense horror is not an affect like any other, but one that precisely marks the extent of what the subject can bear. Horror, that which exceeds narration or speech, is always rendered a property of the other rather than the self, of course, as we know from popular culture. In the horror movie genre, the inexpressible lurks in the imagination and in the homestead. It is that which must be guarded against, but which reveals the faultlines or excesses of the everyday. Crucially, the horror genre has been theorized as revealing cultural anxieties about race, sexuality, and gender (Clover 1993; Creed 1993; Halberstam 1995; Eadie 2001), the half-forgotten others that lurk in the shadows and confront the typically white, heterosexual, and suburban subjects with what it is that they have (sometimes literally) buried. Horror thus marks the return of the repressed and its vanquishing restores harmony, even if only temporarily.[18]

Feminist theorists have similarly theorized horror in terms of temporality, as a sign of a haunting of the subject or narrative that cannot be fully eradicated. Most famously, Julia Kristeva situates horror as a visceral response to abjection, to the remembered connection to others and to the socially unacceptable (1982). The abject must be left behind in the psychic development of the subject if she is to be a proper social being, but its presence lingers of course, producing cultural representations of horror of the kind indicated. For Kristeva, the abject is stored in memory, and thus the boundary between past and present is essential in order to retain present subjective integrity. For postcolonial theorists, in contrast to Kristeva's more limited prototype of the universal subject, the horror expressed at the abject that has been left behind in the Western subject's past is more directly politicized. From Franz Fanon (1991 [1952]) through to Ranjana Khanna (2003), abjection folds the psyche and colonial history together, marking individual and collective development as social as well as familial. For Fanon, the racial unconscious of white and black subjects in colonialism is a mirroring, such that black subjects and collective and political projects must come to terms with self-loathing as part of their constitution in modernity. For Khanna, Western (post)colonial subjects are haunted by a colonial past that cannot be mourned but prevents genuine openness in the present. Further, the political danger lies not in the melancholia of what cannot be incorporated, but in the transformation of that which cannot be mourned into an external object, into *pure past.*

Gayatri Spivak also theorizes a version of the abject that forms part of this postcolonial tradition. For Spivak, "the subaltern" signifies as that which lies outside of the subject/object relation and can be written back into dominant narratives in deconstructive mode (1999b). Spivak reflects most famously on the colonial horror at the figure of the Indian sati (the immolating widow), the one whose death is consistently cited as evidence of pure nature savagery. The sati is, for Spivak, an abject figure that hovers over the Western subject/object relation. She represents a primitive past that must be guarded against for Western subjectivity to retain its sense of itself as civilized. Recognition of the other-subject in the present, here, is thus dependent on his or her being *not-sati,* a subject who has left behind such barbarism, such excessive attachments. Temporality is central to Spivak's understanding of Western subject/object relations, then. Where for Kristeva, the temporality of *individual* development is the primary object of analysis, for Spivak, the temporalities of the subject and colonialism are always intertwined and cannot be thought separately. Indeed she conceives of "the West" itself as having relational meaning to "the Rest" only through its own "willed autobiography . . . [that] still masquerades as disinterested history" (1999b: 208) and considers Kristeva's work to be thus implicated.[19]

The transformation of that which cannot be managed into the subject's past is already familiar from the discussion of agency. Thinking about the temporality of horror via postcolonial theory foregrounds the central role of affect in repeating linear histories of "the West," however. It foregrounds the psychic and political investments of the subject in refusing to accept spaces as shared and narrates subjectivities as linked through violence as much as through empathy. In this respect a focus on a located horror is a similar move to the citation tactics developed in the last chapter. It reveals what is expelled from narrative in order for the political grammar of the subject to remain intact, and it understands that horror as situated and political, rather than abstract and universal in the Kristevan vein.

Postcolonial theorists do not stop at the horror, however, precisely because of its colonial weight and representational force.[20] Thus the abject is both feared and desired because subject status is conditional on creating and recreating a fantasy life for it, one that can never quite carry its excessive burden. For Spivak, failed writing or speech in the Western subject is a site of possibility because of what is thereby revealed, both about what comprises the unspeakable, and also the limits of subject/object relations. The opportunity for transformation lies not in attempts to become or befriend the other (contra Spelman and Lugones), which will always be fraught with misrepresentation, but in attention to "the site where the line between friend and foe is undone" (1999b: 194).[21] And following recitation, here I want both to illuminate what it is that situated horror reveals and to imagine an alternative historiography starting from that point.

AFFECTIVE RESOLUTIONS

Let us now examine some instances in Western feminist theory where horror is used to negotiate the unspeakable that hovers over the subject/object relation and that threatens to undo the certainty of who the Western feminist subject is and where she has come from. In identifying instances of Western feminist horror (rather than horror in general), I have been particularly struck by the expression of "gut reactions" that delimit arguments about recognition, and in this respect the resurgence of bodily knowledge as the basis of judgment, precisely where empathy fails. Indeed, this centring of the body within affective disruptions to narrative coherence constitutes evidence of two kinds. The perceived violation or restriction of the bodily boundaries of another—through obscuring it in relation to religious covering practices, or through direct intervention in the examples of FGC and transsexual surgeries that I discuss here[22]—is frequently the catalyst for empathy. But if it fails, for any of the various reasons already discussed, then a bodily shudder, the experience of horror, closes off empathy and naturalizes the limit of connection across time or space.

The experience of horror that causes a temporary break in Western feminist subject/object relations may precipitate a straightforward judgment of the other-subject or practices concerned as unacceptable. In other words, the experience of horror may well mark the stopping point of the deferral of the limit discussed above. This is very clearly the case in some responses to FGC, in which the horror itself is repeated textually as evidence in several ways. Paradigmatically, Mary Daly's early account of "African Genital Mutilation" designates cutting practices as "Unspeakable Atrocities" in her chapter title (1978), and she begins by stating, "There are some manifestations of the sado-ritual syndrome that are unspeakable —incapable of being expressed in words because they are inexpressibly horrible" (1978: 155). Daly underscores her horror by providing a startling level of detail of different cutting practices in contrast to her declaration of their inexpressibility: she dwells at some length on their relative severity and the forms of individual and collective violence necessary for their enactment. Similarly, Fran Hosken provides example after example of cutting practices worldwide, collected in her extensive, later updated, report (1994 [1982]).[23] The report is filled with detailed eyewitness accounts of FGC practices that teach horror to the reader, if they did not already experience it.

This repetition of the unspeakable has several effects. It transmits the horror to the reader, producing agreement about the limit of who can be considered to possess agency, who and what can be brought intact into the present of feminist subjectivity. But it also constitutes evidence of the harm itself, representing the mutilated as wholly acted upon. On the one hand a portrayal then, and one Chandra Mohanty directly critiques as contributing to hierarchical subject/object relations (2003 [1988]), yet at the same time an affective transfer that catches the reader and precipitates a mirrored encounter with the limit. In similar vein to Mohanty, Martha Nussbaum points out that this representational repetition characteristic of discussions of FGC risks fetishizing the practice, and she endorses the view that on occasion "the fascination with FGM contains at least an element of the sensational or even the prurient" (1998: 126). And this is indeed the contradiction: on the one hand, FGC practices are too horrible to describe; on the other, the reader or audience must be schooled in their horror if they are to take the same stance.[24] Indeed, despite her warning, Nussbaum herself repeats descriptions of scenes of forced cutting of young girls in her short chapter on the subject, a narrative choice in line with her argument against unhelpful dissembling and the importance of a clear stance against cutting practices.

As in Western feminist representations of FGC, the horror of transsexual mutilation is often fetishized through such repetition of detail, most notably in Sheila Jeffreys's work (2002a). Images and descriptions float before the reader's eye, varying only slightly and producing a feeling of nausea that only this level of relentless reiteration can accomplish. To turn away in that moment would, rather ironically, be an admission of lack of care. In a similar vein, Germaine Greer presents what she believes to be a witty account of her own horror when expected to shake a transsexual woman's hand (1974). Importantly, Greer assumes shared feminist revulsion at what she describes as the large, hairy male-to-female transsexual hand that she recoils from touching. For Greer, this horror is both objective—the hand is self-evidently horrible—and subjective—a feminist will know that this is a masquerade and fail to be convinced. The horror itself is enough to justify lack of empathy, since it marks an other already beyond the pale. The irony of course is that the distinction relies on an investment in a natural female body that might otherwise be considered suspect from a feminist perspective, as Myra Hird similarly notes of Tamsin Wilton's over-reliance on a menstruating female subject to mark the trans/woman distinction (Wilton 2000; Hird 2002). The feminist present and future must be spearheaded by a female-bodied subject. The use of horror to mark an absolute distinction between feminists and transsexuals also positions transsexuals as aggressors, as actively seeking to undermine feminism.[25] And in both a Kristevan and Spivakean sense, this is not simply paranoia: Greer's shudder marks the extent of what can be incorporated within a feminist narrative of which she is to remain a coherent subject.

The judgment arising from horror in both examples is of barbarism, the experience of which cannot be transformed into agency; and that barbarism clearly marks the limit of what a Western feminist subject can be expected to "allow for" as part of the feminist present. It highlights a clear limit to empathy and resolves any ambivalence about that relationship. Jo Doezema makes a similar point about Western feminist responses to the position of the "Third World Prostitute," describing the force of horror as creating "wounded attachments" that belie the separation that the affective recoil enacts (Doezema 2001).[26] This mode is extremely common:

one morning in the final stages of editing this book, I awoke to Geraldine Brooks' comment in a broadsheet article on Muslim women's human rights that "I find the kind of moral relativism that justifies practices such as female genital mutilation disgusting and fatuous" (2009). My concern here is not whether or not FGC should be stopped or by whom, but with the affective basis of the judgment. Brooks' somewhat throwaway disgust (the article does not otherwise discuss FGC) marks the limit of Western feminist subjectivity in two ways, in fact. It marks a limit in order to produce clear judgment, and it also frames her more open argument about religious veiling as one that can be taken seriously as nonrelativist. Her affective certainty here allows her reader to consider her less absolute position elsewhere.

Horror not only marks Western feminist narratives in which a final judgment of the limit of the subject / object relation is the result, however. While less likely to utilize the *repetitive* mode discussed above, a more ambivalent position will also mobilize shock or horror in negotiating the limit of how far agency may be extended. Thus, Isabelle Gunning begins her article that argues for the importance of cross-cultural empathy in consideration of FGC with the following preamble:

In the spring of 1990, I re-encountered a practice that I had for many years found distressing, that of female genital surgeries. . . . As I started my research, I continued to feel anger and revulsion at the practice and a strong desire to see it eradicated as quickly as possible. (1992: 189)

In her article, the "distress . . . anger and revulsion" she feels becomes a primary resource for adjudicating between practices, either now or in the past. Her revulsion, then, precipitates a hierarchical and temporal ordering of the kind discussed earlier, so that she can be clear about which practices are acceptable or unacceptable for feminism. There is a similar process at work in Kathy Davis's response to Wairimu Njambi's article in *Feminist Theory*, a piece that focuses on the potential pleasures of FGC in social context (2004). The three theorists asked to respond are broadly sympathetic to her line of argument and mark their appreciation of her insistence on the importance of respect for cultural difference and interpretation in FGC debates (Castañeda 2004; Davis 2004a; Henry-Waring 2004). All three remark too on Njambi's useful emphasis on African women's agency in seeking circumcision, on the ways that such an analysis is helpful for making sense of a range of practices usually thought of as harmful, and for linking histories and forms of cutting cross-culturally. In a supportive tone, then, Kathy Davis confirms that "feminists in the west need to listen to the voices of women who engage in genital cutting, need to involve themselves in self-critical analysis of their own histories of colonialism and racism, and should treat female circumcision as a cultural bodily practice" (2004: 305). Yet all three theorists also stress the importance of "taking a stand" against relativist arguments that suggest *any kind* of FGC practice may be acceptable.

As Gunning did, Davis begins her response with her confession:

Female circumcision—or genital cutting—among African women evokes a contradictory mix of feelings in me, as it does with many feminists, ranging from a vicarious "ouch" to anger at patriarchal structures, which control women's bodies and sexuality, to curiosity about why women defend and even embrace a practice which is painful and dangerous to their health. (2004: 305)

That "vicarious 'ouch'" guides Davis's assessment of certain practices and not others as acceptable within a feminist framework and underwrites her theoretical argument that the alternative to this judgment, namely cultural relativism, encourages an "indifference to the suffering experienced" by women undergoing the practice (2004: 305). Davis's "ouch" is represented as what allows her to empathize with other women's suffering. It links her body to those of others; she experiences their pain at the level of her own body. But this "ouch" also marks off certain practices and bodies as unacceptable prior to the encounter with the other-subject under consideration. It is a response to "female circumcision" in general. It is an anticipated "ouch" that she does not actually experience and that creates for her the requisite distance to inspire curiosity about a practice her affect makes her doubt the ability to defend. In other words, Davis's affect provides conditions—theoretically, an antirelativist stance—that determine the limits of the empathy they also generate.[27]

As Claudia Castañeda suggests in her own response to Njambi's article, the division of practices into the more or less violent, the more or less agented or acceptable, is precisely a way of mediating the horror of "the unspeakable" in work on FGC. Castañeda argues that a focus on practices deemed "less harmful" (2004: 314) allows for comparisons to be drawn between Western and non-Western "speakable" practices, but does not circumvent the question of how to consider "the unspeakable" in ethical or intersubjective terms. Following Castañeda, I contend that it is the ranking of FGC practices via horror that pushes abjection back beyond the subject/object relation where it belongs. Rather than producing clear-cut judgments, as in the examples above, the affectively determined ranking allows for empathy through bodily experience in relation to some practices, but marks a limit beyond which the subject cannot go. It also marks all practices as fully known and readable from the subject position.

As in the FGC debates, horror at transsexual surgery is also expressed by those more generally sympathetic to its subjects and their claims to authenticity. In her argument with Tamsin Wilton mentioned above, for example, Myra Hird defends transsexual subjects against a final judgment of their unnaturalness, but follows in the queer tradition of seeing transgender realignments as more progressive than surgery (2002). Surgery is a self-evident ill that belongs to the past of a progressive feminism that allows a proliferation of genders (Hausman 1995). The agency of the transsexual taking up surgery is certainly avowed, but the contradiction between its horror and its necessity can be resolved in the long run. In the process, it is the other-subject who must transform themselves once again, rather than the empathetic feminist subject.

But horror is not only something experienced by other people, of course. I feel it too. It marks the limits of my own empathetic intersubjectivity just as surely as it does Daly's, Gunning's, Jeffreys's, and Hausman's. I have already mentioned being *startled* and feeling *nauseous* at the repetitions of horror in feminist accounts of both FGC and transsexual surgeries. These are not neutral responses, but draw me into an intersubjective encounter of my own. They confront me with the same potential limit to subjectivity and force me to consider how far my own empathy might extend, and when I will retreat to "save myself." I am as invested as the theorists of FGC I find easiest to critique. I too crave the repetition of the horror, coming back to the texts and experiencing a bodily satisfaction at the certainty of what I will find there. I feel sick. I feel sick at the descriptions, sick at my affect, want to gag. I put the texts down, come back to them later. The same thing happens, and the feeling starts to have a guilty pleasure of its own. Intellectually, I prefer the vacillations of Davis and Henry-Waring, and thus the hold the repetition has on me is amplified by my shame.[28] Shame here relies on those "horrors" I am drawn to not being a part of my subjective present, of course; it marks the temporality of my own subjectivity as surely as it does that of those I have been engaging. We are attached, the fantasy of the other and I.

Engaging the author's horror as I have been produces a relationship to the author in the reader, too, provokes a visceral reaction that reminds me of Susan Stryker's rage at attempts to deny the history and subjects of transgenderism (1994). To continue to think through some of my own affective responses rather than those of other Western feminists, let me try and track my own affect in relation to some of the narratives I have been examining in this section. When reading Sheila Jeffreys I am enraged at the ease of her judgment, protective of the subjects she renders as objects. I am furious, and rightly so I insist, when Tamsin Wilton prefers to reify a menstruating female body rather than conceive of a range of possible bodily "origins" to gender identity. But reading my excessive (and dismissive) affects as altruism or protectiveness as I have oddly phrased it here may be misplaced. I am also astonished that I have to read such nonsense, astonished that such work is published in this day and age. Has this argument not already been had, and been won? The encounter with the author's horror, then, also forces me to come face to face with my own certainty as inheritor of a Western feminist progress narrative, a certainty now tempered with paranoia: perhaps these theorists are making a comeback? Outrage (a kind of combination of rage and astonishment), then, indicates that I am more attached to a progress narrative—within which transsexuals are recognized agents, certainly, but which is much less troubled by transgendered subjects if it is honest—than I might like to admit. The pleasure in occupying that narrative high ground is tempered by the realization that progress narratives emphasizing fragmentation are not necessarily any more appealing to transsexual subjects than loss or return narratives in this respect. My own horror, in other words, also affirms a limit to subject/object relations in Western feminist theory in the face of a possible disruption to my status as its author. Horror intervenes in both contexts to cast out the abject, to reconfigure my feminist subjectivity as coherent, and to mark others as fully readable within its singular temporality.

CONCLUSION

Returning to Spivak's invitation to consider "Europe as Other," we might want to start from these moments of affective rupture in an attempt to trace narrative otherwise. It seems to me that there are two different ways of doing this when we start from what horror forecloses. The first concerns the way in which the other-subjects represented in these affectively overloaded accounts will always be in excess of their descriptions. In this respect, a serious, ethical engagement with transsexual subjectivity might minimally start from an acknowledgment that surgery may be experienced as both past and future freedom for the subjects concerned. What is rarely considered in Western feminist accounts of transsexuality, for example, is the pleasure of transsexual surgery, the inseparable significance of it to becoming a transsexual subject. As Jay Prosser indicates in his reading of transsexual autobiographies, transsexual subjects frequently embrace their surgery, relish the scars, and remember the process as formative of, rather than a by-product of, transsexual subjectivity (1998). In contrast, disgust and horror are reserved for the experience of the wrongly sexed body and its expected relationship to gender. And to return to Njambi, what cannot be contemplated in the range of Western feminist accounts discussed above is that the practice of FGC may be experienced neither as an oppression to be left behind nor as an unspeakable horror or even unpleasant necessity. What is inconceivable is that any FGC practice may be actively embraced, pleasurably anticipated, and experienced as a marker of becoming adult or becoming a member of a desired community. Other subjects have other histories they author, it seems.

But thinking from affect into the other-subject may not only be a question of allowing for subjectivity without the necessity of recognition in extant feminist terms. It may also require an acknowledgment that one is already in the history of the other-subject and not in ways that fit with the desire for heroism. Njambi's and Prosser's pleasures may also remake us *as others* in narratives of subjects with different spatio-temporalities. This points us to the potential importance of a politics of difficulty, of entanglement, in which one is the impediment and not the solution. Is there a way of seeing through another's eyes historiographically rather than empathetically, I wonder? If we think for a moment about the limit figure for Western feminist theory of the fully covered Muslim woman, the one that cannot be incorporated into the comparative Western frame, might we ask how starting from horror alters subject/object relations in a slightly different way. If we imagine the liveliness of this "figure" looking at us, what does she see? Perhaps she sees, as Joan Scott tells us, that a Western feminist narrative of achieved secular gender equality is predicated on our availability to a (structurally) heterosexual male gaze (2007). She no doubt sees that sexual liberation and gender liberation are curiously intertwined in Western feminist subjectivity; and no doubt she sees a denial of that as central to the critique of her covering. Or, in the context of FGC, Western feminist horror that marks the limit to the subject/object relation is attached to the infibulated woman, as we know. But for her, perhaps, a Western feminist narrative requires a life and body unmarked by pain, requires subjection to belong to the past. The horror precludes facing the ways in which we have not left gender inequality behind at all, perhaps. My visceral shudders instantiate an affective fantasy I can live with. Yet in her eyes, I am more similar to the antirelativists or feminist imperialists, perhaps even colonists, than I would like to acknowledge, projecting a fantasy in order to keep my gender and raced subjectivity intact. And what of the transsexual subject? What does s/he see? Perhaps similarity rather than difference between hostile and favorable feminist accounts, both of which rely on a negation of enjoyment of the surgeon's knife. S/he recognizes perhaps instead the surgeon, or the hormone-giver, who recognizes the subject s/he strives to embody as well as be.

But I am getting carried away. These figures do not see me, tell me, warn me, or chide me. They do not reveal layers of history that my subject status requires I deflect. I have, despite Spivak's warnings, raced off to find my "real Caliban . . . forgetting that he is a name in a play" (1999a: 118). Such reversals do little to alter the presumptions of Western feminist subjectivity, overloading the alternative with an excess of intentionality, constructing her or him as peculiarly aggrieved. Such visions require no work, only admission, on my part. I am in danger of inventing another history that tells me the truth about myself. Starting from rather than ending with affect in this chapter certainly indicates a different history to a feminist subject/object relationship and may interrupt the political grammar of the Western feminist subject, even if only for a moment. Recognition of Western feminist horror as another subject's potential pleasure may disrupt spatial and temporal accounts that have a singular subject in the present. But this cannot be the basis for the writing of an alternative, better, history. This would be masochism indeed. But further, it would be to allow other subjects to carry the burden of feminist judgment and of possible feminist futures in ways that refuse accountability for the amenabilities of feminist stories that have been my concern throughout this book.

Instead, what I want my exploration of affect to do here is point to the limit of self-knowledge, and invariably of knowledge of the other, as the starting point of political engagement. I want to point to the entanglement of the space of the present encounter (imagined or real) as the space of work, rather than the space that must be cleaned up in order for judgments to occur. Refusing to resolve the limit, as with recitation, may open up a vision of what is lost when we invest in progress, loss, or return narratives and to remake history from that perspective. Judgments that are based in the protection of a singular vision of a Western feminist past, present, and future are bound to reproduce rather than challenge the amenability of Western feminist political grammar. They make it impossible to challenge assumptions about inequality in anything other than the most banal ways. Staying with the limit, I want to suggest, offers a space for feminist engagement that assumes amenability of feminist stories and subjects rather than seeking first to separate these out from the complex conditions of contemporary gendered meaning. Perhaps we can break with Western feminist narratives of progress, loss, and return, not because we love others as ourselves, but because we would like a present and a future with some unpredictability in them.

NOTES

1 I am grateful to one of the readers of the initial manuscript for the term "political grammar" and to both readers for their thoughtful and generous engagements.

2 I use the terms "story," "narrative," and "grammar" throughout the book. By "stories" I mean the overall tales feminists tell about what has happened in the last thirty to forty years of Western feminist theory and indicate too their status as "myth" or "common opinion." By "narratives" I mean the textual refrains (content and pattern) used to tell these stories and their movement across time and space. By "grammar" I mean the techniques (oppositions, intertextual reference, and so on) that serve as narrative building blocks. I also use the term "political grammar" by which I mean to indicate the stitching together of all these levels as well as the broader political life of these stories. I have tried to be consistent in how these terms are used, but there are moments when of course technique and repetition are not distinct, or where I use other terms such as "history" to get me out of trouble.

3 You will notice that I have not provided references to particular authors in my overview here, relying on an initial sense of these stories as familiar. And it is indeed that familiarity that I am interested in, that motivates the range

of "citation tactics" that I explore throughout, and that I explain later in this introductory chapter.

4 In Western feminist progress, loss, and return narratives postmodernism and poststructuralism are often represented as synonymous, or one or other is understood to stand in for both. I have tried not to reproduce the same slip, in part because I lean towards a poststructural approach myself. In representing my own understanding I tend to mark a (sometimes arbitrary, I admit) distinction by using "poststructuralism" to denote an attitude to text/subject/world over "postmodernism" as a critique of modernism or understanding of the social world as transformed by, for example, reflexive individualism.

5 One effect of postfeminist discourse is that even the most poorly served young women will refer to themselves as liberated and free to choose what they want in life, irrespective of the often woefully limited economic, social, cultural, or interpersonal opportunities available to them (Walkerdine, Lucey et al. 2001; Walkerdine 2003).

6 As a number of theorists have suggested, the desire to symbolically uncouple women's or gender studies from lesbianism (as accusation) assumes a heterosexual subject as the norm and positions lesbian or bisexual women very differently within the field (Munt 1997; Hesford 2005; hoogland 2007).

7 Also focusing on the Dutch example, Rosi Braidotti notes further that this official discourse assumes that "our women . . . are already liberated and thus do not need any more social initiatives or emancipatory policies. 'Their women,' however, . . . are still backwards and need to be targeted for special emancipatory social actions or enforced 'liberation' " (2005: 180).

8 Anne Phillips insists that we thus need "multiculturalism without culture" if the over-association of culture with gender inequality is to be moved on from. She argues, rightly I believe, that this is essential for feminist challenges to global gender inequality (2007).

9 While there have been many critiques of gender studies as itself a move from the political intent of women's or feminist studies (Evans 1991; Richardson and Robinson 1994; Threadgold 2000; Stromquist 2001), others have celebrated gender studies' de-emphasis on woman as the de facto ground of academic feminism (Gillis and Munford 2003; Zalewski 2003), in line with loss and progress narratives, respectively. My point here is not to take a position on these debates, but to highlight one aspect of the institutional life of feminist storytelling.

10 It would seem odd to attempt to cite "feminist history" in a footnote, so let me gesture to one (London-based) project that seeks to enrich our knowledge of the past by focusing on complexities that are often overlooked: "History of Feminism Network: Celebrating, Exploring and Debating the History of Feminism"— http://historyfeminism.wordpress.com/.

11 See also Benita Roth's account of the emergence of a black feminist "vanguard" in the 1960s and 1970s, and Nancy MacLean's work, which links affirmative action

to black and working class women's struggles in the same period (MacLean 1999; Roth 1999).

12 The above theorists all pay careful attention to the role of "the teller of tales" in the process of history making. Not only is the storyteller motivated to tell this history, not that history, but the storytelling subject is also produced, and produces herself, in the process of making that history. As Burton cautions: "If we fail to recognize this dynamic [between historian and archive] we neglect an obligation to investigate our sense of identification with the archive itself" (2001: 67).

13 See Iris van der Tuin's article " 'Jumping Generations,' " which links generation and geography very particularly, and my own response to this tendency in the same special issue of *Australian Feminist Studies* on "Feminist Timelines" (Hemmings 2009; van der Tuin 2009).

14 This may be one historiographical reason why the French Marxist tradition, including Christine Delphy, has been overlooked in preference for the sexual difference tradition more commonly associated with "écriture féminine" (See Braidotti 2000; Delphy 2000; Jackson 2001).

15 Caren Kaplan warns us that this happens when the careful contextualization of feminist positioning is replaced with localized universalisms or aestheticization (Kaplan 1994).

16 This project thus owes a more than considerable debt to the work of Michel Foucault, in terms of my interest in mapping dominant knowledges (1970; 1975; 2000), their production, maintenance, and effects (1972; 1981), the links across discursive forms and functions (1980b), and strategies for imagining otherwise (1980a; 1988). The reason I describe the dominant threads of Western feminist storytelling as narratives rather than discourses for the most part is in order to emphasis their patterning rather than content or context. The close attention to ordering of meaning follows Foucault, as does the focus on oppositions, exclusions, and silences, but my interest remains on their narrative function, the rehearsal, repetition, and rhythm that are so central to the making of feminist community agreement. Where I do use the term "discourse" in the book, my use of it remains fundamentally Foucauldian.

17 Individual chapters in anthologies, or articles in journals I do not directly analyze here, may also reproduce or critique the stories I take as my object of inquiry, and they have had a clear influence on my thinking (Segal 2000; Felski 2001; Wiegman 2002; Moore 2006). And no doubt many readers will be familiar with other texts that endorse cultural and social understandings of feminism as anachronism (Sommers 1994; Hakim 1995; Coward 1999; Sommers 2000).

18 One clear danger of this approach is that it reduces an individual author's right of reply and makes it hard for readers to check the accuracy of my citation, too. I did try other approaches to citation of the journal glosses at one point, but author citation invariably drew me back into engaging with individual arguments, rather than the passing narratives an author might not even wish to claim. So, while

acknowledging that this is a risky strategy in several ways, this aspect of citation practice remains central to this project.

19 My "turn to affect" in this project might strike readers familiar with my earlier critique of this term as rather ironic (Hemmings 2005a). In "Invoking Affect" I intervene in debates that herald the affective turn as a cutting-edge means to move beyond epistemological and political dead-ends. Suggesting that such calls produce a history of poststructuralism stripped of its feminist and postcolonial antecedents, I argue that invoking affect as new fails to provide a history to affect and makes us (as critics) inattentive to affect's intertwining with and production through the social. The tone of this article is so critical that it might easily be read as a dismissal of the importance of affect altogether, although this was never my intention. My focus here then both starts from that interest in the social as lived in affective registers and results in the development of a warmer tone on my part.

20 Here I am making use of Silvan Tomkins' distinction between affects (as states) and emotions (as particular expressions of those states) (1963).

21 Elspeth Probyn understands the tension between the epistemological frames of gender and our ontological experiences of the same as the basis for feminist reflexivity (1993). A focus on affect as that which binds the epistemological and the ontological might also be thought of as part of a reflexive project.

NOTES TO CHAPTER ONE: **PROGRESS**

1 Almost all the extracts I cite in part 1 are included as good or typical examples of a given narrative tendency; other reasons are stated in introducing the extract. I have kept ellipses to a minimum, but have included these where long sections make the point otherwise difficult to follow. Readers will remember, I hope, that my citation practice foregrounds journals and date over author. This may feel odd, or even unethical, but I hope that the importance of this practice in establishing narrative forms within feminist theory will be borne out by my analysis.

2 For Wiegman, one of these effects is the reduction of a contested history to a generationally typecast one in which disagreements are cast as part of the march of time rather than spatially enacted. Generationalism is a consistent aspect of progress, loss, and return narratives, one I flag throughout the book and discuss more fully in my conclusion to part 1.

3 In this respect the object of analysis, e.g., woman, will be understood differently even where it remains in place. The shift is thus as much about what we mean by terms within feminist theory as it is about which terms are cherished or abandoned.

4 The above extract uses the term "post-modernism" to describe a particular set of approaches to research, politics, and culture that I would probably describe as "poststructuralist" myself. As flagged in note 4 of my introduction, in the extracts examined across all three dominant forms of Western feminist storytelling, "post-modern," "poststructuralist," or "deconstructionist," as well as related terms, tend

to be used interchangeably. In loss narratives, these slippages work to homogenize the set of accounts thus denoted; in return narratives all terms are likely to be brought together under the designation "cultural turn" or sometimes "linguistic turn" (again without attention to differences between these).

5   Indeed, so strong is the certainty that certain kinds of Western feminist thought belong in the past, it can be something of a shock to realize that radical feminists, for example, continue to write in the present that has—surely?—successfully debunked their claims to relevance.

6   See Anne Phillips's chapter, "What's wrong with essentialism?" in which she suggests that we need to distinguish between different kinds of essentialist ills at the very least (2010).

7   I return to the importance of the concept of agency in the representation of Western feminist theory as dynamic and open in the last chapter.

8   Jane Gallop argues that there are two distinct stories told about feminist theory in the 1980s: one prioritizing poststructuralism as precipitating a move to difference; the other emphasizing black feminist critiques of the category "woman" in feminism. She suggests that authors frequently struggle to bring these stories together (Gallop, in Lurie, Cvetkovich et al. 2001). For Gallop, the first story is often haunted by the second, where it does not make connections explicit (2001: 688). In my reading, attempts to bring them together are often also marked by an attempt to make sense of the same through temporal displacement.

9   Only occasionally (as in the *Feminist Studies* extract) is the 1980s represented in progress narratives as the decade inaugurating class critiques, despite the accusation of 1970s feminism as middle-class as well as white and heterosexual. No doubt this is due to the association of 1970s feminism with both radical and socialist feminisms, which would make this hard to narrate plausibly. This association does, however, facilitate the location of social concerns and material inquiry in the 1970s for return narratives, as we will see in chapter 3.

10 These comparisons are central to how Western feminist loss and return narratives function as well, and I will track these throughout the book.

11 I am encouraged in my desire to delve into what work "Butler" does for Western feminism storytelling by her own interest in such representations. She asks her reader to consider: "What are the institutional histories . . . that 'position' me here now? If there is something called 'Butler's position,' is this one that I devise, publish, and defend, that belongs to me as a kind of academic property? Or is there a grammar of the subject that merely encourages us to position me as the proprietor of those theories?" (1992: 8–9).

12 For broader social theory, it seems a Western feminist progress narrative has done much of its work for it, providing the perfect rationale—its irredeemable, racist essentialism—for not having to reference or engage feminist theory pre-Butler anymore. Not only that: as a "lesbian" who theorizes the limits of that location and the conditions under which this category operates as foundational for feminism and lesbian and gay politics (1992), Butler can provide a useful alibi, as suggested. Identification with Butler, whatever the sexuality of the author,

transfers responsibility for the consigning of the lesbian feminist subject to the past onto a subject least likely to be accused of homophobia.

NOTES TO CHAPTER TWO: LOSS

1 I am reminded here of the rage often expressed (by students and faculty alike) at, for example, the textual difficulties of Gayatri Spivak's work and at the consistent rendering of this as an aggressivity embedded in the text itself. A similar dynamic may be at play in the anger students express every year at "being forced" to read psychoanalysis and at the secondary texts that only add to their feelings of exclusion. Of course in the latter case particularly, a theory of projection may be helpful, but the case I am making here concerns the necessity of this affective displacement for loss narratives to function historiographically, for "Theory" to come to stand as the opposite of politics.

2 Mary Evans identifies and explores the limits of this opposition in her 1982 article "In Praise of Theory" (1982). In this piece Evans warns of the dangers of setting up a straw trope of the "political" in opposition to the "theory" that it cannot function without. Yet this tension remains one that often unreflexively structures feminist debate.

3 The lament of the loss of the political is familiar from social theory too, though frequently it is feminism (or identity/sectarian fragmentation more generally) that is blamed for its demise. The teleology is similar, though, as is its affect—melancholy—as Wendy Brown has suggested (1999). Paraphrasing and parodying Richard Rorty, Nancy Armstrong writes that what went wrong within the Left was that "a new generation of intellectuals stopped handing out leaflets at factory gates and devoted themselves to cultural politics" (2001: 21).

4 There are by now several texts that attempt to delineate academic feminism as multiply located, characterized by conflict rather than agreement, and as having a traceable history not simply reducible to external politics (e.g., Griffin and Braidotti 2002; Wiegman 2003; Braithwaite, Heald et al. 2004; Davis, Evans et al. 2006). These discussions do nevertheless tend to slip into overarching progress and loss narratives that reproduce rather than analyse these assumptions, or displace disagreements onto the generational presumptions that I discuss throughout part 1 (see also Looser and Kaplan 1997; Braidotti and Colebrook 2009).

5 The Research Assessment Exercise (RAE) was the U.K.'s national evaluation of academic research output, used as the basis for determining the allocation of the overall reduced research money. The exercise was enormously divisive in that it mitigated against projects that take considerable time to set up (Lewis 2000), created a counter-productive culture of competition (Knights and Richards 2003), prioritized conservative, mainstream work over innovation (Lee and Harley 1998), and made interdisciplinary work subject to disciplinary evaluation. The RAE was always considered problematic for Women's and Gender Studies, but the withdrawal of the sub-panel for the 2008 exercise absolutely confirmed this view. The RAE has been replaced by the Research Excellence Framework (REF), which

will evaluate academic work in a similar way (that is, through disciplines and on the basis of submitted outputs). Several factors suggest this is likely to be as, if not more, pernicious an audit: the inclusion of "impact" as a considerable percentage of institutionalized evaluation (where "impact" means "use" outside the academy); the exceptionally quick turnaround (REF submissions are due in December 2013 at time of writing); and the increasing brutal reduction in higher education funding in the U.K. more generally under a coalition government, suggesting we are likely to be competing for crumbs.

6   For direct commentary on the impact of neoliberal education agendas on academic feminism in the U.K. see Beverley Skeggs (1995) and Mary Evans (2006), and for its impact on Australian academic feminism before, during, and after John Howard, see the special themed section of *Feminist Review* "Mainstream or Muzzled?" (Genovese 2010).

7   Embedded in this critique of feminists who have come to feminism through text is an assumption Nina Lykke challenges, namely that feminists were never textually politicized in the 1970s (2004a).

8   Robyn Wiegman suggests in fact that feminist accounts of disciplinary differences are *always* generationally inflected (1999a: 363).

9   Loss narratives prioritize social scientific approaches, particularly sociology, as I have shown. The setting of this against an interdisciplinary humanities that prioritizes theory, however, means that its logic can also be taken up by other disciplines as part of a lament for lost rigour, and also as part of progress narrative where steady fragmentation challenges the need for an interdisciplinary feminist project at all (e.g., Brown 1997). I included two examples of loss narrative glosses that set literary rigour against interdisciplinary, cultural "turns" in feminist theory, but these are much less common than the setting of social science against "poststructuralist" approaches. Importantly, in all these calls for a return to disciplinary certainties, women's and gender studies are not understood as valid *disciplinary* homes in their own right.

10 The volume *Feminism Meets Queer Theory*, taken from a special issue of *Differences*, provides a useful overview of the different positions in this area (Weed and Schor 1997). Feminist work lamenting the substitution of feminist politics with queer approaches includes Jackson 1999 and Jeffreys 2002b. For a more sustained account of the irreconcilable tension between queer theory and sociology see Steven Seidman's *Queer Theory/Sociology* (1996).

11 I am reminded once more of Sabine Hark's reading of feminist resistance to queer theory among German feminist academics, in which queer theory is consistently cast as predator (Hark 2002).

NOTES TO CHAPTER THREE: **RETURN**

1   To avoid too much repetition, while I continue with the familiar focus on journal extracts and their production of a common sense of the recent Western feminist past, I combine this approach with wider-ranging reflections on material

turns and on some of the implications of sexuality's over-association with the cultural turn.

2 These two extracts foreground different conceptions of materiality—as concerned with economic and structural constraint, on the one hand, and ontological form, on the other. These distinctions are not relevant for the general point I am making here, but I discuss these different strands below.

3 My thanks go to one of the readers of this manuscript for helping me clarify this point.

4 As in other Western feminist narratives, return narratives tend to refer to postmodernism, poststructuralism, deconstruction, language, or cultural theory/ turn interchangeably. As in previous chapters, I follow the term used in the textual glosses I am concerned with.

5 As discussed below, materialism may also be the property of philosophy or the arts, where "the material" is more fully theorized in relation to the body and affect. The move remains a disciplinary one, however.

6 The above excerpt is repeated from the last chapter, in which I more fully discuss the disciplinary regulation of loss narratives in particular. I include this extract here as highlighting the overlaps between loss and return narratives in particular, but will not include additional crossover examples to avoid repetition.

7 In return narratives, "representation" refers to textual or visual coding in its proximity to poststructuralism and can also occur as a synonym for "post" theories more broadly. It is usually qualified as "political representation" where it refers to acting on behalf of individuals or groups. See Gayatri Spivak's useful critique of the separation of the two uses of the term in "Can the Subaltern Speak?" (1988).

8 In her discussion of Martha Nussbaum's response to Judith Butler's work, Robyn Wiegman notes that, for the former, poststructuralism may be said to have "domesticated the feminist enterprise, leading to narcissistic performances that parody real feminist struggle" (1999/2000: 110).

9 A special issue of *Body and Society* from 2004 includes a range of positions in this tradition (Berg and Akrich 2004), including Bruno Latour's elaboration of the concept of "levels" to understand the body's insistent materiality (2004).

10 For Braidotti this temporality is shot through with sexual difference and is not a neutral bodily life experienced outside of the sexed body. Recent engagements with Braidotti's work in this vein form the basis of Nigianni and Storr's collection *Deleuze and Queer Theory* (2009) and a special issue of *Australian Feminist Studies* on "Feminist Timelines" (Braidotti and Colebrook 2009).

11 The rest of this chapter primarily interrogates the socially inflected strand of return narratives, although due to the doubled meaning of materiality, and to the overlap of tone and historiography effects between the two strands, these are of course not entirely separable. As discussed in the introduction to the book, I have engaged in a more sustained way with the use new materialist approaches make of "affect" in social theory elsewhere and do not want to repeat this work here (Hemmings 2005a).

12 While there have been multiple attempts to theorize "location" in Western feminist theory (notably, Rich 1986; Haraway 1990; Frankenberg and Mani 1993; Bailey 2000; Collins 2000), where this work focuses on privilege it tends to foreground the importance of undoing the same rather than thinking about privilege as a location from which to speak. Such a desire makes sense, of course; it acknowledges the importance of differential location and access to power. Yet, in many ways, the "difficulties of privilege" are thus circumvented or deflected onto the desire not to have any, or the insistence that one does not, even where such an assertion is absurd. Minnie Bruce Pratt's "Identity: Skin Blood Heart" remains a moving exception, in my view (Bulkin, Pratt et al. 1984).

13 As Vikki Bell has pointed out in relation to Nussbaum's tone, it is her certainty that allows Butler's theoretical approaches to be associated with "evil" (2002: 576–78).

14 My analysis of a formative opposition between "merely cultural" and "culture bound" has been influenced by the wide literature on feminism and multiculturalism (e.g., Cohen, Howard et al. 1999; Gunew 2003; Phillips 2007; Scott 2007). Although I do not engage substantially with this literature here, my work here reflects a debt to Anne Phillips's arguments in *Multiculturalism Without Culture* (2007). Phillips suggests that the "problem of culture" is not whether or not particular cultures are essentially bad for women, but why and how "culture" belongs to racially, ethnically, or religiously marked subjects and communities in Western political theory. Phillips further explores the connections between meanings of culture, gender, feminism, race, ethnicity, and religion in *Gender and Culture* (2010).

15 I borrow the idea of conceptual sticking from Sara Ahmed, who uses it to theorize the sticking of emotion to particular marked bodies (2004c).

16 In this vein, Rosemary Hennessy notes rather early for the literature that "for materialist feminists, sexuality, along with those features that often accompany how it is understood in the West (pleasure, consumption, cultural diversity), is part of a given global reality in which these terms have a very specific and privileged address" (1993: 965).

17 Thanks to Carolyn Williams for helping me think about this point.

18 Similar lines of argument predate my own. Robyn Wiegman has interrogated the presumption that materiality and oppression are co-extensive (Wiegman 1999/2000: 117) and Ratna Kapur asks the pertinent question "Why is 'material condition' assumed to refer only to women's experience of oppression and impoverishment?" (Kapur 2001: 83).

19 See responses to this article in the special issue of the *British Journal of Sociology* in which Butler's piece is published, which further situate the relationship between sexual identity and regulation of citizenship and migration (Ali 2008; Bhatt 2008; Modood 2008; Woodhead 2008), and Butler's engagement with these responses (2008a; 2009). My concern about this work, however, is that it easily slips into a demonization of sexual identity politics as white and Western

again with the trumping of supposed sexual freedoms by a focus on an opposed subjugated migrant.

NOTES TO CHAPTER FOUR: **AMENABILITY**

1 I mentioned the U.K. Research Excellence Framework (REF) in chapter 2, which initially promised to make more extended use of "bibliometrics" in its evaluation of academic work. "Bibliometrics" refers to quantitative indicators of research quality based on citation of work within privileged journal sets. Although its use as part of assessment has been largely abandoned (at time of editing), its threat has already resulted in localized institutional pressure to publish in certain journals and not others.

2 As I have suggested throughout the book, a notable exception to this general lack of attention is Robyn Wiegman's work on institutional battles over the right kind of feminist theory (1999/2000; 2001; 2002; 2004). My own work remains in consistent dialogue with hers.

3 It has sometimes been a struggle to persuade editors and reviewers of journals of the importance of this de-authorization, in part because of the institutional pressures I have indicated and in part, too, because of the ways in which feminist theorists' contributions are too often sidelined in social theory already. I am grateful to the staff and the editors at Duke University Press for recognizing the importance of this tactic and for taking the risk with me.

4 As Lynne Segal has compellingly argued, the "crisis in masculinity" is as old as feminism and its attendant backlashes (Segal 1990; see also McDowell 2002). Discourses of masculine crisis in relation to feminist claims have also been theorized as discourses of white Western masculine crisis in particular (Wiegman 1999b; Robinson 2000).

5 I put "gay couples" in scare quotes here to indicate that these representations tell us little about the identities of those represented.

6 Unlike sexual freedom for men, sexual freedom for women is consistently marked as heterosexual, presumably on the basis that heterosexual freedom for men must already have been universally achieved. Mark Chiang's analysis of *The Wedding Banquet,* in which he critiques the gendered heterosexual presumptions that underpin homosexual liberation for men as always requiring the abandonment of family, is apt in this context (1998). For Chiang the understanding of homosexuality as transnational, and heterosexuality as national, relies on a prior belief in women (as symbols of both nation and family) as structurally and actually heterosexual.

7 I return to what I perceive to be a feminist over-investment in agency as the marker of subject status in considering gendered investment in norms or their transformation in the final chapter of the book.

8 The increase of generational language in accounting for shifts in feminist theory in the last decade may also be an effect of the postmillennium moment. Generational reflections include pre- and postmillennium feminist memoirs (e.g., Brown-

miller 1999; Jay 1999; Rowbotham 2000), and special issues of journals or collections (Hall, O'Sullivan et al. 1999; Howard and Allen 2000; Davis 2004b; Henry 2004) that encourage looking back and forward in generational modes. The proliferation of new feminist work on time must surely also be an effect of this taking stock (Felski 2000; Grosz 2002; Tronto 2003; Grosz 2005), though in a less autobiographical vein.

9 Drucilla Cornell's discussion of the attention to race and class difference central to consciousness raising in the 1970s would be one important exception (2000), as would the Feminist Review Collective's reflections on theoretical and political shifts and continuities across "feminist generations" through its thirty year history (2005).

10 Iris van der Tuin has made efforts to think about generation in a nonheteronormative, anoedipal way, arguing for "generation" as transposition rather than as inheritance within feminist theory. Yet the term itself is caught in its own history, and van der Tuin's own theorization substitutes geographical succession (of continental sexual difference over Anglo-American epistemologies) whatever her intentions, a point I have argued elsewhere (Hemmings 2009; van der Tuin 2009).

11 For a sense of these various circumstances see *The Making of European Women's Studies* journals vols. I–VIII and Gabriele Griffin and Rosi Braidotti's European women's studies reader, *Thinking Differently* (2002). Braidotti's chapter in this anthology importantly maps not just these differences across time and space, but their impact for feminist epistemology and institutional politics (2002b).

12 I use the term "Third Wave" here as distinct from "postfeminism," though the two are sometimes used co-extensively. "Third wavers" identify with feminist aims even as they may differentiate themselves from earlier theoretical or political endeavours (Heywood 2006); "postfeminism" usually marks a break from feminism, irrespective of potential shared agendas (Heywood and Drake 1997; Gillis, Howie et al. 2004). It is, in fact, rare for individuals to identify as postfeminist, and in this sense the latter term tends to describe a social or discursive formation rather than individuals or groups (Brooks 1997; Braithwaite 2002).

13 There is a further call that has gained recent institutional purchase, and that is to designate the project "women's and gender studies." While I have some sympathy with the choice not to choose, this attempt at inclusion reproduces theoretical and historical assumptions that the two refer to different projects in the first instance, and thus, in the context of my own interests, does not resolve (as it seems to) the historiographic issues embedded in these questions of nomenclature.

14 The Gender Institute's institutional history is recorded in a working paper published to celebrate its 15th anniversary (Armitage and Pedwell 2005).

15 In this respect I have been profoundly influenced by poststructuralist historians of the relationship between subject and object of both gender and feminism, such as Denise Riley (1988) and Joan Scott (1999) as well as Gayatri Spivak (1999b).

16 Unlike Janet Halley, for example, who has advocated taking "a break from femi-

nism" because of its inability to take account of sexual politics outside its own frames of recognition and because of its failure to reflect sufficiently on its own power (2006). There is much I agree with in Halley's argument, not least her attention to authority as part of, rather than antithetical to, feminist interventions. But in suggesting a "break" as a solution, my feeling is that Halley fixes feminism's meanings as those she identifies as institutionally compromised, while allowing queer sexual politics to emerge as the current saviour in the face of critical and political difficulty.

NOTES TO CHAPTER FIVE: CITATION TACTICS

1 Poststructuralism and feminism are separated in social theory more generally, too. In work like Anthony Giddens's on the transformation of intimacy (1992), or Michael Hardt's and Antonio Negri's on new forms of "Empire" in the context of neoliberal globalization (2000), the lack of citation of feminist poststructuralists allows these (male) theorists to "rediscover" gender equality as pertinent in the present (in the case of Giddens), or to overlook feminist work that has made similar arguments (in the case of Hardt and Negri).

2 Sara Ahmed also argues that the erasure of black feminism from poststructuralism is fundamental to the "rediscovery" of the body in feminist theory after the cultural turn (2008).

3 Who is cited will be highly discipline specific, of course. Historian colleagues have indicated that Joan Scott is consistently given this role in feminist history journals, for example.

4 This section builds on my initial discussion of citation of Butler in chapter 1. I use a different range of extracts in this chapter to avoid repetition.

5 Because of Butler's inimitable influence beyond feminist theory, and in order to highlight further the overlaps between Western feminist storytelling and social theory more broadly, this chapter draws more than the others on both interdisciplinary feminist theory journals and other interdisciplinary theory journals such as *Body & Society*, *Critical Inquiry*, and *Theory, Culture and Society*.

6 As discussed more fully in the last chapter, the citation of feminist, women's, or gender studies as the proper name of the field is often a chronological indicator (from women's studies to gender studies) even though this is not always an accurate description of shifts in the naming of the field in a given location.

7 As one of the initial readers of this manuscript helpfully pointed out, the positioning of Foucault as "poststructuralist" is odd in these glosses in itself. Neither Foucault nor Butler have ever so identified themselves. But the focus of my analysis is on their citation in progress, loss, and return narratives, and part of this process is so to designate them. Indeed that characterization is key to the temporalities I am tracing here.

8 David Halperin's loving and ironic homage, *Saint Foucault*, makes the nature of this relationship most explicit (1995).

9 As above, there is enough intertextual evidence for reading this second extract as invoking, if not directly citing, Butler.

10 This ontological exploration might explain the otherwise odd insistence (given Butler's prominent position in the field) that queer theory is too *male* for feminist theory (e.g., Martin 1994; Jeffreys 2002b).

11 I am adapting Luce Irigaray's term "hom(m)osexuality" here (1985b). Irigaray uses the term to indicate proximity between male sociality and sexuality in the ordering of the social world. I use "hom(m)o-citational" to emphasize Butler's masculinization in feminist citation practices and to queer this attempt to domesticate her relationship with Foucault.

12 In addition to Sara Ahmed's article, see the following: (Ermarth 2000; Lorber 2000; Winter 2000). Related debates concern the exclusive nature of feminist production within academic hierarchies in terms of power relations and access to theory (see Skeggs 1997; 2004).

13 In line with Terry Lovell, then, I understand what "stars" mean and how they are represented as motivated rather than descriptive (2000).

14 Published sequentially in the journal *Gender Issues* and later collected in the collection *The Straight Mind and Other Essays* (Wittig 1992).

15 I would now be more inclined to think of Wittig's privileging of the category "lesbian" in terms of political provocation, rather than incitement to identity, and in this respect as elaborating Adrienne Rich's insistence on all women having lesbian attachments (1980).

16 Most famous among these critiques of Irigaray's essentialism, perhaps, is Gayatri Spivak's "French Feminism in an International Frame" (1981), later revisited less harshly in "French Feminism Revisited" (1993). More recently, Rosi Braidotti and Christine Delphy, among others, have sought to resituate "French" feminism's reception by a U.S. audience as a function and effect of international power relations (Braidotti 1991; Delphy 2000).

17 Robyn Wiegman makes a similar point in "Un-Remembering Monique Wittig" (2007). As part of *GLQ*'s commemorative special issue on Wittig, Wiegman takes queer feminist theory to task for its privileging of less troublesome theorists within a queer canon, but warns against simple reclamation as well. For Wiegman, Wittig might remind us of the importance of critique in both intellectual and institutional life and of the productive nature of discomfort in working through rather than dismissing epistemological (more than ontological) difference.

18 It is thus also not surprising that Butler's work in *The Psychic Life of Power* (1997b) is rarely cited in these narratives, since this would make it difficult to sustain her position as "carrier of culture" over materiality, or as representative of a reductive attention to constraint over proliferation.

19 Adapted definition from Word "Reference Tools."

20 The three literary examples I have cited here are all concerned with rewriting colonial literary narratives from the perspective of marginal figures, whose racialized, sexualized, and gendered stereotyping in the original stories is turned to give these characters depth and visibility.

21 My thanks to Lisa Duggan for raising this issue in response to a lecture on recitation in Tampere, Finland, in November 2006.

22 While the process of developing this citation tactic involved experimenting with as many examples from the journals as possible, here I only include those that have already been mentioned in this chapter, so that readers can contextualize them in relation to my earlier argument, should they so wish.

23 I have included Irigaray as Wittig's partner in the last two extracts in order to respect Butler's engagement with her in *Gender Trouble*, the text most commonly alluded to in the glosses I am reciting. Irigaray's reanimation here also has the potential to reposition new materialism's framing of Butler and Irigaray only as antagonists.

24 In both Wittig and Butler I would argue the relationship between sexual identity and social reality remains in tension. Wittig sees the distinction between man and woman as a power-effect of heteronormativity and thus considers identities embedded in this distinction as social rather inevitable (1982). Butler insists that "lesbian" as an identity should be permanently called into question, but does not suggest that it should be abandoned (1992; 2004b).

25 This argument echoes Rosemary Hennessy's that materialist and what we now call queer perspectives have not always been anathema to one another (1993). It also invites a re-reading of the debates between Nancy Fraser and Judith Butler I discussed in the previous chapter (Butler 1997a; Fraser 1997).

26 As Rosi Braidotti enjoins, a new, creative space of possibility may be the only politically progressive imagination we can fully grasp at present (2006).

NOTES TO CHAPTER SIX: AFFECTIVE SUBJECTS

1 Thus recitation might be thought of as a more politically attached variant of genealogy (Foucault 1972; 1980a).

2 This is rather different use of the term "limit" than that proposed by Rosi Braidotti in *Transpositions* (2006), although her use has certainly influenced my thinking in this respect. Braidotti focuses on the importance of "knowing one's own limits" in thinking through sustainable critical and political practice. Here, I focus on the historiographic and textual limit to the extension of the subject in relation to others, which is, I believe, embedded in our own capacity to think intersubjectively as feminists. Thanks to the readers of the original manuscript for suggesting I make the issue of "limit" more visible.

3 Empathy is thus closely tied to standpoint theories of a variety of kinds, where knowledge is understood as a struggle for visibility of hitherto excluded perspectives and meanings (Harding 1991; Harding 1993; Hartsock 1998). From a feminist standpoint perspective the success of a standpoint epistemology can be judged on the basis of whether marginalized subjects are (a) given a voice, and (b) recognize themselves in a given standpoint account (Smith 1987; Mies 1991). Standpoint has been critiqued on the basis of its universal claims about women's status, among other reasons (Hekman 1997; Stoetzler and Yuval-Davis 2002), but

one might see a more open "politics of location" (the term coined by Adrienne Rich [1986]) as an adaptation of standpoint theory. Important to Rich's delineation of this approach is her insight that one must start from where one is, but not place that view at the center of a given account. In this respect her approach is also concerned with shifting the centrality of a Western feminist subject.

4 One could consider the range of work on intersectionality currently popular as one example of this challenge to the idea of "common interest" on the basis of gender alone (e.g., McCall 2005; Yuval-Davis 2006). Interestingly, some work in this area expresses concern about the ways in which this term fixes rather than opens up complexity in the subject (Staunæs 2003; Brah and Phoenix 2004).

5 The questions of intention and implementation in respect of empathy are already contained in the dictionary definition, where to empathize with someone is "to identify with and understand another person's feelings or difficulties," or to "transfer . . . your own feelings and emotions to an object such as a painting" (OED). Within the feminist literature one might say that the first definition is understood as "good empathy" (Code 1995a), while the second might translate into Dean's "lazy and false empathy" (Dean 2003: 96).

6 The "ethic of care" (most famously delineated by Carol Gilligan [1982]) has been similarly critiqued for reinforcing the naturalizing association of women with qualities of care. Rather differently, Nancy Fraser has argued that instead of rejecting these qualities we should seek to make them universal (1994; 1996).

7 Donna Haraway's "Manifesto for Cyborgs" (1985), and *The Companion Species Manifesto* (2003), might be read as extending the understanding of good empathy still further to include the non-human, as might Rosi Braidotti's insistence on a non-anthropomorphic, posthumanist feminist ethics (2006).

8 And as I discuss later in this chapter, when empathy fails to manage these relations, affect comes right to the fore in justifying distinctions made.

9 Beverley Skeggs (2004) similarly critiques Anthony Giddens's (1991; Beck, Giddens et al. 1994) celebration of the reflexive subject of globalization, arguing that while reflexivity suggests an increasing flexibility on the part of Western, middle-class subjects, that flexibility does little to ameliorate (in fact it relies upon or extends) inequality between highly skilled subjects of globalization and working class subjects who are becoming more and more marginal.

10 My thinking about the interruption of grammatical temporality through refusal on the part of the "other-subject" has been developed in part out of shared insights from a reading group on performativity at the LSE. In reading J. L. Austin, several members of the group were particularly taken by the character of "George" who refuses to abide by the grammatical rules of performatives, who takes himself off, and, in Austin's vexed childhood scenarios does not cooperate. My favorite: "For example, at a party, you say, when picking sides, 'I pick George': George grunts, 'I'm not playing.' Has George been picked?" (1975: 28) The relationship between Austin's querying of the nature of the performative and my own interest in refusals is not a direct one, but I have still been interested in imagining a George in relation to my own concerns with empathetic grammar.

11 See Terry Lovell (2003) and Lois McNay (2000; 2003) for useful broad discussions of agency in Western feminist theory.

12 More recent articles in *Feminist Review* by both authors concern dominant representations of trafficked "sex slaves" in Europe and critique feminist approaches that reproduce understandings of trafficked women as victims (O'Connell Davidson 2006b; Andrijasevic 2007). Instead, both authors call for a nuanced contextualization of sex trafficking in relation to migration and citizenship.

13 See Catalina MacKenzie and Natalie Stoljar's collection that develops the idea of "relational autonomy" as a way of retaining the concept of autonomy as central for agency, while acknowledging the problems of liberal conceptions of the bounded individual (2000).

14 In the French context most infamously, feminists were split in this way over the "headscarf debates," which successfully sought to ban young women's wearing of religious head coverings in schools (Scott 2007: 21–41).

15 For scholars concerned with asylum seekers (Khanna 2007), camp detainees (Agamben 1998), migrant workers (Andall and Puwar 2007; Andrijasevic 2007), and targets of war (Butler 2004a), among others, a perceived lack of agency can often result in a diminution of a sense of ethical obligation to the other. One must first be understood as human enough to possess agency.

16 Volpp's comparisons between forced marriage (in India) and low legal ages of consent (in the United States) provoke a useful consideration of why some practices are considered "cultural" and others are not.

17 In work comparing Western body modification with female genital cutting, for example, and as Carolyn Pedwell has argued (2008), the former is understood as less extreme than the latter, but as providing a comparative basis for empathy.

18 There must be considerable pleasure to be had in the repeated resurgence of horror and its management, indeed, if the proliferation of sequels in this genre is anything to go by.

19 Spivak's critiques of Kristeva have focused on her failure to reflect on the consequences of her own "disinterested history" and her exoticization of "others" as less encumbered by, e.g., the limits of Western linguistic frames (Spivak 1981). More recently she has challenged Kristeva's acceptance of an East-West opposition that continues to find in favor of the latter term and thus reproduces its imagined conceptual, political, and gendered history (1999: 66).

20 Bliss Cua Lim draws together postcolonial theory and horror criticism in her discussion of temporalities (2009). Lim highlights ways in which "the supernatural" in horror movies, understood as remainder, can serve as a useful starting point for an ethics of temporality beyond national boundaries.

21 Spivak makes this argument via her discussion of J. M. Coetzee's *Foe* (1987). For Spivak, Coetzee's political integrity lies in his refusal to take the easy route of the guilty colonizer, and she defends him against critics who prefer their postcolonial fiction less allegorical or ambiguous.

22 Carolyn Pedwell warns us about the dangers of comparative approaches to

practices or subjects that are similar only because of the Western feminist perspective that binds them together (2007; 2008). Indeed she particularly singles out comparisons between FGC and body modifications (including transsexual surgeries) as problematic. My aim here is not to compare practices, though, but to highlight the similar use of horror as the basis of feminist judgment of these practices.

23 Hosken coined the phrase "female genital mutilation" (1981) to describe what later others have called "female genital surgery" or "female genital cutting," where the latter are considered less sensationalizing.

24 For Silvan Tomkins, the father of cognitive affect theory, it matters little whether affective response is innate or learned, since it can be taught by repetitive example (1963).

25 Janice Raymond's *The Transsexual Empire,* in which transsexuality allows men to move into the last women-only space—the female body—introduces this tradition (1980).

26 Doezema draws on Wendy Brown's (1993) development of the idea of "Wounded Attachments" in the latter's article of the same name.

27 Likewise, Millsom Henry-Waring's response fuses affect and theoretical judgment in his response to Njambi's article, stating that "there is a gut response as it is hard to view such specific acts of cliterodectomy to infibulation as acceptable" (2004: 319).

28 I am inspired in this reading of my own affect by Gilles Deleuze's account of T. E. Lawrence's experience of being raped: "In the midst of his tortures, an erection; even in the state of sludge, there are convulsions that jolt the body" (1997: 123). For Deleuze, such moments exemplify the unpredictable autonomy of the body. As in my own account, Laurence's experience of shame is not at the event itself but as a judgment on his own affective response.

BIBLIOGRAPHY

Adkins, L. (2002). "Sexuality and Economy: Historicisation vs. Deconstruction." *Australian Feminist Studies* 17(37): 31–41.

——. (2004). "Passing on Feminism." *European Journal of Women's Studies* 11(4): 427–44.

Afshar, H. (1993). *Women in the Middle East: Perceptions, Realities and Struggles for Liberation*. Basingstoke: MacMillan.

——. (1998). *Islam and Feminisms: an Iranian Case-Study*. Basingstoke: MacMillan.

Agamben, G. (1998). *Homo Sacer: Sovereign Power and Bare Life*. Stanford: Stanford University Press.

Agustin, L. (2007). *Sex at the Margins: Migration, Labour Markets and the Rescue Industry*. London: Zed Books.

Ahmed, S. (2000a). *Strange Encounters: Embodied Others in Post-Coloniality*. London: Routledge.

——. (2000b). "Whose Counting?" *Feminist Theory* 1(1): 97–103.

——. (2004a). "Affective Economies." *Social Text* 22(4): 117–39.

——. (2004b). "Collective Feelings: Or, the Impressions Left by Others." *Theory, Culture and Society* 21(2): 25–42.

——. (2004c). *The Cultural Politics of Emotion*. Edinburgh: Edinburgh University Press.

——. (2008). "Open Forum—Imaginary Prohibitions: Some Preliminary Remarks on the Founding Gestures of the 'New Materialism.'" *European Journal of Women's Studies* 15(1): 23–39.

Al-Ali, N. (2005). "Reconstructing Gender: Iraqi Women between Dictatorship, War, Sanctions and Occupation." *Third World Quarterly* 26(4–5): 739–58.

Al-Ali, N., and N. Pratt (2008). "Women's Organizing and the Conflict in Iraq Since 2003." *Feminist Review* 88: 74–85.

Alcoff, L. (1995). "The Problem of Speaking for Others." In *Who Can Speak: Authority and Critical Identity*, ed. J. Roof and R. Wiegman, 97–119. Champaign: University of Illinois Press.

Alcoff, L., and E. Potter, eds. (1993). *Feminist Epistemologies*. New York: Routledge.

Alexander, J. (1994). "Not Just (Any) Body Can Be a Citizen: The Politics of Law, Sexuality and Postcoloniality in Trinidad and Tobago and the Bahamas." *Feminist Review* 48: 5–23.

——. (2005). *Pedagogies of Crossing: Meditations on Feminism, Sexual Politics and the Sacred*. Durham: Duke University Press.

Ali, S. (2008). "Troubling Times: a Comment on Judith Butler's 'Sexual Politics, Torture and Secular Time.'" *British Journal of Sociology* 59(1): 35–39.

Andall, J., and N. Puwar, eds. (2007). "Italian Feminisms." Special Issue, *Feminist Review* 87.

Andrijasevic, R. (2003). "The Difference Borders Make: (Il)legality, Migration and Trafficking in Italy among Western European Women in Prostitution." In *Unrootings/Regroundings: Questions of Home and Migration*, ed. S. Ahmed, C. Castaneda, A.-M. Fortier, and M. Sheller, 251–71. Oxford: Berg.

——. (2007). "Beautiful Dead Bodies: Gender, Migration and Representation in Anti-Trafficking Campaigns." *Feminist Review* 86: 24–44.

Ang, I. (2001). *On Not Speaking Chinese: Living Between Asia and the West*. London: Routledge.

Anim-Addo, J. (2003). "Imoinda: Or She Who Will Lose Her Name—A Play for Twelve Voices in Three Acts." In *Voci femminili caraibiche e interculturalità*, ed. G. Covi, 1–155. Trento, Italy: I Labirinti, Pubblicazioni Università di Trento.

Annfelt, T. (2002). "More Gender Equality—Bigger Breasts? Battles Over Gender and the Body." *Nora: Nordic Journal of Women's Studies* 10(3): 127–36.

Armitage, F., and C. Pedwell (2005). "Putting Gender on the Map: The LSE Gender Institute's First Fifteen Years." *Working Papers in Gender Studies*. London: London School of Economics.

Armstrong, N. (2001). "Who's Afraid of the Cultural Turn?" *Differences* 12(1): 17–49.

Austin, J. L. (1975). *How to Do Things With Words*. Cambridge, Mass.: Harvard University Press.

Bailey, A. (2000). "Locating Traitorous Identities: Toward a View of Privilege-Cognizant White Character." In *Decentering the Center: Philosophy for a Multicultural, Postcolonial, and Feminist World*, ed. U. Narayan and S. Harding, 283–98. Bloomington: Indiana University Press.

Bal, M. (2002). *Travelling Concepts in the Humanities: A Rough Guide*. Toronto: University of Toronto Press.

Bar On, B.-A. (1993). "Marginality and Epistemic Privilege." In *Feminist Epistemologies*, ed. L. Alcoff and E. Potter, 83–100. New York: Routledge.

Bartky, S. (2002). *'Sympathy and Solidarity' and Other Essays.* Lanham, Md.: Rowman and Littlefield.

Bashford, A. (1998). "The Return of the Repressed: Feminism in the Quad." *Australian Feminist Studies* 13(27): 47–53.

Beck, U., A. Giddens, and S. Lash (1994). *Reflexive Modernization: Politics, Tradition and Aesthetics in the Modern Social Order.* Stanford: Stanford University Press.

Bell, V. (2002). "Feminist Thought and the Totalitarian Interloper: On Rhetoric and the Fear of 'Dangerous Thinking.'" *Economy and Society* 31(4): 573–87.

Berg, M., and M. Akrich (2004). "Introduction—Bodies on Trial: Performances and Politics in Medicine and Biology." *Body and Society* 10(2–3): 1–12.

Berlant, L. (1997). *The Queen of America Goes to Washington City: Essays on Sex and Citizenship.* Durham: Duke University Press.

——. (2004). *Intimacy.* Chicago: University of Chicago Press.

——. (2007). "Nearly Utopian, Nearly Normal: Post-Fordist Affect in 'La Promesse' and 'Rosetta.'" *Public Culture* 19(2): 273–301.

——. (2008). *The Female Complaint: The Unfinished Business of Sentimentality in American Culture.* Durham: Duke University Press.

Bhatt, C. (2008). "The Times of Movements: a Response." *British Journal of Sociology* 59(1): 25–33.

Bhavnani, K.-K., J. Foran, and P. Kurian (2003). *Feminist Futures: Re-imagining Women, Culture and Development.* London: Zed Books.

Bordo, S. (1993). *Unbearable Weight: Feminism, Western Culture, and the Body.* Berkeley: University of California Press.

Boyce, P. (2006). "Moral Ambivalence and Irregular Practices: Contextualizing Male-to-Male Sexualities in Calcutta." *Feminist Review* 83: 79–98.

Brah, A., and A. Phoenix (2004). "Ain't I a Woman? Revisiting Intersectionality." *Journal of International Women's Studies* 5(3): 73–86.

Braidotti, R. (1991). *Patterns of Dissonance: A Study of Women in Contemporary Philosophy.* Cambridge: Polity.

——. (2000). "The Way We Were: Some Post-Structuralist Memoirs." *Women's Studies International Forum* 23(6): 715–28.

——. (2002a). *Metamorphoses: Towards a Materialist Theory of Becoming.* Cambridge: Polity Press.

——. (2002b). "The Uses and Abuses of the Sex/Gender Distinction in European Feminist Practices." In *Thinking Differently: A Reader in European Women's Studies.* G. Griffin and R. Braidotti, 285–307. London: Zed Books.

——. (2005). "A Critical Cartography of Feminist Post-Postmodernism." *Australian Feminist Studies* 20(47): 169–80.

——. (2006). *Transpositions: On Nomadic Ethics.* Cambridge: Polity Press.

Braidotti, R., E. Chrakiewicz, S. Hausler, and S. Wieringa (1994). *Women, the Environment and Sustainable Development: Towards a Theoretical Synthesis.* London: Zed Books with INSTRAW.

Braidotti, R., and C. Colebrook, eds. (2009). "Feminist Generations: Special Issue." *Australian Feminist Studies* 24(59).

Braithwaite, A. (2002). "The Personal, the Political, Third-Wave and Postfeminisms." *Feminist Theory* 3(3): 335–44.

Braithwaite, A., S. Heald, S. Luhmann, and S. Rosenberg (2004). *Troubling Women's Studies: Pasts, Presents, Possibilities*. Toronto: Sumach Press.

Bronfen, E., and M. Kavka (2001). *Feminist Consequences: Theory for the New Century*. New York: Columbia University Press.

Brooks, A. (1997). *Postfeminisms: Feminism, Cultural Theory and Cultural Forms*. London: Routledge.

Brooks, G. (2009). "Finger-Wagging Won't Help Muslim Women," *The Guardian*, London.

Brown, W. (1993). "Wounded Attachments." *Political Theory* 21(3): 390–410.

——. (1997). "The Impossibility of Women's Studies." *Differences* 9(3): 79–90.

——. (1999). "Resisting Left Melancholy." *Boundary 2* 26(3): 19–27.

Brownmiller, S. (1999). *In Our Time: Memoir of a Revolution*. London: Aurum, 2000.

Buchanan, I., and C. Colebrook (2000). *Deleuze and Feminist Theory*. Edinburgh: Edinburgh University Press.

Bulkin, E., M. B. Pratt, and B. Smith (1984). *Yours in Struggle: Three Feminist Perspectives on Anti-Semitism and Racism*. New York: Long Haul Press.

Burton, A. (2001). "Thinking Beyond the Boundaries: Empire, Feminism and the Domain of History." *Social History* 26(1): 60–71.

Butler, J. (1990). *Gender Trouble: Feminism and the Subversion of Identity*. New York: Routledge.

——. (1992). "Contingent Foundations." In *Feminists Theorize the Political*, ed. J. Butler and J. Scott, 3–21. New York: Routledge.

——. (1997a). "Merely Cultural." *Social Text*: 265–77.

——. (1997b). *The Psychic Life of Power: Theories in Subjection*. Stanford: Stanford University Press.

——. (1999). "Revisiting Bodies and Pleasures." *Theory, Culture and Society* 16(2): 11–20.

——. (2004a). *Precarious Life: The Powers of Mourning and Violence*. London: Verso.

——. (2004b). *Undoing Gender*. New York: Routledge.

——. (2008a). "A Response to Ali, Beckford, Bhatt, Modood and Woodhead." *British Journal of Sociology* 59(2): 255–60.

——. (2008b). "Sexual Politics, Torture, and Secular Time." *British Journal of Sociology* 59(1): 1–23.

——. (2009). *Frames of War: When is Life Grievable?* New York: Verso.

Calloni, M. (2003). "Interview: Feminism, Politics, Theories and Science." *European Journal of Women's Studies* 10(1): 87–103.

Campt, T. (2004). *Other Germans: Black Germans and the Politics of Race, Gender, and Memory in the Third Reich*. Ann Arbor: University of Michigan Press.

Castañeda, C. (2004). "Entering the Dialogue." *Feminist Theory* 5(3): 311–17.

Chiang, M. (1998). "Coming out into the Global System: Postmodern Patriarchies and Transnational Sexualities in 'The Wedding Banquet.'" In *Q and A: Queer in Asian America*, ed. D. L. Eng and A. Hom, 374–95. Philadelphia: Temple University Press.

Chow, R. (1994). "Where Have All the Natives Gone?" In *Contemporary Postcolonial Theory: A Reader*, ed. P. Mongia, 123–45. London: Arnold.

Clover, C. (1993). *Men, Women, and Chain Saws: Gender in the Modern Horror Film.* Princeton: Princeton University Press.

Code, L. (1993). "Taking Subjectivity into Account." In *Feminist Epistemologies*, ed. L. Alcoff and E. Potter, 15–48. New York: Routledge.

——. (1995a). "I Know Just How You Feel: Empathy and the Problem of Epistemic Authority." In *Rhetorical Spaces: Essays on Gendered Locations*, 120–43. New York: Routledge.

——. (1995b). *Rhetorical Spaces: Essays on Gendered Locations.* New York: Routledge.

Coetzee, J. M. (1987). *Foe.* London: Penguin.

Cohen, J., M. Howard, and M. Nussbaum eds. (1999). *Is Multiculturalism Bad for Women?* Princeton: Princeton University Press.

Collins, P. H. (2000). *Black Feminist Thought: Knowledge, Consciousness, and the Politics of Empowerment.* New York: Routledge.

Cornell, D. (2000). "Las Greñudas: Reflections on Consciousness-Raising." *Signs* 25(4): 1033–39.

Cornwall, A., E. Harrison, and A. Whitehead, eds. (2007). *Feminisms in Development: Contradictions, Contestations and Challenges.* London: Zed Books.

Corrêa, S., and R. P. Petchesky (1994). "Reproductive and Sexual Rights: a Feminist Perspective." In *Population Policies Reconsidered: Health, Empowerment and Rights*, ed. G. Sen, A. Germain and L. C. Chen, 107–23. Cambridge, Mass.: Harvard University Press.

Coward, R. (1999). *Sacred Cows: Is Feminism Relevant to the New Millennium?* London: Harper Collins.

Creed, B. (1993). *The Monstrous-Feminine: Film, Feminism, Psychoanalysis.* New York: Routledge.

Cruz-Malave, A., and M. F. Manalansan IV, eds. (2002). *Queer Globalizations: Citizenship and the Afterlife of Colonialism.* New York: New York University Press.

Daly, M. (1978). "African Genital Mutilation: The Unspeakable Atrocities." In *Gyn/ecology: The Metaethics of Radical Feminism*, 153–77. Boston: Beacon Press.

Davis, K. (1994). *Reshaping the Female Body: The Dilemma of Cosmetic Surgery.* London: Routledge.

——. (2003). *Dubious Equalities and Embodied Differences: Cultural Studies on Cosmetic Surgery.* Lanham, Md.: Rowan and Littlefield.

——. (2004a). "Between Moral Outrage and Cultural Relativism." *Feminist Theory* 5(3): 305–11.

——. (2004b). "Editorial: 'Passing on Feminism.'" Special issue, *European Journal of Women's Studies* 11(4): 1–5.

Davis, K., M. Evans, and J. Lorber, eds. (2006). *The Handbook of Women's and Gender Studies.* London: Sage.

Dean, C. J. (2003). "Empathy, Pornography, and Suffering." *Differences* 14(1): 88–124.

Deem, M. (2003). "Disrupting the Nuptial at the Town Hall Debate: Feminism and the Politics of Cultural Memory in the USA." *Cultural Studies* 17(5): 615–47.

Deleuze, G. (1997). *Essays Critical and Clinical*. Minneapolis: University of Minnesota Press.

Delphy, C. (2000). "The Invention of French Feminism: An Essential Move." *50 Years of* Yale French Studies: *A Commemorative Anthology, Part 2: 1980–1998. Yale French Studies* 97: 166–97.

Demoor, M., and K. Heene (2002). "State of the Art: Of Influences and Anxieties— Sandra Gilbert's Feminist Commitment." *European Journal of Women's Studies* 9(2): 181–98.

Derrida, J. (1997). *The Politics of Friendship*. New York: Verso.

Doezema, J. (2001). "Ouch! Western Feminists' 'Wounded Attachment' to the 'Third World Prostitute.'" *Feminist Review* 67: 16–38.

Duggan, L. (2003). *The Twilight of Equality? Neoliberalism, Cultural Politics, and the Attack on Democracy*. Boston: Beacon Press.

Duhaček, D. (2006a). "Feminist Perspectives on Democratization in Serbia/Western Balkans." *Signs* 31: 923–28.

———. (2006b). "The Making of Political Responsibility: Hannah Arendt and/in the Case of Serbia." In *Women and Citizenship in Central and Eastern Europe*, ed. J. Lukič, J. Regulska, and D. Zavirsek, 205–23. Burlington, Vt.: Ashgate.

DuPlessis, R. B., and A. Snitow, eds. (2007). *The Feminist Memoir Project: Voices from Women's Liberation*. New Brunswick, N.J.: Rutgers University Press.

Eadie, J. (2001). "Shivers: Race and Class in the Emperilled Body." In *Contested Bodies*, ed. R. Holliday and J. Hassard, 61–80. London: Routledge.

Ebert, T. L. (1996). *Ludic Feminism and After: Postmodernism, Desire, and Labor in Late Capitalism*. Ann Arbor: University of Michigan Press.

Ermarth, E. (2000). "What Counts as Feminist Theory?" *Feminist Theory* 1(1): 113–18.

Evans, M. (1982). "In Praise of Theory: The Case for Women's Studies." *Feminist Review* 10: 61–74.

———. (1991). "The Problem of Gender for Women's Studies." *Out of the Margins: Women's Studies in the Nineties*, ed. J. Aaron and S. Walby, 67–74. London: Falmer Press.

———. (2006). "Did I Sign Up for This? Comments on the New Higher Education." In *The McDonaldization of Higher Education*, ed. D. Hayes and R. Wynyard, 159–66. Charlotte, N.C.: Information Age Publishing.

Faludi, S. (1992). *Backlash: The Undeclared War against Women*. London: Chatto and Windus.

Fanon, F. (1991 [1952]). *Black Skins, White Masks*. London: Pluto Press.

Felski, R. (2000). *Doing Time: Feminist Theory and Postmodern Culture*. New York: New York University Press.

———. (2001). "Feminist Futures." *International Journal of Cultural Studies* 4(2): 238–45.

Feminist Review Collective. (2005). "A 'Feminist Review' Roundtable on the Un/certainties of the Routes of the Collective and the Journal." *Feminist Review* 80: 198–219.

Fernández-Kelly, P. (2000). "Reading the Signs: the Economics of Gender Twenty-five Years Later." *Signs* 25(4): 1107–12.

Ferrier, C. (2003). "Is Feminism Finished?" *Hecate* 29(2): 6–22.

Foucault, M. (1970). *The Order of Things: An Archaeology of the Human Sciences*. London: Tavistock.

——. (1972). *The Archaeology of Knowledge and the Discourse on Language*. New York: Pantheon.

——. (1975). *Discipline and Punish: The Birth of the Prison*. Harmondsworth: Penguin.

——. (1980a). *Language, Counter-Memory, Practice: Selected Essays and Interviews*. Ithaca, N.Y.: Cornell University Press.

——. (1980b). *Power/Knowledge: Selected Interviews and Other Writings 1972–1977*, Brighton: Harvester Press.

——. (1981). *The History of Sexuality, Vol 1: An Introduction*. Harmondsworth: Penguin.

——. (1988). *Technologies of the Self: A Seminar with Michel Foucault*. Amherst: University of Massachusetts Press.

——. (2000). "Governmentality." In *Power: Essential Works of Foucault 1954–1984 Vol. 3*, ed. J. D. Faubion, et. al., 201–22. New York: New Press.

Frankenberg, R., and L. Mani (1993). "Crosscurrents, Crosstalk—Race, 'Postcoloniality,' and the Politics of Location." *Cultural Studies* 7(2): 292–310.

Fraser, M. (1999). "Classing Queer: Politics in Competition." *Theory, Culture and Society* 16(2): 107–31.

Fraser, N. (1994). "After the Family Wage: Gender Equity and the Welfare State." *Political Theory* 22(4): 591–618.

——. (1996). *Justice Interruptus: Critical Reflections on the "Postsocialist" Condition*. New York: Routledge.

——. (1997). "Heterosexism, Misrecognition, and Capitalism: A Response to Judith Butler." *Social Text* 52–53: 279–89.

——. (2001). "Recognition Without Ethics." *Theory, Culture and Society* 18(2–3): 21–42.

——. (2005). "Mapping the Feminist Imagination: From Redistribution to Recognition to Representation." *Constellations* 12(3): 295–307.

Gal, S., and G. Kligman (2000). *The Politics of Gender after Socialism*. Princeton: Princeton University Press.

Genovese, A. (2010). "Mainstream or Muzzled? Australian Academic Feminism." *Feminist Review* 95: 69–131.

Giddens, A. (1991). *Modernity and Self-Identity: Self and Society in the Late Modern Age*. Stanford: Stanford University Press.

Giddens, A. (1992). *The Transformation of Intimacy: Sexuality, Love and Eroticism in Modern Societies*. Cambridge: Polity Press.

Gill, R. (2000). "Review of 'The New Feminism' and 'Postfeminisms.'" *Feminist Review* 64: 139–42.

———. (2007). *Gender and the Media.* Cambridge: Polity.

Gilligan, C. (1982). *In a Different Voice: Psychological Theory and Women's Development.* Cambridge, Mass.: Harvard University Press.

Gillis, S., G. Howie, and R. Munford eds. (2004). *Third Wave Feminism: A Critical Exploration.* London: Palgrave MacMillan.

Gillis, S., and R. Munford (2003). "Introduction: Special Issue—Harvesting Our Strengths: Third Wave Feminism and Women's Studies." *Journal of International Women's Studies* 4(2): 1–11.

Gordon, A. (1997). *Ghostly Matters: Haunting and the Sociological Imagination.* Minneapolis: University of Minnesota Press.

Greer, G. (1974). "Review of 'Conundrum' by Jan Morris." In *The Madwoman's Underclothes: Essays and Occasional Writings.* London: Pan Books.

Grewal, I. (2005). *Transnational America: Feminisms, Diasporas, Neoliberalisms.* Durham: Duke University Press.

Grewal, I., and C. Kaplan (1994). *Scattered Hegemonies: Postmodernity and Transnational Feminist Practices.* Minneapolis: University of Minnesota Press.

Griffin, G., and R. Braidotti, eds. (2002). *Thinking Differently: A Reader in European Women's Studies.* London: Zed Books.

Griffin, G., and J. Hanmer (2001). "Employment and Women's Studies: The Impact of Women's Studies Training of Women's Employment in Europe." Hull: University of Hull.

Grosz, E. (2000). "Histories of a Feminist Future." *Signs* 25(4): 1017–21.

———. (2002). "Feminist Futures?" *Tulsa Studies in Women's Literature* 2(1): 13–20.

———. (2005). *Time Travels: Feminism, Nature, Power.* Durham: Duke University Press.

Gunew, S. (2003). *Haunted Nations: The Colonial Dimensions of Multiculturalisms.* London: Routledge.

Gunning, I. (1992). "Arrogant Perception, World Travelling and Multicultural Feminism: The Case of Female Genital Surgeries." *Columbia Human Rights Law Review* 23: 189–248.

Hakim, C. (1995). "Five Feminist Myths about Women's Employment." *British Journal of Sociology* 46(3): 429–55.

Halberstam, J. (1995). *Skin Shows: Gothic Horror and the Technology of Monsters.* Durham: Duke University Press.

———. (1998). *Female Masculinity.* Durham: Duke University Press.

Hall, C., S. O'Sullivan, A. Phoenix, M. Storr, L. Thomas, and A. Whitehead, eds. (1999). "Snakes and Ladders: Reviewing Feminisms at Century's End." *Feminist Review* 61: 1–3.

Halley, J. E. (2006). *Split Decisions: How and Why to Take a Break from Feminism.* Princeton: Princeton University Press.

Haraway, D. (1985). "Manifesto for Cyborgs: Science, Technology, and Socialist Feminism in the 1980s." *Socialist Review* 80: 65–108.

——. (1990). "Situated Knowledges: The Science Question in Feminism and the Privilege of Partial Perspective." *Feminist Studies* 14(3): 575–99.

——. (2003). *The Companion Species Manifesto: Dogs, People, and Significant Otherness.* Chicago: University of Chicago Press.

Halperin, D. (1995). *Saint Foucault.* Oxford: Oxford University Press.

Harding, S. (1991). *Whose Science? Whose Knowledge? Thinking from Women's Lives.* Milton Keynes: Open University Press.

——. (1993). "Rethinking Standpoint Epistemology: What is 'Strong Objectivity'?" In *Feminist Epistemologies*, ed. L. Alcoff and E. Potter, 49–82. New York: Routledge.

Hardt, M., and A. Negri (2000). *Empire.* Cambridge, Mass.: Harvard University Press.

Haritaworn, J., T. Tauquir, and E. Erdem (2008). "Gay Imperialism: Gender and Sexuality Discourse in the 'War on Terror.'" In *Out of Place: Interrogating Silences in Queerness/Raciality*, ed. A. Kuntsman and E. Miyake, 71–95. York: Raw Nerve Books.

Hark, S. (2002). "Disputed Territory: Feminist Studies in Germany and Its Queer Discontents." *American Studies Quarterly* 46(1): 87–103.

Hartsock, N. (1990). "Foucault on Power: A Theory for Women?" *Feminism/Postmodernism*, ed. L. J. Nicholson, 157–75. New York: Routledge.

——. (1998). *The Feminist Standpoint Revisited and Other Essays.* Boulder, Col.: Westview Press.

Hausman, B. L. (1995). *Changing Sex: Transsexualism, Technology, and the Idea of Gender.* Durham: Duke University Press.

Hawkesworth, M. (2004). "The Semiotics of Premature Burial: Feminism in a Postfeminist Age." *Signs* 29(4): 961–85.

Hekman, S. J. (1990). *Gender and Knowledge: Elements of a Postmodern Feminism.* Cambridge: Polity Press.

——. (1997). "Truth and Method: Feminist Standpoint Revisited." *Signs* 22(2): 341–65.

——. (1999). *The Future of Differences: Truth and Method in Feminist Theory.* Cambridge: Polity Press.

Hemmings, C. (2005a). "Invoking Affect: Cultural Theory and the Ontological Turn." *Cultural Studies* 19(5): 548–67.

——. (2005b). "Telling Feminist Stories." *Feminist Theory* 6(2): 115–39.

——. (2006). "The Life and Times of Academic Feminism: Checking the Vital Signs of Women's and Gender Studies." In *The Handbook of Women's and Gender Studies*, ed. K. Davis, M. Evans, and J. Lorber, 14–34. London: Sage.

——. (2007a). "What is a Feminist Theorist Responsible For? Reply to Torr." *Feminist Theory* 8(1): 69–76.

——. (2007b). "What's in a Name? Bisexuality, Transnational Sexuality Studies and Western Colonial Legacies." *International Journal of Human Rights* 11(1/2): 13–32.

——. (2009). "Generational Dilemmas: A Response to Iris van der Tuin's 'Jumping Generations: On Second- and Third-Wave Feminist Epistemology.'" *Australian Feminist Studies* 24(59): 33–37.

Bibliography

Hennessy, R. (1993). "Queer Theory: A Review of the 'Differences' Special Issue and Wittig's 'The Straight Mind.'" *Signs* 18(4): 964–73.

——. (2000). *Profit and Pleasure: Sexual Identities in Late Capitalism.* New York: Routledge.

Henry, A. (2004). *Not My Mother's Sister: Generational Conflict and Third-Wave Feminism.* Bloomington: Indiana University Press.

Henry-Waring, M. (2004). "Commentary." *Feminist Theory* 5(3): 317–23.

Hesford, V. (2005). "Feminism and Its Ghosts: The Spectre of the Feminist-as-lesbian." *Feminist Theory* 6(3): 227–50.

Heywood, L. (2006). *The Women's Movement Today: An Encyclopaedia of Third-Wave Feminism.* Westport, Conn.: Greenwood Press.

Heywood, L., and J. Drake (1997). *Third Wave Agenda: Being Feminist, Doing Feminism.* Minneapolis: University of Minnesota Press.

Hird, M. J. (2002). "Out/performing Our Selves: Invitation for Dialogue." *Sexualities* 5(3).

——. (2004). "Feminist Matters: New Materialist Considerations of Sexual Difference." *Feminist Theory* 5(2): 223–32.

hoogland, r. (2007). "Feminist Theorizing as 'Transposed Autobiography.'" *Journal of Lesbian Studies* 11(1–2): 153–60.

Hosken, F. P. (1981). "Female Genital Mutilation and Human Rights." *Feminist Issues* 1(3): 3–23.

——. (1994 [1982]). *The Hosken Report: Genital and Sexual Mutilation of Females.* Lexington, Mass.: Women's International Network News.

Howard, J., and C. Allen, eds. (2000). "Feminisms at a Millennium." Special issue, *Signs* 25(4).

Hsieh, L. (2008). "Interpellated by Affect: The Move to the Political in Brian Massumi's 'Parables for the Virtual' and Eve Sedgwick's 'Touching Feeling.'" *Subjectivity* (23): 219–35.

Hughes, C. (2004). "Open Forum: Perhaps She Was Just Having a Bad Hair Day! Taking Issue with Ungenerous Readings of Feminist Texts—An Open Letter." *European Journal of Women's Studies* 11(4): 103–109.

Irigaray, L. (1985a). *Speculum of the Other Woman.* Ithaca, N.Y.: Cornell University Press.

——. (1985b). *This Sex Which Is Not One.* Ithaca, N.Y.: Cornell University Press.

Jackson, S. (1993). *Women's Studies: A Reader.* Hemel Hempstead: Harvester Wheatsheaf.

——. (1999). *Heterosexuality in Question.* London: Sage.

——. (2001). "Why a Materialist Feminism is (Still) Possible and Necessary." *Women's Studies International Forum* 23(3–4): 283–93.

——. (2007). "Gender, Sexuality and Heterosexuality: The Complexity (and Limits) of Heteronormativity." *Feminist Theory* 7(1): 105–21.

Jay, K. (1999). *Tales of the Lavender Menace: A Memoir of Liberation.* New York: Basic Books.

Jeffreys, S. (2002a). "FTM Transsexualism and the Destruction of Lesbians." In *Unpacking Queer Politics: A Lesbian Feminist Perspective*, 122–43. Cambridge: Polity.

——. (2002b). *Unpacking Queer Politics: A Lesbian Feminist Perspective*. Cambridge: Polity.

Jones, M. (1998). "Historicising Feminist Knowledge: Notes toward a Genealogy of Academic Feminism in the 1970s." *Australian Feminist Studies* 13(27): 117–28.

Kaplan, C. (1994). "The Politics of Location as Transnational Feminist Critical Practice." In *Scattered Hegemonies: Postmodernity and Transnational Feminist Critical Practice*, ed. I. Grewal, and Caren Kaplan, 137–52. Minneapolis: University of Minnesota Press.

Kapur, R. (2001). "Imperial Parody." *Feminist Theory* 2(1): 79–88.

——. (2005). *Erotic Justice: Law and the New Politics of Postcolonialism*. London: The Glass House Press.

Kašić, B. (2004). "Feminist Cross-Mainstreaming within 'East-West' Mapping." *European Journal of Women's Studies* 11(4): 473–85.

Khanna, R. (2003). *Dark Continents: Psychoanalysis and Colonialism*. Durham: Duke University Press.

——. (2007). "Indignity." *Ethnic and Racial Studies* 30(2): 257–80.

King, K. (1994). *Theory in Its Feminist Travels: Conversations in U.S. Women's Movements*. Bloomington: Indiana University Press.

Klein, R. D. (1991). "Passion and Politics in Women's Studies in the 1990s." In *Out of the Margins: Women's Studies in the Nineties*, ed. J. Aaron and S. Walby, 75–89. London: Falmer Press.

Knights, D., and W. Richards (2003). "Sex Discrimination in UK Academia." *Gender, Work and Organization* 10(2): 213–39.

Kristeva, J. (1981). "Women's Time." In *The Kristeva Reader*, ed. T. Moi, 187–214. Oxford: Basil Blackwell.

——. (1982). *Powers of Horror: An Essay on Abjection*. New York: Columbia University Press.

Latour, B. (2004). "How to Talk about the Body: The Normative Dimension of Science Studies." *Body and Society* 10(2–3): 205–29.

Lee, F. S., and S. Harley (1998). "Peer Review, the Research Assessment Exercise and the Demise of Non-Mainstream Economics." *Capital and Class* 66: 23–51.

Lewis, J. (2000). "Funding Social Science Research in Academia." *Social Policy and Administration* 34(4): 129–52.

Liinason, M., and U. M. Holm (2006). "PhDs, Women's/Gender Studies and Interdisciplinarity." *Nora: Nordic Journal of Women's Studies* 14(2): 115–30.

Lim, B. C. (2009). *Translating Time: Cinema, the Fantastic, and Temporal Critique*. Durham: Duke University Press.

Looser, D., and E. A. Kaplan (1997). *Generations: Academic Feminists in Dialogue*. Minneapolis: University of Minnesota Press.

Lorber, J. (2000). "Using Gender to Undo Gender: A Feminist Degendering Movement." *Feminist Theory* 1(1): 79–95.

Lovell, T. (2000). "Thinking Feminism with and against Bourdieu." *Feminist Theory* 1(1): 11–32.

———. (2003). "Resisting with Authority: Historical Specificity, Agency and the Performative Self." *Theory, Culture and Society* 20(1): 1–17.

Lugones, M. C. (1990). "Playfulness, 'World'-Travelling, and Loving Perception." In *Making Face, Haciendo Caras: Making Soul*, ed. G. Anzaldúa, 390–402. San Francisco: Aunt Lute Press.

Lugones, M. C., and E. Spelman (1983). "Have We Got a Theory for You! Feminist Theory, Cultural Imperialism and the Demand for 'The Woman's Voice.'" *Women's Studies International Forum* 6(6): 573–81.

Luibhéid, E., ed. (2008). "Queer/Migration." Special Issue, *GLQ* 14(1).

Luibhéid, E., and L. Cantú Jr, eds. (2005). *Queer Migrations: Sexuality, U.S. Citizenship and Border Crossings*. Minneapolis: University of Minnesota Press.

Lurie, S., A. Cvetkovich, J. Gallop, T. Modleski, and H. Spillers (2001). "Roundtable: Restoring Feminist Politics to Poststructuralist Critique." *Feminist Studies* 27(3): 679–707.

Lykke, N. (2004a). "Between Particularism, Universalism and Transversalism: Reflections on the Politics of Location of European Feminist Research and Education." *Nora: Nordic Journal of Women's Studies* 12(2): 72–82.

———. (2004b). "Women's/Gender/Feminist Studies—A Post-Disciplinary Discipline?" *The Making of European Women's Studies* 5: 91–101.

MacKenzie, C., and N. Stoljar, eds. (2000). *Relational Autonomy: Feminist Perspectives on Autonomy, Agency, and the Social Self*. Oxford: Oxford University Press.

MacLean, N. (1999). "The Hidden History of Affirmative Action: Working Women's Struggles in the 1970s and the Gender of Class." *Feminist Studies* 25(1): 42–75.

Madhok, S. (2007). "Autonomy, Gendered Subordination and Transcultural Dialogue." *Journal of Global Ethics* 3(3): 335–57.

Mahmood, S. (2005). *Politics of Piety: The Islamic Revival and the Feminist Subject*. Princeton: Princeton University Press.

Martin, B. (1994). "Sexualities without Genders and Other Queer Utopias." *Diacritics* 24(2/3): 104–21.

Massad, J. A. (2007). *Desiring Arabs*. Chicago: Chicago University Press.

Massumi, B. (2002). *Parables for the Virtual: Movement, Affect, Sensation*. Durham: Duke University Press.

McCall, L. (2005). "The Complexity of Intersectionality." *Signs* 30(31): 1771–802.

McDowell, L. (2002). "The Trouble with Men? Young People, Gender Transformations and the Crisis of Masculinity." *International Journal of Urban and Regional Research* 24(1): 201–209.

McMahon, E. (2005). "'Puberty Blues' Takes Feminist Generationalism to the Beach." *Australian Feminist Studies* 20(48): 281–89.

McNay, L. (1999). "Subject, Psyche and Agency: the Work of Judith Butler." *Theory, Culture and Society* 16(2): 175–93.

———. (2000). *Gender and Agency: Reconfiguring the Subject in Feminist and Social Theory*. Cambridge: Polity Press.

———. (2003). "Agency, Anticipation and Indeterminacy in Feminist Theory." *Feminist Theory* 4(2): 139–48.

McRobbie, A. (2000). *Feminism and Youth Culture*. Basingstoke: Macmillan.

———. (2004). "Feminism and the Socialist Tradition . . . Undone?" *Cultural Studies* 18(4): 503–22.

———. (2008). *The Aftermath of Feminism: Gender, Culture and Social Change*. London: Sage.

Merck, M. (2004). "Sexuality, Subjectivity and . . . Economics?" *New Formations* 52: 82–93.

Messer-Davidow, E. (2002). *Disciplining Feminism: From Social Activism to Academic Discourse*. Durham: Duke University Press.

Mies, M. (1991). "Women's Research or Feminist Research?" In *Beyond Methodology: Feminist Standpoint as Lived Experience*, ed. M. M. Fonow and J. A. Cook, 60–84. Bloomington: Indiana University Press.

Miller, A. M., and C. S. Vance (2004). "Sexuality, Human Rights, and Health." *Health and Human Rights* 7(2): 5–15.

Modood, T. (2008). "A Basis for and Two Obstacles in the Way of a Multicultural Coalition." *British Journal of Sociology* 59(1): 47–52.

Mohanty, C. T. (2003 [1988]). "Under Western Eyes: Feminist Scholarship and Colonial Discourses." In *Feminism without Borders: Decolonizing Theory, Practicing Solidarity*, 17–42. Durham: Duke University Press.

Moore, H. (2006). "The Future of Gender or the End of a Brilliant Career?" In *Feminist Anthropology: Past, Present and Future*, ed. P. L. Gellerand M. K. Stockett, 23–42. Philadelphia: University of Pennsylvania Press.

Munt, S. R. (1997). "'I Teach Therefore I Am': Lesbian Studies in the Liberal Academy." *Feminist Review* 56: 85–100.

Narayan, U. (1997). "Contesting Cultures." In *Dislocating Cultures: Identities, Traditions and Third-World Feminism*, 2–39. New York: Routledge.

———. (2000). "Undoing the 'Package Picture' of Cultures." *Signs* 25(4): 1083–86.

Nicholson, L. J. (1996). *Second Wave: A Reader in Feminist Theory*. New York: Routledge.

Nigianni, C., and M. Storr, eds. (2009). *Deleuze and Queer Theory*. Edinburgh: Edinburgh University Press.

Njambi, W. N. (2004). "Dualisms and Female Bodies in Representations of African Female Circumcision: a Feminist Critique." *Feminist Theory* 5(3): 281–303.

Nussbaum, M. C. (1998). *Sex and Social Justice*. New York: Oxford University Press.

———. (1999). "The Professor of Parody." *The New Republic*: 37–45.

Oakley, A. (1997 [1981]). "Interviewing Women: A Contradiction in Terms." In *Doing Feminist Research*, ed. H. Roberts, 30–61. London: Routledge.

O'Barr, J. F. (2000). "My Master List for the Millennium." *Signs* 25(4): 1205–207.

O'Connell Davidson, J. (1998). *Prostitution, Power and Freedom*. Ann Arbor: University of Michigan Press.

———. (2006a). "Men, Middlemen, and Migrants: The Demand Side of 'Sex Trafficking.'" *Eurozine*, http://eurozine.com.

———. (2006b). "Will the Real Sex Slave Please Stand Up?" *Feminist Review* 83: 4–22.

O'Sullivan, S. (1999). "What a Difference a Decade Makes: 'Coming to Power' and 'The Second Coming.'" *Feminist Review* 61: 97–126.

Ousmanova, A. (2003). "On the Ruins of Orthodox Marxism: Gender and Cultural Studies in Eastern Europe." *Studies in East European Thought* 55(1): 37–50.

Özdalga, E. (1998). *The Veiling Issue, Official Secularism and Popular Islam in Modern Turkey*. Richmond: Curzon Press.

Paglia, C. (1992). *Sex, Art and American Culture: Essays*. New York: Vintage.

Parati, G., and R. J. West (2002). *Italian Feminist Theory and Practice: Equality and Sexual Difference*. Madison: Fairleigh Dickinson University Press.

Pedwell, C. (2007). "Theorising 'African' Female Genital Cutting and 'Western' Body Modification: A Critique of the Continuum and Analogue Approaches." *Feminist Review* 86: 45–66.

———. (2008). "Weaving Relational Webs: Theorizing Cultural Difference and Embodied Practices." *Feminist Theory* 9(1): 87–107.

Petchesky, R. P. (2000). "Sexual Rights: Inventing a Concept, Mapping an International Practice." In *Framing the Sexual Subject: the Politics of Gender, Sexuality and Power*, ed. R. G. Parker, R. M. Barbosa, and P. Aggleton, 81–103. Berkeley: University of California Press.

Peterson, V. S. (2003). *A Critical Rewriting of Global Political Economy: Integrating Reproductive, Productive and Virtual Economies*. New York: Routledge.

Phillips, A. (2007). *Multiculturalism without Culture*. Princeton: Princeton University Press.

———. (2010). "What's Wrong with Essentialism?" In *Gender and Culture*, 69–82. Cambridge: Polity Press.

Probyn, E. (1993). "Speaking the Self and Other Feminist Subjects." In *Sexing the Self: Gendered Positions in Cultural Studies*, 1–6. London: Routledge.

———. (1998). "Re: Generation—Women's Studies and the Disciplining of Ressentiment." *Australian Feminist Studies* 13(27): 129–36.

Prosser, J. (1998). *Second Skins: The Body Narratives of Transsexuality*. New York: Columbia University Press.

Puar, J. (2005). "Queer Times, Queer Assemblages." *Social Text* 23(3–4): 121–39.

———. (2007). *Terrorist Assemblages: Homonationalism in Queer Times*. Durham: Duke University Press.

Puri, J. (2002). "Nationalism Has a Lot to Do With It! Unravelling Questions of Nationalism and Transnationalism in Lesbian / Gay Studies." In *The Handbook of Lesbian and Gay Studies*, ed. D. Richardson and S. Seidman, 427–42. London: Sage.

———. (2006). "Stakes and States." *Feminist Review* 83: 139–48.

Puwar, N. (2005). "The Future of 'Feminist Review' and Feminisms: Un/becomings and Possibilities." *Feminist Review* 81: 15–19.

Ramazanoğlu, C., and J. Holland, eds. (1993). *Up against Foucault: Explorations of Some Tensions between Foucault and Feminism*. London: Routledge.

Raymond, J. G. (1980). *The Transsexual Empire*. London: Women's Press.

Rhys, J. (2000 [1966]). *Wide Sargasso Sea*. London: Penguin.

Rich, A. (1980). "Compulsory Heterosexuality and Lesbian Existence." In *Women— Sex and Sexuality*, ed. C. Stimpson and E. S. Person, 62–91. Chicago: University of Chicago Press.

——. (1986). "Notes Toward a Politics of Location." In *Blood, Bread and Poetry: Selected Prose 1979–1985*, 210–31. London: Virago.

Richardson, D., and V. Robinson (1994). "Theorizing Women's Studies, Gender Studies and Masculinity: The Politics of Naming." *European Journal of Women's Studies* 1: 11–27.

Riley, D. (1988). *"Am I That Name?": Feminism and the Category of "Women" in History*. Basingstoke: Macmillan.

Robinson, S. (2000). *Marked Men: White Masculinity in Crisis*. New York: Columbia University Press.

Robinson, V., and D. Richardson (1997). *Introducing Women's Studies: Feminist Theory and Practice*. New York: New York University Press.

Roiphe, K. (1993). *The Morning After: Sex, Fear, and Feminism on Campus*. Boston: Little, Brown and Co.

Roof, J. (1996). *Come As You Are: Sexuality and Narrative*. New York: Columbia University Press.

——. (1997). "Generational Difficulties; or, The Fear of a Barren History." In *Generations: Academic Feminists in Dialogue*, ed. D. Looser and E. A. Kaplan, 69–87. Minneapolis: University of Minnesota Press.

Roof, J., and R. Wiegman, eds. (1995). *Who Can Speak? Authority and Critical Identity*. Urbana-Champaign: University of Illinois Press.

Roth, B. (1999). "The Making of the Vanguard Center: Black Feminist Emergence in the 1960s and 1970s." In *Still Lifting, Still Climbing: African American Women's Contemporary Activism*, ed. K. Springer, 70–90. New York: New York University Press.

Rowbotham, S. (2000). *Promise of a Dream: A Memoir of the Sixties*. London: Allen Lane.

Sawicki, J. (1991). *Disciplining Foucault: Feminism, Power, and the Body*. New York: Routledge.

Sayeed, A. (2006). "Making Political Hay of Sex and Slavery: Kansas Conservatism, Feminism and the Global Regulation of Sexual Minorities." *Feminist Review* 83: 119–31.

Scharff, C. (2009). "Young Women's Dis-Identification with Feminism: Heteronormativity, Neoliberalism and Difference." PhD dissertation, Gender Institute, London School of Economics and Political Science.

Scott, J. (1999). "Gender as a Useful Category of Historical Analysis." In *Gender and the Politics of History*, 28–50. New York: Columbia University Press.

——. (2007). *The Politics of the Veil*. Princeton: Princeton University Press.

Sedgwick, E. K. (1987). "A Poem Is Being Written." *Representations* 17(winter): 110–43.

——. (1991). *Epistemology of the Closet*. London: Harvester Wheatsheaf.

———. (2003). *Touching Feeling: Affect, Pedagogy, Performativity.* Durham: Duke University Press.

Segal, L. (1990). *Slow Motion: Changing Masculinities, Changing Men.* New Brunswick, N.J.: Rutgers University Press.

———. (2000). "Only Contradictions on Offer." *Women: A Cultural Review* 11(1–2): 19–36.

———. (2007). *Making Trouble: Life and Politics.* London: Serpent's Tail Press.

Seidman, S. (1996). *Queer Theory/Sociology.* Oxford: Blackwell.

Sherry, A. (2000). "Building the Bridge: Taking Feminism into the Twenty-First Century." *Australian Feminist Studies* 15(32): 221–26.

Skaerbaek, E. (2004). "It Takes Two to Tango: On Knowledge Production and Intersubjectivity." *Nora: Nordic Journal of Women's Studies* 12(2): 93–101.

Skaerbaek, E., D. Duhaček, E. Pulcini, and M. Richter (2006). *Common Passion, Different Voices: Reflections on Citizenship and Intersubjectivity.* York: Raw Nerve Books.

Skeggs, B. (1995). "Women's Studies in Britain: Entitlement Cultures and Institutional Constraints." *Women's Studies International Forum* 18(4): 475–85.

———. (1997). *Formations of Class and Gender: Becoming Respectable.* Thousand Oaks, Calif.: Sage.

———. (2004). *Class, Self, Culture.* London: Routledge.

Smith, D. (1987). "Women's Perspective as a Radical Critique of Sociology." In *Feminism and Science,* ed. E. Fox Keller and H. Longino, 17–27. Oxford: Oxford University Press.

Sommers, C. H. (1994). *Who Stole Feminism? How Women Have Betrayed Women.* New York: Simon and Schuster.

———. (2000). *The War against Boys: How Misguided Feminism is Harming Our Young Men.* New York: Simon and Schuster.

Spivak, G. C. (1981). "French Feminism in an International Frame." *Yale French Studies* 62: 154–84.

———. (1988). "Can the Subaltern Speak?" In *Colonial Discourse and Post-Colonial Theory,* ed. P. Williams and L. Chrisman, 66–111. New York: Columbia University Press.

———. (1993a). "French Feminism Revisited." In *Outside in the Teaching Machine,* 141–72. New York: Routledge.

———. (1993b). "The Politics of Translation." In *Outside in the Teaching Machine,* 179–200. New York: Routledge.

———. (1999a). *A Critique of Postcolonial Reason: Toward a History of the Vanishing Present.* Cambridge, Mass.: Harvard University Press.

———. (1999b). "History." In *A Critique of Postcolonial Reason: Toward a History of the Vanishing Present,* 198–311. Cambridge, Mass.: Harvard University Press.

Stanley, E., and S. Wise (2000). "But the Empress Has No Clothes! Some Awkward Questions about the 'Missing Revolution' in Feminist Theory." *Feminist Theory* 1(3): 261–88.

Staunaes, D. (2003). "Where Have All the Subjects Gone? Bringing Together the

Concepts of Intersectionality and Subjectification." *Nora: Nordic Journal of Women's Studies* 11(2): 101–10.

Stoetzler, M., and N. Yuval-Davis (2002). "Standpoint Theory, Situated Knowledge and the Situated Imagination." *Feminist Theory* 3(3): 315–33.

Stromquist, N. (2001). "Gender Studies: A Global Perspective of Their Evolution, Contribution, and Challenges to Comparative Higher Education." *Higher Education* 51: 373–87.

Stryker, S. (1994). "My Words to Victor Frankenstein above the Village of Chamounix: Performing Transgender Rage." *GLQ* 1(13): 237–54.

Suleri, S. (1992). "Woman Skin Deep: Feminism and the Postcolonial Condition." *Critical Inquiry* 18(4): 756–69.

Sylvester, C. (1995). "African and Western Feminisms: World-Traveling the Tendencies and Possibilities." *Signs* 20(4): 941–69.

Terry, J. (1991). "Theorizing Deviant Historiography." *Differences* 3(2): 55–74.

——. (1999). *An American Obsession: Science, Medicine, and Homosexuality in Modern Society*. Chicago: University of Chicago Press.

Tétreault, A. M. (2006). "The Sexual Politics of Abu Ghraib: Hegemony, Spectacle and the Global War on Terror." *NWSA Journal* 18(3): 1–19.

Thompson, B. (2002). "Multiracial Feminism: Recasting the Chronology of Second Wave Feminism." *Feminist Studies* 28(2): 337–61.

Thorne, B. (2000). "A Telling Time for Women's Studies." *Signs* 25(4): 1183–87.

Threadgold, T. (2000). "Gender Studies and Women's Studies." *Australian Feminist Studies* 15(31): 39–48.

Tomkins, S. (1963). *Affect Imagery Consciousness, Vol 2: The Negative Affects*. New York: Springer Publishing.

Torr, R. (2007). "What's Wrong with Aspiring to Find Out What Has Really Happened in Academic Feminism's Recent Past? Response to Clare Hemmings' 'Telling Feminist Stories.'" *Feminist Theory* 8(1): 59–67.

Treacher, A., H.-H. Pai, L. Khalili, and P. Alldred, eds. (2008). "Editorial: The Gendered Embroilments of War." *Feminist Review* 88: 1–6.

Trinh, M.-H. (1989). *Woman, Native, Other: Writing Postcoloniality and Feminism*. Bloomington: Indiana University Press.

Tronto, J. (2003). "Time's Place." *Feminist Theory* 4(2): 119–38.

Van der Tuin, I. (2009). "'Jumping Generations': On Second- and Third-Wave Feminist Epistemology." *Australian Feminist Studies* 24(59): 17–31.

Vasterling, V., E. Demény, C. Hemmings, U. M. Holm, P. Korvajärvi, and T-S. Pavliodou (2006). *Practising Interdisciplinarity in Gender Studies*. York: Raw Nerve Books.

Venn, C. (2007). "Cultural Theory and Its Futures: Introduction." *Theory, Culture and Society* 24: 49–54.

Volpp, L. (2001). "Feminism versus Multiculturalism." *Columbia Law Review* 101(5): 1181–218.

Walby, S. (2000). "Beyond the Politics of Location: The Power of Argument in a Global Era." *Feminist Theory* 1(2): 189–206.

Walkerdine, V. (2003). "Reclassifying Upward Mobility: Femininity and the Neo-Liberal Subject." *Gender and Education* 15(3): 237–48.

Walkerdine, V., H. Lucey, and J. Melody, eds. (2001). *Growing Up Girl: Psychosocial Explorations of Gender and Class*. Basingstoke: Palgrave.

Ware, V. (2006). "Info-War and the Politics of Feminist Curiosity." *Cultural Studies* 20(6): 526–51.

Weed, E., and N. Schor, eds. (1997). *Feminism Meets Queer Theory*. Bloomington: Indiana University Press.

Wekker, G. (2004). "Still Crazy after All These Years . . . Feminism for the New Millennium." *European Journal of Women's Studies* 11(4): 487–500.

White, H. V. (1992). *Tropics of Discourse: Essays in Cultural Criticism*. Baltimore: Johns Hopkins Press.

Wiegman, R. (1999a). "What Ails Feminist Criticism? A Second Opinion." *Critical Inquiry* 25: 362–79.

———. (1999b). "Whiteness Studies and the Paradox of Particularity." *Boundary 2* 26(3): 115–50.

———. (1999/2000). "Feminism, Institutionalism, and the Idiom of Failure." *Differences* 11(3): 107–36.

———. (2001). "Statement: Women's Studies—Interdisciplinary Imperatives, Again." *Feminist Studies* 27(2): 514–18.

———. (2002). "Academic Feminism against Itself." *NWSA Journal* 14(2): 18–37.

———, ed. (2003). *Women's Studies on Its Own: A Next Wave Reader in Institutional Change*. Durham: Duke University Press.

———. (2004). "On Being in Time with Feminism." *Modern Language Quarterly* 65(1): 161–76.

———. (2007). "Un-Remembering Monique Wittig." *GLQ* 13(4): 505–18.

Wilson, R. K. (2008). "Reclaiming 'Agency,' Reasserting Resistance." *IDS Bulletin* 39(6): 83–91.

Wilton, T. (2000). "Out/Performing Our Selves: Sex, Gender and Cartesian Dualism." *Sexualities* 3(2): 237–54.

Winter, B. (2000). "Who Counts (or Doesn't Count) What as Feminist Theory? An Exercise in Dictionary Use." *Feminist Theory* 1(1): 105–11.

Wittig, M. (1980). "The Straight Mind." *Gender Issues* 1(1): 103–11.

———. (1982). "The Category of Sex." *Gender Issues* 2(2): 63–68.

———. (1985). "The Mark of Gender." *Gender Issues* 5(2): 3–12.

———. (1992). *The Straight Mind, and Other Essays*. London: Harvester.

Woodhead, L. (2008). "Secular Privilege, Religious Disadvantage." *British Journal of Sociology* 59(1): 47–52.

Yuval-Davis, N. (2006). "Intersectionality and Feminist Politics." *European Journal of Women's Studies* 13(3): 193–209.

Zalewski, M. (2003). "Commemorating Women's Studies?" *Feminist Theory* 4(3): 339–42.

———. (2007). "Do We Understand Each Other Yet? Troubling Feminist Encounters

With(in) International Relations." *British Journal of Politics and International Relations* 9(2): 302–12.

Zimmerman, B. (1997). "Confessions of a Lesbian Feminist." In *Cross-Purposes: Lesbians, Feminists, and the Limits of Alliance*, ed. D. Heller, 159–68. Bloomington: Indiana University Press.

INDEX

1970s: essentialism in, 39–40, 66, 162, 168; as heteronormative, 66; lesbian feminism in, 51–52; as politically radical, 64–66, 74, 100, 162; racism and, 13, 66, 168; radical feminism in, 6, 49, 239 n. 9; socialist feminism in, 6, 239 n. 9

1980s: black feminism in, 6, 22, 43–53, 162–63, 231 n. 8; difference and, 5, 40–48; identity and, 5, 47, 162; lesbian feminism in, 6, 43, 48–57, 162–63; as politically radical, 66, 74, 162; poststructuralism and, 45–46, 67, 231 n. 8; as pro-sex, 6, 49–51; as transitional decade, 40–43, 49

1990s: as depoliticized, 67, 162; difference and, 5, 40–41, 46–48, 50–52; intersectionality and, 48; poststructuralism and, 6, 89–93; queer and, 6, 50, 89–93, 162

2000s (noughts), 5, 99

Abu Ghraib, 143
academia: use of abstract language in, 67–69, 185, 232 n. 1; as agent of feminist theory, 34–35; depoliticization and, 4, 6, 26, 67–93, 232 n. 3; elitism and, 67–69, 76–78; feminist generations and, 63–64, 76–84; institutional politics of, 10–11, 74–80, 134–35, 149–55, 232–33 n. 5; "star system" in, 76, 175–76, 239 n. 12. *See also* disciplinarity; interdisciplinarity
accountability, 150–51, 176–77
Adkins, Lisa, 73
affect: ambivalence as, 63; anger as, 24, 26, 63, 78–81, 223; discomfort as, 200–202; as distinct from emotion, 230 n. 20; enthusiasm as, 106, 108; friendship as, 149, 202–3; generational, 150–51, 156; horror and, 197, 215–23, 242 n. 20; identification and, 24, 62–63, 180, 191–92, 195; importance of, 230 n. 19; intersubjectivity and, 25; in loss narratives, 21, 62–63, 68–69, 72–73, 78–83; as narrative technique, 20–21, 23–27, 133–37; passion as, 3, 23–24, 68, 108; in progress

CLARE HEMMINGS is a reader in feminist theory and the director of the Gender Institute at the London School of Economics. She is the author of *Bisexual Spaces* (2002), co-author of *Practising Interdisciplinarity in Gender Studies* (2006), co-editor of *Travelling Concepts in Feminist Pedagogy* (2006) and *The Bisexual Imaginary* (1997), and editor of "Transforming Academies" for *Feminist Review* (2010).

Library of Congress Cataloging-in-Publication Data

Hemmings, Clare.
Why stories matter : the political grammar of feminist theory / Clare Hemmings.
p. cm.—(Next wave)
Includes bibliographical references and index.
ISBN 978-0-8223-4893–1 (cloth : alk. paper)
ISBN 978-0-8223-4916-7 (pbk. : alk. paper)
1. Feminist theory. 2. Women's studies. 3. Culture—Study and teaching.
I. Title. II. Series: Next wave.
HQ1190.H466 2011
305.4201—dc22   2010028813